Women's Literary Portraits in the Victorian and Neo-Victorian Novel

Women's Literary Portraits in the Victorian and Neo-Victorian Novel

An Intertextual Study

Aleksandra Tryniecka

LEXINGTON BOOKS
Lanham • Boulder • New York • London

Published by Lexington Books
An imprint of The Rowman & Littlefield Publishing Group, Inc.
4501 Forbes Boulevard, Suite 200, Lanham, Maryland 20706
www.rowman.com

86-90 Paul Street, London EC2A 4NE

Copyright © 2023 by The Rowman & Littlefield Publishing Group, Inc.

All rights reserved. No part of this book may be reproduced in any form or by any electronic or mechanical means, including information storage and retrieval systems, without written permission from the publisher, except by a reviewer who may quote passages in a review.

British Library Cataloguing in Publication Information Available

Library of Congress Cataloging-in-Publication Data

ISBN 978-1-66690-577-9 (cloth: alk. paper)
ISBN 978-1-66690-579-3 (paper : alk. paper)
ISBN 978-1-66690-578-6 (electronic)

∞™ The paper used in this publication meets the minimum requirements of American National Standard for Information Sciences—Permanence of Paper for Printed Library Materials, ANSI/NISO Z39.48-1992.

For Professor Anna Kędra-Kardela, with sincere gratitude for many years of a precious literary and scholarly journey which will be always present in my heart.

Contents

Preface	ix
Acknowledgments	xiii
PART I: BETWEEN THE PAST AND THE PRESENT	1
Chapter One: Dialogue in Revisionary Fiction	3
Chapter Two: Intertextuality: Creating Theoretical Framework for a Literary Debate	9
Chapter Three: Intertextuality in Practice: Examining the Literary World	17
Chapter Four: The Novel Domesticated in the Victorian World	21
Chapter Five: The Victorian Novel and Social Debate	31
Chapter Six: Profits, Ideals, and the "Self": Victorian Ambiguities Rediscovered in Literature	49
Chapter Seven: The Woman Question or Women Questions?	61
Chapter Eight: The Ethics of the Past and the Present: The Nineteenth Century Reimagined in the Modern World	79
Chapter Nine: Beyond Nostalgia: Filling the Modern Culture with Victorianism	87
Chapter Ten: Women and Spiritual Revival	101
Chapter Eleven: Women and Family in the Neo-Victorian Novel	105

PART II: DIVING INTO THE NEO-VICTORIAN NOVEL — 107

Chapter Twelve: The New Woman Restaged: The Madwoman in the Library and the Man in Ruskin's Garden in Gail Carriger's *Soulless* — 109

Chapter Thirteen: Women and their Apparel in Victorian and Neo-Victorian Texts: Constructing Women Characters by Means of Fashion — 149

Chapter Fourteen: Diving Deeper into Fashion: Clothes in Wilkie Collins's *The Woman in White* and in Gail Carriger's *Soulless* — 169

Chapter Fifteen: Voice and Identity in the Victorian and Neo-Victorian Novel: Charlotte Brontë's *Jane Eyre*, Jean Rhys's *Wide Sargasso Sea,* and Clare Boylan's *Emma Brown* — 183

Chapter Sixteen: Nameless and Voiceless: Clare Boylan's *Emma Brown* and Jean Rhys's *Wide Sargasso Sea* — 195

Chapter Seventeen: Neo-Victorian Biofiction: Syrie James's *The Secret Diaries of Charlotte Brontë* and the Biography Retold — 211

Epilogue — 227

Bibliography — 233

Index — 243

About the Author — 247

Preface

Dear Reader,

This book is the fruit of my interest in and love for literature, especially the Victorian novel and its present-day literary reworkings. The aim of this work lies in examining how the nineteenth-century novel emerged and interacted with the Victorian sociocultural world, how it portrayed women in the nineteenth-century sociocultural context, and how these literary portrayals contributed to and influenced what we currently understand as neo-Victorian revisionary fiction. Women's roles and their place in Victorian society are especially interesting and fascinating to trace in the literary context since, as I believe, women have always been located at the center of social discourse and interaction, skilfully balancing between the public sphere and domestic realm with the latter, at least traditionally, ascribed to them. From their social position, through their private lives, to the choices of their attire, Victorian women pave the way for our understanding of Victorian society at large, with its conflicts, dualisms, ambiguities, double standards, dreams, hopes, aspirations, ambitions, and moral dilemmas. Moreover, literary portrayals of Victorian women allow one to re-create the vision of the past and restore the back-then marginalized voices in revisionary fiction of the twentieth- and twenty-first century. This revisionary fiction—the neo-Victorian novel—offers not only a rearview-mirror perspective of the bygone, but also provides a vast commentary on the present-day society. In the neo-Victorian novel, it is through the prism of the twentieth- and twenty-first century gaze that Victorian narratives concerning women are re-analyzed and brought back to light with a new, transformed, and powerful message. In effect, revisionary narratives project the Victorian past and nineteenth-century women from the current sociocultural angle. Hence, rewriting the Victorian past is not only an undertaking enriching one's understanding of the nineteenth-century world, but also a self-explanatory process concerning the present-day society, its cultural structure and moral condition. As I believe, this literary, self-explanatory process epitomized by the rise of the neo-Victorian novel is necessary for the functioning of the present-day society, as every society at a given historical time searches for a point of reference in order to establish its similarities and differences with the bygone world. The interest in rewriting the Victorian past in the modern vein testifies to the fact that the nineteenth-century world is still vital for the understanding of the present, while the present-day society is, essentially, a continuation of this historical time line.

The two cutting-edge, pioneering works of the 1960s engaging in a dialogical exchange with the past are: Jean Rhys's *Wide Sargasso Sea* (1966) and John Fowles's *The French Lieutenant's Woman* (1969). In time, the neo-Victorian revisionary genre tremendously expanded, including, among many others, such works as: Peter Ackroyd's *Dickens* (1990), Antonia S. Byatt's *Possession* (1990), Michèle Roberts's *In the Red Kitchen* (1990), Sarah Water's famous *Affinity* (1999), Belinda Starling's *The Journal of Dora Damage* (2006), and Lloyd Jones's *Master Pip* (2007). These acclaimed works introduce historical figures into literary contexts (Ackroyd's *Dickens*) or place fictional nineteenth-century characters in innovative settings (Jones's *Master Pip*). They also shed light on the so far marginalized voices (Waters's *Affinity*), incorporate postmodern discourses into the Victorian world (Starling's *The Journal of Dora Damage*) or switch between the historical and temporal planes (Byatt's *Possession* and Roberts's *In the Red Kitchen*).

Even though this book is a work maintained within the framework of academic discourse, my hope is that it can reach the readers not only strictly associated with the academic world, but also literature enthusiasts, as well as students of literature and those readers who hope to explore literary history from a more academic angle. After all, literature is the key to understanding the past, as well as our current historical placement and sociocultural values. In this sense, it is the key to understanding the self.

The initial chapters of this book offer analysis of Bakhtin's dialogism and intertextual theories, as it is indispensable to place the concept of the novel in theoretical frameworks with a special emphasis on its dialogical and intertextual nature. The readers especially interested in the nineteenth century and its sociocultural landscape can readily dive into chapter 4, which explores the sociocultural and literary contexts in which the Victorian novel emerged. Furthermore, my work discusses the placement of women in nineteenth-century society and their ambivalent and complex portraits preserved on the pages of the Victorian novel. The literary portrayals of women are reimagined on the pages of neo-Victorian, revisionary fiction. Finally, the readers will find dialogical analysis of the selected Victorian and neo-Victorian novels with literary portraits of women at the center of this discussion. The novels discussed in my book are, essentially, those texts which have been close to my heart as a reader, student, and teacher and, thus, I hoped to share them with my readers as well, together with the joy of reading and rereading these works in the Victorian and neo-Victorian light. The neo-Victorian novels analyzed in this book include: Jean Rhys's *Wide Sargasso Sea* (1966), Clare Boylan's *Emma Brown* (2003), Syrie James's *The Secret Diaries of Charlotte Brontë* (2009), and Gail Carriger's *Soulless* (2009). These selected texts are essentially discussed in an intertextual dialogue, while corresponding with one another on different layers of the literary debate. As mentioned before, my analyses are based on the principles of dialogism and intertextuality—presented in detail in chapter 1. This choice has been vital to me, as my hope was to present a continuity between the literary past and the present, as well as the coexistence of sometimes contrasting, yet always complementary discourses related to the novelistic portrayals of Victorian and neo-Victorian women. There are numerous academic works dedicated to the literary portrayals of women in the Victorian novel which exclusively draw on gender and feminist theories—while I immensely value this approach and find it indispensable for the understanding of the culturally embedded past, I decided to create a work fully based on dialogical/intertextual perspectives which would enable me to swiftly bind together the fascinating polyphony of literary voices emerging both in the past and the present. It is this choir of literary voices—oftentimes diversified, divided by time and historical perspectives, yet always interrelated—which fascinates me the most. Hence, I decided to draw on dialogical/intertextual perspectives in order to present to you this book: the result of my personal journey with the Victorian and neo-Victorian novel. Once more, I would like to highlight that even though the major theory applied in this study is not feminism, the concluding messages stemming from my analyses are pointing in the same direction in which feminism does—thus proving the validity of feminist discourse as well: in the Victorian past and, still, in the current-day era, women are balancing between the public and private spheres, striving to assert themselves and speak with their own individualized voices. Interestingly enough, the conventional social roles ascribed to women in Victorian times are simultaneously criticized and perpetuated in the present-day era. The ambiguities of the twenty-first century relate to the ambivalences of the Victorian past, showing that the past and the present should be still discussed and, hopefully, discussed by means of a literary dialogue.

While the novels discussed in my work deal with the issues of women's complexity and marginalization as well, they primarily celebrate the possibilities and little victories of neo-Victorian women. Tracing the opportunities of neo-Victorian heroines appears especially vital in the current times, which are primarily concentrated on excavating the ordeals and horrors of the past, leaving no room for hope. Therefore, I will try to present neo-Victorian literary women as figures who "redeem" the past and offer a more reassuring and optimistic version of the bygone and, thus, a more optimistic outlook for the future. May "literary lessons" of the past assist us in the creation of the more empathetic present.

With best wishes, or, resorting to the nineteenth-century letter-writing convention:

Ever Your Affectionate Friend and Author,
Aleksandra Tryniecka

Acknowledgments

If it were not for the fortunate circumstances which allowed me to develop my love for literature and, most importantly, if it were not for the kindness, encouragement, and constant support of my friends and colleagues, this book would not be here. I am very grateful to my parents, friends, and colleagues for their support and unceasing encouragement on this literary journey. I am also very grateful to Professor Anna Kędra-Kardela for her untiring patience, kindness, commitment, continuous support, and invaluable advice. I would also like to thank the Professors Evangelia Sakelliou-Schultz, Maria Pirgerou, Anna Despotopoulou, Aleksandra Kędzierska, Marta Komsta, Gregory Papanikos, Czesław Grzesiak, and Andrzej Kowalczyk for their kindness, support, and helpful advice. I am very grateful to Holly Buchanan for her continuous support while this book was coming to life. Moreover, I am grateful to the librarians at Maria Curie-Skłodowska University in Lublin for offering me their help, guidance, and constant kindness. Last but not least, I would like to express my sincere gratitude to the Faculty of English Language and Literature at the National and Kapodistrian University of Athens: thank you for providing me with innumerable sources to carry out my research and allowing me to daydream for hours about the Victorian past in your beautiful library in Athens.

PART I

Between the Past and the Present

Chapter One

Dialogue in Revisionary Fiction

"Do we begin with texts and produce theories about them after we have read them? Or do we begin with theories about texts and then read specific texts in the light of those theories?," inquires Graham Allen in his *Intertextuality* (132).[1] While this fundamental query remains unsolved, the modern literary scene hosts a growing number of revisionary works which re-narrate the previously existent texts in the modern vein and which demand a fresh theoretical outlook highlighting their simultaneous innovative and derivative character. The focus of this book is particularly on selected Victorian and neo-Victorian novels. The latter, Hadley observes, "do not merely replicate Victorian narrative modes, but rather transform them" (147). In this light, intertextuality, the popular critical idiom in recent scholarly analysis, appears to constitute an appropriate theoretical tool for the study of Victorian literary revision. While the term "intertextual" can be ascribed to literature as well as to arts and visual media, in this book it is applied exclusively to the analysis of the literary text, with the text standing for "whatever meaning is generated by the intertextual relations between one text and another and the activation of those relations by a reader" (Allen, 220).[2] Hence, textual meaning is developed as a result of the reader's unique interpretation of texts.

Importantly, intertextual theories proliferate and blur: Bożena Kucała describes this phenomenon in *Intertextual Dialogue with the Victorian Past in the Contemporary Novel* as the "theoretical instability" of intertextuality (33). Whereas, on the one hand, intertextuality serves as an effective theoretical framework applied in the modern analysis of literary texts, the proliferating definitions of the term create confusion, on the other. As she aptly argues,

> the ambiguous status of the concept of intertextuality in contemporary critical discourse stems, on the one hand, from the contrast between the relatively long history of the term and the substantial body of theoretical work done on it, and, on the other hand, from the persistent questioning of the validity and usefulness of the concept. (Kucała, 31)

The theoretical foundation of intertextuality can be credited to Bakhtin's profound study of a dialogue and the novel as a dialogical genre. Coining the term *dialogism*, Bakhtin placed the novel—the only dialogical genre according to him—in the center of his attention. In his essay "Epic and Novel" (published in 1970, hence thirty years after its original presentation), Bakhtin stresses the relevance of the so-called Socratic dialogues, pointing out that they paved the way for the prototypical novelistic genre: "we possess a remarkable document that reflects the simultaneous birth of scientific thinking and of a new artistic-prose model for the novel," he argues, "these are the Socratic dialogues" (Bakhtin, *Dialogic Imagination*, 24). The Socratic dialogues, a genre of prose which originated in Greece in the fourth century BCE, features Socrates as the protagonist and discusses philosophical problems by means of the "Socratic method" ("Socratic elenchus"), which encourages critical and reflective thinking, fully relying on questions and answers contributing to the growth of new ideas. According to Charles H. Kahn, "the Socratic elenchus is a successful technique for revealing ignorance in the interlocutors" (201). The method is based on the subsequent questioning of the interlocutor in order to enhance one's awareness of the world and "reality."

Bakhtin highlights the fact that the Socratic dialogues are necessarily responsive to the "real" world, hence contrasting with the notions of the *absolute past*[3] and conclusiveness. The Socratic dialogues are constantly seeking answers; they are open to change, undermining dogmas and conventions in the same way that the novel does through its narrative and inquisitive nature, whereas the *absolute past* signifies a complete and irrefutable record of events which carry a unified and closed message beyond the Reader's questioning and influence. Characteristic for the epic, the *absolute past* is the domain of such universal protagonists as Odysseus (Homer's Odyssey) or Roland (*The Song of Roland*), whose fates are predestined from the beginning until the last words.

Similarly, the concept of "conclusiveness" is built upon the tradition of the high genres, directed toward resolution and closure through one dominant voice instead of a dialogue of equally privileged voices (the trait of the novel).

Whereas the epic entirely belongs to the past, the novel figures as an open, constantly developing genre open to a constant debate. Bakhtin compares the language of the epic to the "language [used for speaking] about the dead" which "is stylistically quite distinct from language about the living" (*Dialogic Imagination*, 20). As he remarks, the language of the high genres is permanently suspended in the worship of the bygone—in a narrative that cannot be revived. Thus, a seeming completeness and conclusiveness dominates the literary history of mankind. "The temporal valorized categories of absolute beginning and absolute end are extremely significant in our sense of time and in the ideologies of past times," Bakhtin observes, "the beginning is idealized, the end is darkened" (*Dialogic Imagination*, 20). Apparently, this type of nostalgia and longing for the past are both inscribed in human nature and transferred into the literary canon of high genres which exemplify these yearnings. However, according to Bakhtin, the high genres hinder the development of free and varied literature: guided by the canon, they avoid dialogue, thus never letting the potential object of interest come close enough to the reader's zone. This "zone" is the space within which the readers are allowed to find alternative meanings within the text, redefine protagonists and reimagine them in the modern vein, as well as redefine the text and place it within the current context.

Essentially, "the novel . . . has no canon of its own," Bakhtin posits, "it is, by its very nature, not canonic. It is plasticity itself. It is a genre that is ever questioning, ever examining itself and subjecting its established forms to review" (39). The same postulates—rejection of the concepts of absolute narrative and conclusive ending—propel modern authors to rewrite Victorian works in order to expose and enhance their textual dialogue with the present. In the light of the Bakhtinian thought, neo-Victorian fiction thrives on the colloquy of perspectives (without the emphasis on conclusion).

Both Socrates and Bakhtin reject universal definitions and rhetoric as well, believing them to be hazardous tools hindering dialogue and independent thought. According to Zappen, "like the early Bakhtin, Socrates of the early dialogues felt the burden of cultural values that were not his own" (*Dialogic Imagination*, 13). Importantly, the art of the Socratic dialogues rejects the imposition of one's authoritarian voice on another. The dialogues provoke one to reflect on the world and life in a non-schematic, individualistic way (Zappen, 13). They serve as an initial point for facing the conflict between one and the world of unquestioningly traditional, but oftentimes destructive values and behavioral patterns. The Socratic dialogue anticipates the "questioning" of the "universal definitions" and "cultural values." Essentially, the dialogue in such form lies at the heart of the neo-Victorian literary revision, where nineteenth-century texts are evoked and revisited in the contemporary light and where the so-far omitted or unheard nineteenth-century voices come to the surface in order to spring into a new literary existence.

All in all, according to Bakhtin, the novel attains literary perfection as a dialogized genre filled with a plurality of voices, and thus devoid of the "dominant force or truth" (Bakhtin, 20). The Bakhtinian notion of dialogue not only enables the excavation of the literary past in the modern vein, but also facilitates self-criticism of the novelistic genre. Accordingly, neo-Victorian texts reach beyond the mere nostalgia for the past and provide a commentary on both the past and the present. For instance, in John Fowles's *The French Lieutenant's Woman* (1969), the novel acknowledged as one of the forerunners of the revisionary genre, the past and the present collide: the protagonist, Sarah Woodruff, epitomizes both the nineteenth-century gender struggle for equality and the proto-feminist perspective. In his novel, Fowles purposefully draws on Victorian conventions and plots including, among many others, those derived from Dickens or Thackeray. Christian Gutleben aptly observes that neo-Victorian texts emerge in the "polarity between nostalgia and subversion," while inherently drawing on the narratives from the past:

> the fascination with Victorianism seems inevitably to come with a temptation to denounce the injustice towards some of its ill-used of forgotten representatives. . . . This paradoxical form of wistful revisionism eventually leads to an aesthetic and ideological deadlock. Contemporary fiction advocates social, sexual and sometimes aesthetic advancement, and yet to do so it appropriates, reverts to and builds on a model of the past. (10)

According to Gutleben, it is only possible to address the past while returning to it and building upon it. Yet, it might result in an "ideological deadlock" (10), as not only the literary past could be unjustly appropriated, but also it might direct literary discussions toward the starting point, without bringing in novelty or fresh perspectives. To avoid such aesthetic and ideological standstill, one could analyze Victorian and neo-Victorian texts side by side. Such approach implements the concept of Bakhtin's *dialogism*, which signifies "the characteristic epistemological mode of a world dominated by heteroglossia," the state in which "everything means, is understood, as a part of a greater whole—there is a constant interaction between meaning, all of which have the potential of conditioning others" (Bakhtin, 426). In simple words, heteroglossia is "language's ability to contain within it many voices, one's own *and* other voices" (Allen 2000, 29). Michael Holquist highlights in *Dialogism* that heteroglossia indicates "many-languagedness" (1990, 1):

> dialogism's drive to meaning should not be confused with the Hegelian impulse toward a single state of higher consciousness in the future. In Bakhtin there is no one meaning being striven for: the world is a vast congeries of contesting meanings, *a heteroglossia so varied* that no single term capable of unifying its diversifying energies is possible. [emphasis added] (22)

Neo-Victorian texts inherently coexist in a dialogic relation with their Victorian predecessors, creating such "vast congeries of contesting meanings" (22). In neo-Victorian texts, the literary past becomes almost tangible—it can be formed into a new shape molded by the current sociocultural context. Such molding can be perceived as a kind of "domestication" of the past eradicating its initial unfamiliarity. The neo-Victorian novel foregrounds new aspects of the bygone, with the past no longer understood as something complete, but rather as a fluid, inconclusive entity endowed with fuzzy boundaries. As we move through the history and time, so do the boundaries change. Understanding the literary past always requires a point of reference, a comparison *with* other texts, because, as was mentioned before, the past cannot be understood in isolation. Since the point of view changes simultaneously with the passing époques, the visions of the past become multifaceted. Thus, the neo-Victorian novel offers yet another perception of Victorian England. However, this literary vision is not taken for granted, as it is investigated anew and approached creatively from a topical cultural viewpoint. Hence, neo-Victorian literature offers a proposal of the past rather than what one may call the historical "truth." Investigating this proposal is conducted by means of a dialogue. Consequently, neo-Victorian fiction is inhabited by numerous dialogically interacting and equally important voices. The Bakhtinian dialogue of voices provides an opportunity to explore the nineteenth-century literary realm with its complex, multifaceted dimensions. Victorian and neo-Victorian texts coexist, "being for Bakhtin is thus already 'being with,' or, '*co*-being,'" Michael Eskin observes (71). The Bakhtinian "co-being" implies that texts cannot exist in isolation: neo-Victorian texts are indebted to their predecessors, creating new meanings while revisiting the previous sources and responding to their content. For instance, Syrie James's autobiographical fiction, *The Secret Diaries of Charlotte Brontë* (2009), introduces Brontë's biography from a fresh, first-person stance while remaining fully indebted to the previously available texts, including Gaskell's and Gérin's seminal biographies.

Eskin observes that "in view of the perpetual task of co-existing, it is impossible for the human being to assume a neutral stance" (72). The dialogical coexistence of the Victorian and neo-Victorian texts proves that a "neutral stance" toward the literary past is simply unattainable. Revisioning and rereading of the Victorian texts is always intentional and subjective, performed from a given sociocultural perspective, which precludes the possibility of "assuming a neutral" view. Each act of coexistence is prone to judgment, and there are no objective revisions of the past. Yet, as mentioned before, dialogism opposes conclusive revisions. Undoubtedly, Bakhtin's thought provokes one to consciously rethink and reconfigure the bygone from miscellaneous literary angles.

NOTES

1. A part of this chapter was published in the article "Bakhtin's Dialogism, Intertextual Theories and Neo-Victorian Fiction" in *Annales Universitatis Mariae Curie-Sklodowska (section Philologiae)*, A. Tryniecka, January 2020, vol. 38, 171–85.

2. For Bakhtin, reading a literary text involves communication based on the reader's knowledge: "literary texts are utterances, words that cannot be divorced from particular subjects in specific situations. In other words, literature is another form of communication, and, as such, another form of knowledge. Literary texts, like other kinds of utterance, depend not only on the activity of the author, but also on the place they hold in the social and historical forces at work when the text is produced and when it is consumed" (Holquist 1990, 66).

3. The concept of the "absolute past" appears also in Goethe's and Schiller's terminology and signifies "the subject for the epic." It is "closed and completed in the whole as well as in any of its parts. It is, therefore, possible to take any part and offer it as the whole" (Hoffman, Murphy, 51).

Chapter Two

Intertextuality

Creating Theoretical Framework for a Literary Debate

Intertextuality, the term which "slipped into an outline of Bakhtinian dialogism" (Kucała, 31), similarly binds the Victorian and neo-Victorian texts into the integral whole, as it

> replaces the search for meaning as generated by the unity of an individual text (. . .) with analysis of meaning as "something which exists between a text and all the other texts to which it refers and relates, moving out from the independent text into a network of textual relations." [Allen 2002:1] (Kucała, 37)

Thus, while dialogism binds texts together in a dialogue of equally privileged voices, intertextuality explores the meanings originating between texts. In *History and Poetics of Intertextuality*, Marko Juvan investigates the sources of the term "intertextuality." He understands intertextuality "by its natural linguistic logic" as "relations between texts," "interweaving of texts," "weaving of one text into another," "connectedness and interdependence of at least two related texts," "the characteristic of a text of establishing a relation with (an)other text(s) or having another or multiple texts woven into it" or "inter-relatedness or interaction of texts" (13).[1]

According to Kucała, intertextual approaches generally branch out into those focusing on the all-encompassing fragmentation of texts (disintegrative orientations) and those acknowledging the codependent textual affinity of works originating from the authorial impulse (integrative orientations) (38). "The former," Kucała claims,

> initiated and developed by the French theorists, stresses the role of textual relations as a centrifugal force, decentring the text and disintegrating its meaning. The latter, centripetal orientation, while acknowledging the basic role of textual

relations in constituting the meaning of an individual text, nevertheless strives to consolidate this meaning by focusing the analysis back on the given text and delineating its limits, if only for the sake of analytical viability. (38)

The term "intertextuality," in its "centrifugal," disruptive form, was used by Julia Kristeva in her "Word, Dialogue, and Novel" in 1966. Drawing on Bakhtin's thought, Kristeva argues that each text—perceived as a signifying structure—carries a plurality of meanings while analyzed (each time) against a different background. According to Kristeva, the "stabilization" of meaning implies a serious threat manifesting itself in the birth of ideology. It appears to be the cornerstone which draws Bakhtin's philosophy and Kristeva's thought together. Yet, although decidedly influenced by Bakhtin, Kristeva derives the basis for her theory from various sources. She builds her new mode of semiotics—semianalysis—based not only on Bakhtin's "double-voicedness," but also on Ferdinand de Saussure's study of anagrams, Sigmund Freud's psychoanalysis, and Karl Marx's notion of production (Allen, 34). Such diversity of sources allows Kristeva to expand her study beyond the boundaries of the literary world, as she refuses to work with the term "literature" as such. For Kristeva, the term "literature" appears to be loaded with ideological weight and burdened with the process of inevitable selection, while "poetic language" embraces the layers of meanings that she strives to discover (Kristeva, 5). The vast discrepancy between Bakhtin's concern with the novel and Kristeva's preoccupation with the "poetic language" is thus discernible prima facie. Kristeva employs original Bakhtinian thought in the intertextual context which steps beyond the literary framework, reaching toward the vast area of semiotic research. While incorporating intertextuality into the overly broad theoretical spectrum, Kristeva questions the safe assumption that the origins of a given work can be attributed to an individual. Marko Juvan maintains that the vision of the text unleashed from the temporal and spatial dimension, devoid of authorship and creative influence, may be threatening to those readers who are accustomed to the "traditional" perception of the reading process:

> it would be difficult to convince such a reader, hardbound book in hand, that the text is boundless and that other texts and discourses intrude amid the printed lines. . . . A book functions as a clearly delimited whole and presence. (1)

According to Kucała, Gérard Genette's intertextual theory appears to be "the most systematic and elaborate methodology for studying intertextuality" (40). I also believe that Genette's theory enables a thorough yet flexible classification and analysis of Victorian and neo-Victorian novels. Genette assumes that literary works are, in a specific sense not original and should be treated as specimens of a confined system (Allen, 96). His theory is based on the assumption that, even though authors create and bring to literary life their individual, unique plots, characters, ideas, and perspectives, these had already appeared in literary history in some form or emerged as a consequence of a conscious or unconscious dialogue with previous texts. Genette coins the term "open structuralism," described by Allen as

> a poetics which gives up on the idea of establishing a stable, ahistorical, irrefutable map or division of literary elements, but which instead studies the relationships (sometimes fluid, never unchanging) which link the text with the architextual network out of which it produces its meaning. (100)

As Genette states in *Palimpsests*, open structuralism offers an opportunity for the "relational reading" (399), the concept which appears equally valid in the process of re-narrating the Victorian works in the neo-Victorian vein. The title of Genette's work (*Palimpsests*) stems from his assumption concerning the palimpsestuous nature of texts: "on the same parchment, one text can become superimposed upon another, which it does not quite conceal but allows to show through" (398–99). The palimpsestuous nature of neo-Victorian texts is also recognized by Mark Llewellyn in his article "What is Neo-Victorian Studies?" Genette's palimpsestuous vision of texts appears congruent with Llewellyn's perception of neo-Victorian fiction and can be readily applied to the analysis of the neo-Victorian genre.

Genette investigates the interdependency between the emerging texts and the notion of the "architext"—the "basic, unchanging" concept of the text embodying the foundation of the literary system (Allen, 100).

In *Palimpsests*, he introduces the notion of transtextuality, the concept of apparent or veiled relationality between texts, dividing it respectively into five subcategories: architextuality, intertextuality,[2] metatextuality, paratextuality,

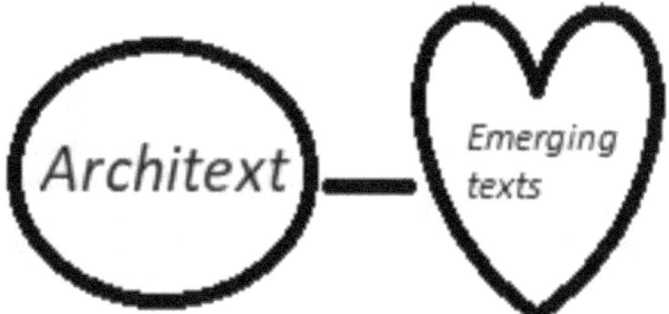

Figure 2.1. Architext vs. Emerging Texts—*sensu* Genette. *Drawing by Aleksandra Tryniecka.*

and hypertextuality. In *The Architext*, Genette comments on transtextuality in the following manner: "*for the moment* the text interests me (only) in its *textual transcendence*—namely, everything that brings it into relation (manifest or hidden) with other texts" (81). Architextuality stands for Genette's paramount term regulating the relations between the entire range of texts. As he states in *Palimpsests*, it is the category "the most abstract and implicit of all" (4). Architextuality recognizes texts as belonging to genres and categories. Importantly, Genette negates the structuralist notion of the closed, orderly relations between the "building blocks" of the text by describing the architext as a semi-web endowed with fuzzy boundaries.

Another subcategory, metatextuality, Genette indicates, "is the relationship most often labeled as 'commentary.' It unites a given text to another, of which it speaks without necessarily citing it (without summoning it), in fact sometimes even without naming it" (4). The function of metatextuality proves invaluable in the process of internalizing texts by the reader, since metatextuality prepares one for the reception of the text and, simultaneously, forms expectations and reading strategies. The insertion of a metatextual commentary appears especially significant in neo-Victorian works which require from the potential reader specific background knowledge in order to become thoroughly "appropriated" and "absorbed."

Naturally, it is possible to read and appreciate neo-Victorian works without knowledge of the previous texts to which they are referring, yet full appreciation of modern, revisionary work, as well as full appreciation of the literary Victorian past, comes with the broader understanding of metatextual commentaries. Such is the case with Charlotte Brontë's *Jane Eyre* and Jean Rhys's *Wide Sargasso Sea*, where the latter offers a metatextual commentary on the previous text. In Rhys's novel, there are no direct references to Charlotte Brontë or to the title of her work, yet there is a constant literary dialogue maintained through the plot, symbols, and characters, pointing directly at *Jane Eyre*. Even though it is Rhys's text commenting on Brontë's novel, I call this metatextual commentary a "dialogue," because both of the texts are transformed and enriched in this process. Metatextual commentaries appear in the text either as clear indicators or subtle hints, yet always remodeling the architextual web; that is, reorganizing texts. Another subcategory of transtextuality is paratextuality: "the paratext . . . marks those elements which lie *on the threshold of the text* and which help to direct and control the reception of a text by its readers" [emphasis added] (Allen, 103). Paratexts also involve: "a title, a subtitle, intertitles; prefaces, postfaces, notices, forewords, etc; marginal, infrapaginal, terminal notes; epigraphs; illustrations; blurbs, book covers, dust jackets, and many other kinds of secondary signals" (Genette, *Palimpsests*, 3). Even though the reader tends to omit these elements, thus treating them in a "secondary" manner, they might be, in fact, of the utmost importance for the understanding of a given text. The notion of paratextuality is especially relevant in the study of neo-Victorian texts, where it can be applied, for example, to the analysis of prefaces (*peritexts*). Preface in the neo-Victorian novel orientates one in the reading process—it provides an intentional hint regarding the reading of the text. For instance, in Syrie James's semibiographical novel *The Secret Diaries of Charlotte Brontë*, the preface provides a direct clue that the text should be read as a fictionalized biography. Moreover, preface reflects on the nature of neo-Victorian texts, highlighting their attempt at revisioning the precedent narratives. In neo-Victorian novels, the paratext is usually created intentionally by the author, acting as a deliberate and integral part of the novel. In this sense, it is not detached from the overall work. Hence, I propose my own term—"authorial paratextuality"—to indicate the paratexts intentionally created by authors that draw the reader's attention to the revisionary task of the neo-Victorian genre and, simultaneously, constitute an indissoluble and integral part of the main text. In his work *Paratexts: Thresholds of Interpretations*, Genette uses a term similar to "authorial paratextuality." Mainly, he discusses "*authorial*, or *autographic*, preface" (178).[3]

Hypertextuality constitutes yet another variant of transtextuality. "By hypertextuality," Genette states in *Palimpsests*, "I mean relationship uniting a text B (which I shall call the *hypertext*) to an earlier text A (I shall, of course, call it the *hypotext*), upon which it is grafted in a manner that is not that of commentary" (5).[4] Hypertextuality can be used for the investigation of the differences underlying neo-Victorian and Victorian texts. Hypertextuality may be theoretically confused with architextuality, as both these notions deal with references to previous texts. However, architextuality designates texts belonging to a particular genre, while hypertextuality deals with the relations between the texts where the subsequent one is modified for a certain reason; (resulting, for instance, in a parody or pastiche) (Allen, 108). Genette emphasizes that certain *hypotexts* (the texts to which *hypertexts* respond) appear to be lost and cannot be rediscovered with ease. However, he assumes that hypertextuality is present in all literary works.

It appears that Genette's theory has a substantial potential for linking the Victorian texts with neo-Victorian works. Genette's theory does not insist on the ultimate classification of texts. Still, it operates within the boundaries of scientific classification, while hypothesizing that each *hypertext* possesses its *hypotext*, while the entire literary system is founded on the architextual basis. While Genette introduces other extensive theoretical divisions, their concerns go beyond the subject of this work. However, the notion of transtextual interrelationship between texts appears especially significant in my study of women literary characters in both Victorian and neo-Victorian novels, because it allows for constructing interdependent relations between the nineteenth-century and modern characters.

The notion of intertextuality has been widely discussed by Polish scholars as well, including Michał Głowiński, Ryszard Nycz, Henryk Markiewicz, and Stanisław Balbus. In *Tekstowy Świat: Poststrukturalizm a wiedza o literaturze (Textual World: Post-Structuralism and Literary Criticism)*, Ryszard Nycz discusses three fundamental intertextual relations: "text-text," "text-genre," and "text-reality" (95). The third relation deserves particular attention, as it touches upon the notion of "reality," which can be understood as the subject's experience. As Nycz argues, one can detect in the "text-reality" dependency the opportunity to analyze associations of literary texts with social, historical, and cultural contexts (95). Marko Juvan argues that "Ryszard Nycz . . . concludes justly that intertextual research is a good example of postmodern theoretical discourse: today literary theory is decidedly displaced from the position of objective and universal knowledge to the relative periphery of historically contingent utterances" (6). A similar conclusion stems from Kucała's observation: "defending intertextuality, Ryszard Nycz argues that its rapid entry into the critical vocabulary seems to testify to a previous terminological void exposing the insufficiency of the traditional study of influence (2000: 79–82)" (33). Whereas "influence" indicates a one-directional impact, intertextuality entails the codependent existence of the anterior and subsequent texts.[5]

In light of Nycz's treatment of intertextuality, texts can be perceived as representations of individual experiences framed by the sociocultural and historical context. Arguing along these lines, Victorian fiction immortalizes these experiences from the nineteenth-century standpoint, while neo-Victorian texts mirror and revive these experiences in the modern vein.

A similar notion of intertextuality as a "dialogic relationship" is offered in Heidi Hansson's study. Moreover, Hansson stresses the involvement of the reader in the act of assimilating the text: "without the reader's desire for complete comprehension, intertextual play cannot exist" (22). In Hansson's view, the potential reader is expected to be acquainted with the previous and subsequent text in order to form possible associations between the two. What is more, Hansson claims, the working of intertextuality can entirely escape the reader's attention, particularly while it is not "physically locatable," but can also represent "cultural phenomena or genre-based criteria as well as actual texts" (24) (cf. Nycz).[6]

While Hansson points to these theoretical shortcomings of the term, Marko Juvan examines both the transforming power and limitations of intertextuality:

on the one hand, [intertextuality] has functioned as a law, a historical code, and a prisonhouse that controls cultural ideology, dictating semantic and structural dispositions to each new text; on the other, it has been a key to transgression, a means of undoing conventions. (14)

Discussing the "double-facedness" of intertextuality, Juvan's considerations imply the question of ideology. Intertextuality—the notion seemingly liberating from the chains of a dominant discourse—appears equally enslaved by it, Juvan posits. According to Juvan, as soon as intertextuality enters a given scientific discourse, it becomes classified and defined. In this sense, it reshapes into an ideology itself. Yet, Juvan also suggests that relying on conventions appears indispensable for the formation of any future concepts and for the sake of structuring ideas (15). Thus, on the one hand, intertextuality falls into a trap of what it tries to avoid—its reliance on the previously sanctioned discourse. On the other hand, this reliance contributes to the establishment of new discourses as well.

NOTES

1. As Juvan indicates, "although the word intertextuality can be attributed to Kristeva, forms from the same word family are much older and were attested in classical Latin; however, these words never functioned as abstract nouns, a fact that was essential for the modern conversion of the word into a theoretical concept in Kristeva's work. The words intertextus, -a, -um ('woven in, tied in, woven through') are past participles of the verb intertexto ('weave in, place inside, join') and were in their adjectival forms associated with literature (Arrivé 13)" (12). According to Juvan, the term "intertext" initially appears in Ovid's story of Arachne.

2. Positioning intertextuality as another form of transtextuality, Genette apparently expurgates Kristeva's concept, constricting it to the narrow literary scope of "quotation, plagiarism and allusion" (Allen, 101): "*intertextuality* in the strict (and, since Julia Kristeva, the 'classical') sense—that is, the literal presence (more or less literal, whether integral or not) of one text within another. Quotation—that is, the explicit summoning up of a text that is both presented and distanced by quotation marks—is the most obvious example of this type of function, which comprises many others as well" (Genette, *The Architext*, 81–82).

3. In *Paratexts*, Genette examines different kinds of prefaces which are dependent on the figure of the author: "the alleged author of a preface may be the author (real or alleged, hence some twists and turns in perspective) of the text: this very common situation we will call the *authorial*, or *autographic* preface. Or the alleged author of a preface may be one of the characters in the action, when there are characters and action: this is the *actorial* preface. Or the alleged author of a preface may be a wholly different (third) person: the *allographic* preface. . . . A preface may be attributed to a real person or to a fictive person. If the attribution to a real person is confirmed

by some other (if possible, by *every* other) paratextual sign, we will call the preface *authentic*. If the attribution to a real person is invalidated by some paratextual sign, we will call the preface *apocryphal*. And if the person to whom the preface is attributed is fictive, we will call the attribution, and therefore the preface, *fictive*" (178–79).

4. While Kristeva's intertextuality deals with the inclusion of the traces of earlier texts within the space of the subsequent one, Genette clearly points out to the *text A—text B relation*, highlighting both the separateness and interdependence of these texts.

5. Heidi Hansson addresses the distinction between intertextuality and "other kinds of associations between texts," including the concept of influence: "if a writer is influenced by previous writing, or uses an older text as a source, does that constitute an intertextual connection? Certainly, but the terminology is misleading. 'Influence' is generally understood as one-directional, whereas intertextuality affects both the dominant and the incorporated text. Influence, moreover, can be pure imitation without making a point, whereas a consciously installed intertext will add something to the primary text." (25)

6. Following this line of argumentation, it seems that the text is what originates in the space between the written lines and the reader's mind. For instance, Clare Boylan's neo-Victorian novel, *Emma Brown* (2003), includes two chapters originally written by Charlotte Brontë in 1853 and meant to begin her never-finished novel *Emma*. The title of the novel encourages one to form connections between Brontë's unfinished work and Boylan's elaboration on the initial plot. Nevertheless, in order to recognize the intertext, the potential reader is expected to possess sufficient knowledge of Charlotte Brontë's life and literary creations. Hence, the readers acquainted with the story of Brontë's unfinished novel will read Boylan's text differently from those ignorant of the context in which the novel appeared. Describing her work, Boylan remarks that the character of Mrs. Chalfont (the leading narrator of the plot) bears resemblance to Charlotte Brontë and to Charlotte's friend, Ellen Nussey. Boylan explains that while introducing Mrs. Chalfont's exquisite narrative, she had in mind Brontë's brilliant correspondence. Therefore, as the author, she strove to endow the novel with "some of [Charlotte's] tone" (*Emma Brown*, 444). However, the "reading" and decoding of the references appearing in the text strictly depends on the reader's knowledge.

Chapter Three

Intertextuality in Practice
Examining the Literary World

In this book, I shall implement Nycz's intertextual approach including three types of relations between the texts, texts-genres and texts-reality. Moreover, I shall adopt Genette's transtextual classification, which offers a practical tool for the analysis of the selected, intertextually-positioned works. I shall also draw on Heidi Hansson's understanding of intertextuality as a "dialogue between texts" which originates as a result of the reader's active and conscious engagement in the reading process (22). The connections between the Victorian and neo-Victorian works discussed in this book are based on the *intertextually generated context, intertextually triggered correlations*, and *bidirectional influence* between the texts. This work is narrowed down to a selected number of texts which, as I believe, mirror the literary transitions of the novelistic genre, reaching from the nineteenth-century literary environment toward the modern revisionary landscape.

In my analysis, Wilkie Collins's *The Woman in White* (1959) serves as an iconic example of the nineteenth-century novel portraying the uniqueness and unconventionality of the woman character in a protomodern vein. Collins, alongside with Anthony Trollope, counted among the few of the Victorian male writers who profoundly engaged in the subject of socially restrained femininity. Whereas Collins's protagonist, Anne Catherick, may be perceived as an outsider and an insane individual unleashed from safeguarding social constraints, she may as well epitomize women's struggle for independence and self-reliance. Currently, this struggle is relocated to modern texts which adhere to the problematique from the nineteenth century in order to transcribe the present.

The bidirectional influence stemming from the "text *versus* text" relation is easily discernible in Jean Rhys's postcolonial novel, *Wide Sargasso Sea* (1966), in which the protagonist, Antoinette, stands for the textual reincarnation of Bertha Mason—the so-far ignored "prisoner in the attic" from

Charlotte Brontë's *Jane Eyre* (1847). While, on the one hand, *Jane Eyre* influenced the creation of *Wide Sargasso Sea*, Rhys's novel endowed Brontë's work with a fresh, revisionary meaning, on the other. By re-narrating the story of a forsaken and supposedly insane character, Rhys demonstrates that intertextual influence remains essentially bidirectional, reaching both toward the past and the future.

The intertextual relations between texts established on the generic level can be re-created on the example of neo-Victorian biofiction, which, drawing on the historical sources, constructs fictionalized narratives of the Victorian historical figures. Syrie James's *The Secret Diaries of Charlotte Brontë* (2009) skillfully merges Charlotte Brontë's biographical sources with a fictionalized narrative. At the same time, James makes efforts not to extend her narrative beyond the a priori existent biographical "facts." The fictionalized biography of Charlotte Brontë bridges the gap between the past and the present, portraying the heroine as an ordinary woman who struggles with everyday problems. The first-person narration (Charlotte speaking "for herself") approximates the reader to the heroine's nineteenth-century zone and allows for the historical recognition of Brontë as an actual Victorian writer.

The "text-reality" relation is discernible on the pages of Gail Carriger's *Soulless* (2009),[1] as the novel offers a futuristic blend of the twenty-first century high-tech landscape with the conventional Victorian environment. Although the blend results in a surrealistic vision of nineteenth-century London, it also creates an innovative, literary world from the "patchwork" of the past and present textual landscapes. Hence, Carriger's fiction highlights the transformative impact of intertextual literary reworkings.

The "paratextual intertextuality," which enriches such works as Clare Boylan's *Emma Brown* (2003) and the aforementioned *The Secret Diaries*, also presents neo-Victorian writing in its transformative context, reaching directly toward the past in order to invite the reader to dialogically embrace the text. Both *Emma Brown* and *The Secret Diaries* are endowed with prefaces that allow one to consciously approach these works from an intertextual angle.

The works discussed here not only reflect the transformative potential of the novelistic genre per se, but also highlight the diversity of authors participating in the revisionary, modern writing. Neo-Victorian literary revision developed into a worldwide phenomenon: for instance, it currently engages such American writers as Syrie James or Gail Carriger. Whereas James recounts the life of one of the most ingenious English female novelists, Carriger reaches for a nineteenth-century London setting in order to fill it with the twenty-first-century thought. It is especially intriguing to think about neo-Victorian texts as interwoven into the steampunk genre (as in the case of Carriger's fiction), which blends the use of futuristic technology with an unquenched longing for the bygone. As Jeff VanderMeer briefly puts it, steampunk equals

> Mad Scientist Inventor [invention (steam x airship or metal man/ baroque stylings) x (pseudo) Victorian setting] + progressive or reactionary politics x adventure plot. (9)

Such "steampunk equation" confirms the validity of Gutleben's claim that in order to reach further into the future, one needs to move backward and draw from the literary past: it is the point that both halts and inspires one to engage in the modern, intertextual exchange of literary voices. Carriger's literary success can be encapsulated in the statement featured on her official website:

> *The Parasol Protectorate* books have been translated into over a dozen different languages, won several awards, turned into graphic novels, and been optioned for TV. They have made appearances on the Mass Market, Manga, Combined Print and eBook, and eBook New York Times Bestseller lists. (http://gailcarriger .com/series/the-parasol-protectorate/)

Hence, since steampunk fiction makes its way into the metamorphosing literary culture, it appears indispensable to acknowledge its expanding existence. The postmodern landscape relocates the "Victorians" into other regions (such as America), eagerly embracing ongoing transformations in the readerly culture (for instance, the appearance of graphic novels, ebooks, and manga which elaborate on the Victorian era).

Importantly, in this work, the intertextual portraits of literary women, emerging from the dialogue between the selected Victorian and neo-Victorian texts, provide an apt commentary on the readers' and authors' changing perspectives. The women characters presented in this book epitomize the Victorian/neo-Victorian dialogue since, in their case, the intertextual "exchange" finds expression on numerous levels: in the depiction of their mental constitution, in their social position, and in the projection of their textual garments. Therefore, I argue that the literary female characters exemplify the ever-developing, open concept which readily responds to the transforming sociocultural environment outside the literary boundaries as well. Modern transformations of female characters in neo-Victorian fiction exemplify the changes in twenty-first-century society. Hence, as this dialogically constructed study shall argue, neo-Victorian women are "self-made" and fully independent from others (in contrast to their Victorian counterparts, molded within the context of their nineteenth-century family). Moreover, as this study shows, neo-Victorian female characters are capable of constructing their own lives and narratives without the involvement of the third party, as happens in the case of nineteenth-century female protagonists.

There have been a number of studies devoted to Victorian and neo-Victorian fiction, based on the intertextual and dialogical approach. However, while offering an overview of critical issues related to the Victorian and neo-Victorian texts, these studies very often fail to focus on the relation between the nineteenth-century and modern literary heroines. The aim of my work therefore is to add a new perspective to the existing Neo-Victorian body of research. While employing dialogism and intertextuality, the study is meant not to merely bridge the gap between the Victorian and modern times, but, in particular, to offer a unique portrait of the literary femininity. It is important to note that while we are fully aware of the existence of gender theories and the wide body of feminist criticism, this study adopts, let us reiterate, an intertextual, dialogical perspective on Victorian and neo-Victorian literary women—the perspective concentrating on different aspects of femininity, including identity, voice, apparel, and social context. On the whole, the aim of this work is to offer an expanded vision of literary femininity as portrayed on the pages of selected Victorian and neo-Victorian texts.

NOTES

1. The first, opening novel from *The Parasol Protectorate* series.

Chapter Four

The Novel Domesticated in the Victorian World

Undoubtedly, neo-Victorian discourse has gradually become the part of our readerly reality. Books situated in the nineteenth-century context, prequels, sequels, and plots referring to the Victorian past are becoming increasingly popular. What is it that we, the readers from the twenty-first century, are feeling drawn to the Victorian past?

Neo-Victorian discourse initially subverts the literary past, yet its ultimate task lies in the restoration of this past to the present-day readerly consciousness. Thus, it re-creates the past, placing it within the present-day context, furthermore molding our understanding of both the past and the present. On the other hand, diving into the literary Victorian world allows one to catch a glimpse of the sociocultural context of the era. In order to better understand the phenomenon of neo-Victorian literature, it is indispensable to return to the nineteenth century and to the history of the novel itself—the novel which re-creates the multifaceted image of the Victorian woman as perceived by nineteenth-century society.

Contemporary reading habits were formed, to a large extent, in the Victorian age. They originated in an expanding, class-divided society and thus remained responsive to social issues. "The most interesting form of the nineteenth century . . . is 'society' itself," Elizabeth Deeds Ermarth observes (123) and, in the nineteenth century, it is precisely society which turned into the central force driving the development of the novel, as well as the context of its origins. In her preface to *The English Novel in History: 1840–1895*, Ermarth states that the Victorian novel treats the "construction of history as a social common denominator" (vii). Furthermore, she notices that "novels especially constitute experimental laboratories for defining and exploring a new construction of corporate order" (vii). Novels allow one to characterize, construct, and reconstruct social realities and historical moments defining cultures and nations. It is from the literary sources that we derive information about the Victorian past and it is through literature that we shape our understanding of the past oftentimes unreachable in other ways. Similarly, Patrick Brantlinger and William B. Thesing posit in *A Companion to the Victorian Novel* that nineteenth-century fiction "has influenced and will continue to influence modern and postmodern culture and society" (7). The interplay between the past and the present provides an inspiring ground for exploring the Victorian period afresh, with a view to finding common links binding contemporaneity with the bygone.

The Victorian era conventionally stretches between 1837 and 1901,[1] highlighting the years of Queen Victoria's reign. As aptly noted by Charles Dickens, "it was the best of times, it was the worst of times" (Dennis, 10). As the "best of times," the Victorian age witnessed sweeping socio-technological changes which encouraged new forms of mobility. As the "worst of times," it was marked by double standards, cultural crisis, uncertainties, and sociopolitical unrest. Victorian anxieties, daily concerns, and significant changes—including social struggles, economic unrest, the appearance of liberalism, and a free market, but also homelessness or displacement—were meticulously reflected in the novel of the epoch. The Victorian period witnessed the emergence of the readerly "novel-oriented community," as novels became the mainstay of nineteenth-century publishing, offering a new literary experience in the private sphere of life[2] (Brantlinger, 3). The rising interest in the realist novel was especially marked by the nineteenth-century industrial revolution, the expansion of the press, and the rise of the middle class, which triggered the emergence of a new protagonist with whom the new readers could identify. As Ian Watt posits,

> the novel is the form of literature which most fully reflects this individualist and innovating reorientation. Previous literary forms had reflected the general tendency of their cultures to make conformity to traditional practice the major test of truth: the plots of classical or renaissance epic, for example, were based on the past history or fable, and the merits of the author's treatment were judged largely according to a view of literary decorum derived from the accepted models in the genre. This literary traditionalism was first and most fully challenged by the novel, whose primary criterion was truth to individual experience. (13)

Despite their focus on relatable, individual experiences, novels still had been looked upon as controversial until the beginning of the Victorian era and even years later.[3] Brantlinger and Thesing argue that only "by the 1840s novel-reading was growing more socially acceptable" (3). As acknowledged by Firdous Azim in her *The Colonial Rise of the Novel*, reading habits evolved together with the transformation of the novelistic content: "the leap from *Robinson Crusoe* (1719) to *Pamela* (1740–1) or *Clarissa* (1748–9) marks the transition of the novel into the more domestic and homely domain" (61). Consequently, she posits, "the novel has been seen as a heterogeneous form of writing, straddling 'fictional' and 'factual' discursive terms" (93): it presented the inner (fictional, imaginary) reality of the characters, as well as the outer (factual, nineteenth-century) world.

The positive change in the perception of the novel in the Victorian era was initiated by the establishment of Mudie's Select Circulating Library (1842) (Brantlinger, Thesing, 3). Charles Edward Mudie's library collection included novels which both cultivated the reader's mind and were appropriate for family reading. According to Barbara Dennis, Mudie's lending library presented an opportunity for middle-class readers to indulge in the literary world at an affordable price (Dennis, 64).

Yet, alongisde "respectable literary works," another branch of novels appeared in the form of "downscale street literature" referred to as "broadsides," evoking both thrill and indignation (Brantlinger, 4). Paradoxically, the "downscale novels" enjoyed good publicity and incorporated such "bestsellers" as G. W. M. Reynolds's *Mysteries of London* (1840s), in which the author regaled his readers with a "muckraking tourguide of London's underworld and nightlife" (4).

As Dennis argues, the development of reading habits was simultaneously enhanced by the growth of the new means of transportation: "'the railway boom' between 1844 and 1847 gave a great boost to the fortunes of the lending library and a captive market to Mudie" (64). As a result, books became an easily available commodity. The novelistic market grew competitive and gradually prepared to cater to diversified kinds of recipients, including middle-class readers as well as the members of the lower classes. The readerly expansion paved the way for another competing "subcategory": the so-called "railway novels" or "yellowbacks," which generally constituted "translations or reprints" of other works (Brantlinger and Thesing, 5). Together with "railway novels," there appeared "railway bookstalls," established by Mudie's competitor, W. H. Smith.[4]

The above-mentioned developments contributed to the transformation of Victorian society. The novel not only offered the lure of income to potential authors and publishing companies but also shaped the sociocultural mood of the period. The economically and mentally transforming society played an active part in the writerly process as well, providing a repository of ideas for the authors, while eagerly discussing their works. At last, novel-reading began to reign in the center of the sociocultural world and, as Brantlinger and Thesing pertinently remark, it "was as controversial as television-watching today" (2); or, shall we say, it was as popular as streaming movies these days. Furthermore, they claim that "although we now take for granted that libraries should have novels in their collections, for the Victorians, whether or not the

Figure 4.1. "Going to Mudie's." *London Society* v. 16, no. 95, November 1869.

Figure 4.2. Opening number of G. W. M. Reynolds's *Mysteries of the Court of London* (1849-1856).

first public libraries should acquire works of fiction was hotly debated" (2). Novel-reading triggered a new set of habits and social behaviors: it resulted in establishing a special bond between readers, authors, and critics. Society began to play the role of a literary critic as well, contributing thereby to the author's potential failure or success. As Azim observes, "the shift from eighteenth-century novelistic concepts of reality to the nineteenth-century emphasis on social realism, is extended to include the reader in active collusion with the writing" (98). The author-reader relationship was particularly strong in the case of those novels which appeared in installments (as, for example, Dickens's *Pickwick Papers*). Installments prompted the anticipation of the so-far unpublished parts of the novel and reshaped the reading process into a confidential "encounter" with the author, as it was often possible for the readers to influence the future plot. The author-reader relations were reciprocal: Victorian readers would discuss the appearing novels, while writers would offer "guidance and direction" on the pages of their literary creations: "through the imaginative depiction of other worlds and characters, the Victorian reader was given access to the reality of feelings and moral issues outside his/her individual experience. Novelists offered reassurance, and often took on the role of sage and mentor," Dennis posits (53).

Such bidirectional exchange between authors and readers can be observed in Charlotte Brontë's life: while the publications of Brontë's works were eagerly anticipated and prompted animated discussions, she felt anxious about them, especially worrying that the texts might reveal too much about her private affairs, or even reveal some traces of her personality. After the first publication (1847), Charlotte Brontë wrote: "*Jane Eyre* will be read by J—B—, by Mrs T—, and B—. Heaven help, keep and deliver me!" (Gaskell, 396).

Indeed, there were investigative readers who evinced a particular interest in the authoress's life, trying to combine the novelistic events with the "facts" concerning Brontë's life. After the publication of *Shirley* (1849), Catherine Winkworth (a reader) wrote to her friend, commenting on the "unhappy tone" of the novel:

> That is not . . . so much to be wondered at, when one knows that the author is *herself* threatened with consumption at this time, and has lost *her* two sisters, Ellis and Acton Bell by it. Their real name is Brontë, they are of the Nelson family. (Gérin, 402–3)

Oftentimes, the plot of the novel, as well as authorial identity, would prove equally important to the readers. The Victorian era witnessed the rise of several literary superstars, including Charles Dickens and Oscar Wilde, who played active roles in their readers' lives not only through the "written word," but also through interactions with the reading audience. The celebrated Victorian writers were vivid and unforgettable figures not to be mistaken for anyone else. They inscribed themselves into literary history thanks to their indelible personalities and unmatched brilliance—not only as writers, but also as individuals. For instance, Dickens, one of the currently most iconic and recognizable representatives of the Victorian literary world, "was invariably the leader whose energy and purposefulness would have irritated less tractable companions," states Peter Ackroyd while discussing Wilkie Collins's holiday with the Dickens family in Boulogne in 1853, "he was the inspirer, the organiser, of the enterprise" (55). Dickens's radiating energy, his intended perfectionism, and his sense of purpose are discernible both in his

Figure 4.3. Charlotte Brontë. Nineteenth-century engraving by William Jackman (Public Domain).

life and in his writing. The Victorian writers were as fascinating to their readers as the works they produced. Not influenced by such contemporary means of communication as social media or film industry, the nineteenth-century literary world thrived on interconnections between authors, their works, and the reading audience.

Reading enabled one not only to catch a glimpse of the author's life, but also to relocate to fictional "reality" and experience this reality by means of imagination. The quality of "mental travel" made the novel attractive enough to enter the domestic sphere and bring the Victorian family together through a shared reading. The inner, mental journey proved to be a rare opportunity for those Victorian women whose world revolved around the "domestic bliss" and daily pastime in a parlor.[5]

In the nineteenth century, the novel gradually attained the function of the major social mentor initiating vivid social discussions over the pending issues. As already indicated, the novel was no longer a literary work removed from the actual world. Instead, it mimicked social reality and offered guidance concerning the norms of behavior. Thus, Victorian fiction enabled the reader to negotiate its culturally invested meaning. During the nineteenth century, it dialogically mirrored the Victorian world, stepping in on educational grounds as well and criticizing the tyrannical didactic methods which often relied, according to Nicholas Dame, on "brutal and repetitive ways . . . 'associations' or mental pathways" (O'Gorman, 95). "Associations," in Victorian terms, signified the processes generated in the mind by the senses rather than by cognitive actions (O'Gorman, 96–97). This assumption lent support to the claim that adolescent minds resembled unwritten pages gradually filled with content (by educational institutions). Such an approach offered teachers infinite power over pupils, propounding that "mental life consist[ed] entirely of sensory data which, via a vast series of associations with other sensations, became 'ideas'" and could be trained by means of repetitive actions (95).[6]

At the end of the century, associationism[7] shifted toward yet another view, asserting a "gradual declension in the power and centrality of conscious processes and the human will" (O'Gorman, 110). This claim, portraying one's inner life as suspended in a doubtful and elusive existence, resulted in such creations as Thomas Hardy's *Tess of the d'Urbervilles* (1891) and *Jude the Obscure* (1895). The conviction concerning one's precarious fate and the lack of control over one's existence influenced the general understanding of the concept of nature which suddenly reshaped into a hostile and unpredictable phenomenon. As noted by Ermarth,

> before mid-century, "nature" generally appears in novels as something hospitable to human aspirations. Fifty years later, nature generally appears in narrative, to the extent it appears at all, as something inhospitable to human meaning. . . . Great moralists like Charlotte Brontë or William Thackeray seek

justification in nature, while George Eliot or Anthony Trollope refer all questions of moral agency and social justice to entirely socialized human action. Towards the end of the century, these ambiguities between natural and social explanation resurface in Thomas Hardy to serve an essentially tragic vision of nature. (3)

This despondent attitude toward the concept of nature resulted in a literary debate over one's fate and place in the socially constructed, yet nature-dependent world. The growing interest in reading was combined with the Victorian fascination with psychology, which encompassed a profusion of disciplines, including "natural history, Lockean philosophy, chemistry, evolutionary science, medicine, . . . fiction and literary criticism" (O'Gorman, 93). These "psychological" studies, as mentioned before, were soon married to education, and the novel began to signify a "part of the story of psychology" (O'Gorman, 94). Simultaneously, fiction became responsible for shaping the reader's mind. According to Dame, in the Victorian age, "the importance given to the educator, the power he or she theoretically possessed, was potentially infinite" (O'Gorman, 95). The novel was gradually exerting such power as well, as it finally reshaped into a respected component of the Victorian social life.

NOTES

1. In the literal, formal sense, the Victorian era is associated with the time of Queen Victoria's reign. Yet, "Victorian traces" can be found in the 1830s, as well as after Queen Victoria's death. The Victorian era, as any other epoch, is characterized by "fuzzy" boundaries. Francis O'Gorman postulates in the introduction to *The Cambridge Companion to Victorian Culture* that the adjective "Victorian" remains "parochial" (3). According to him, "it is monarchical, too—it suggests an aristocratic history rather than one about all classes and social divisions. It is plainly fortuitous rather than necessary: why should the reign of a single constitutional monarch, albeit a long one, cover a period that was distinctive from what came before and what came after?" (3). Furthermore, O'Gorman posits: "what is 'history,' what makes up the contents of a 'historical' account, is the product of after-the-event decisions about the objects of analysis: 'history' as a discourse is created by the act of drawing out a narrative or structuring an argument from particular sets of data, from particular objects of concern" (4). O'Gorman points to a number of ways in which one can define the "Victorian." It can be achieved through, among many others, the analysis of the print culture, the "rise of the national newspaper" (4), the role and development of the middle class, the change in "an individual's sense of connections with others" (8), and the shift toward the scientific perception of the world (10). O'Gorman draws one's attention to dialogically cooperative narratives that mold the term "Victorian" while "propos[ing] different possible avenues into the stretch of historical time between 1830–1900" (10–11).

2. Mudie's Circulating Library "helped make novel-reading an acceptable family activity for many Victorians" (Brantlinger, 4).

3. Novel-reading was often regarded as "a waste of time" by even such enlightened figures as Thomas Carlyle (Brantlinger, 4). Much earlier, in the period between the 1760s and the 1830s, reading activity was treated as a "frivolous entertainment" (Brantlinger, 3).

4. Smith's young age during the time of his investment indicated a shift in the business prospects of the nineteenth-century burgeoning investors (Dennis, 64)—these were the budding and promising individuals who catered to the needs of the newly developing readerly community.

5. In Brontë's *Jane Eyre*, the heroine studies Bewick's *History of the British Birds* and is mentally transferred to a different realm, as the text shows: "the words in these introductory pages connected themselves with the succeeding vignettes, and gave significance to the rock standing up alone in a sea of billow and spray; to the broken boat stranded on a desolate coast; to the cold and ghostly moon glancing through bars of cloud at a wreck just sinking. . . . Each picture told a story; mysterious often to my undeveloped understanding and imperfect feelings, yet ever profoundly interesting" (7). The words evolve into vivid sketches in the heroine's mind, allowing her to participate in a mental, spiritually refining journey—an ennobling inner quest. Such a quest was possible for numerous women of the Victorian era who became avid readers.

6. A substantial critique of the education system can be found in Brontë's *Jane Eyre*, where the educational sphere represented by the Lowood school remains hostile and inhabited by narrow-minded, ruthless educators. In his study of "Psychology in the Victorian Novel," Dames propounds Dickens as another writer who argues in *Hard Times* (1854) along similar lines against the "dictatorial ambitions of teachers who believed in the passive blank slates of their pupils" (O'Gorman, 95).

7. Associationism relies on the idea that each thought originates from experience, whereas mental processes are triggered by means of associations. One of the representatives of the British "Associationist School," David Hume, advocated "a subtly constructivist theory of identity" (Garratt, 65). Associationism "gained support among the 'emergent community of middle-class, freethinking, urban radicalism' to which George Eliot and her contemporaries belonged" (Garratt, 64). At the same time, the notion of associationism disabled the advocacy of free will, as its "unbroken chain of ideas and impressions, causes and effects, appeared to leave no room for human agency, and in fact Hume explicitly referred to the synthesizing ego as a fiction. If the self was no more than the sum of its parts, . . . then all the volitional aspects of the human species—capacities such as will, choice and intention—could be explained away by the vagaries of associational trains and, by extension, the material social world responsible for impressing them. This picture of the mind (and, more broadly, the self or soul, was then, doubly deterministic, sacrificing personal agency to both psychological and environmental imperatives" (Garratt, 64).

Chapter Five

The Victorian Novel and Social Debate

> I think, too, that honest manliness is as necessary to us as feminine grace, and that vicious teaching mars the one as completely as it effaces the other. Does the reading of novels tend to mar the one or to efface the other? If so, for the love of heaven, let us have no more novel-reading. Let us, at any rate, make up our minds about it.
>
> —Anthony Trollope, *An Autobiography: And Other Writings* (244)

The Victorian age mirrors our present-day era in a number of ways. Taking into account the dialogue between the past and the present, it appears that, just like our society, nineteenth-century society was an ambivalent structure undergoing transformative changes especially visible at the end of the century. To some extent, it resembled our present-day society with its ambiguities and double standards, theatrical demands, and simultaneous hopes of honesty and authenticity, as well as with identity crises and moral dilemmas influencing economic choices and vice versa. While reflecting and commenting upon these ambiguities, the nineteenth-century novel continuously testifies to the Victorian nature of the modern world.

As mentioned in the previous chapter, in this book, literature comes into view as a sociocultural tool of standardization. "Literature, at one level, can be seen as history, as the fictions it creates reflect and express the stories and myths through which a nation and a culture choose to express themselves," Azim notes (214). As already argued, the relationship between society (nation) and the novel remains essentially reciprocal: whereas the emerging realist novel mirrors the reader's concerns, the nineteenth-century reader shapes its content through individual expectations, experiences, and perspectives.

The dominant social theme in Victorian fiction provides, as Ermarth claims, an "experiment" (123), since "thousands of social narratives exploring new social possibilities depended on a critical new sense of separation between society and 'nature'" (125). According to Ermarth, nineteenth-century fiction embraced the concept of "society," concentrating on its preliminary transformation and detachment from the natural world based on classifications and hierarchies. While at the onset of the nineteenth century the definition of "society" applied to those who were undisputedly "well-born" and "well-behaved" (123), this notion expanded in the 1850s, accommodating, as Ermarth posits, an "autonomous 'human' entity composed of the entire range of social groups and constituencies" (123):

> like a planetary body condensed from a cloud of cosmic dust, society appears in nineteenth-century narrative as an entity, and no longer as a hierarchical collection of sites in a "natural" order. Such a construction provides a new horizon of definition for individual and collective life. (125)

The Victorian novel significantly contributed to this transformation, creating common ground for negotiation between the concept of the fossilized class hierarchy and the notion of the new, emerging society—a fluid and changing entity created at that time. Such is the society mirrored in Anthony Trollope's 1871 *Lady Anna*, where aristocratic structures are reluctantly yet gradually giving way to the middle-class idea of a self-made man, and where the notion of marriage based on obligations and social status slowly yet surely reshapes into the idea of marriage based on one's choices.

Moreover, as numerous modern scholars highlight, including R. M. Friars and B. Ayers in their 2020 *Neo-Victorian Madness*, the Victorian period abounded in "ideological disparities" (58) especially externalized by the back then marginalized voices, currently resurrected in the neo-Victorian fiction. The marginalized voices of the Victorian era, including those of women, greatly contributed to the complex vision of the nineteenth-century society which, although gradually liberated from the fossilized hierarchy, still appeared to be a largely conflicted and transforming unit.

This new, dynamic notion of society triggered the literary interest in the so-far unexplored lifestyle: nineteenth-century writers depicted the new urban mode of life and the advanced possibilities of commuting, reflecting the expanding expectations of Victorian men and women. As the new urban lifestyle relied on movement, a regular railway passenger service was introduced in 1830. The year 1836 marked the appearance of the first train in London operating between London Bridge and Greenwich (O'Gorman, xv).

Although social mobility proved both promising and intimidating, it decidedly opened up new prospects not only for men, but also for some of the

Victorian women. The possibility of commuting and changing places temporarily allowed women to obtain a partial sense of privacy, independence and social unattainability. Such change is depicted, for example, in Wilkie Collins's *The Woman in White* (1859), where the heroine, Anne Catherick, escapes from the lunatic asylum and travels incognito to avoid social scrutiny. In Hardy's *Jude the Obscure* (1895), Sue Bridehead's commuting also introduces into her life the feeling of autonomy, but also that of restlessness. Commuting by train defines Sue as an unsettled character, without stable roots or the place of her own. In her case, the feeling of belonging is gradually lost in lonely escapism, which she nurtures as long as it imparts the longed-for autonomy. Consequently, since the railway system enhanced traveling possibilities, it also contributed to women's uprootedness: their growing independence mingled with seclusion and withdrawal from the safety of the domestic world. The new, urban world was not yet prepared to define clearly the woman's position in the transforming society. Although those women who traveled by train crossed domestic boundaries, they occupied a liminal, undetermined social position at the same time. Whereas being confined to the domestic sphere signified a lack of professional possibilities, commuting carried with itself a sense of displacement, thus women occupied an ambivalent, uprooted position in nineteenth-century society.

Technological growth and the industrial revolution (initiated in Britain and lasting until 1840), influenced the development of the new standards

Figure 5.1. Illustration of Power Loom Weaving by T. Allom (1835). *History of the Cotton Manufacture in Great Britain* by Sir Edward Baines (1835) (Public Domain).

of collective morality. Together with the economically motivated morality, social divisions were perpetuated.

Accordingly, the novel became engaged with the idea of an "individual" suspended between idealistic (fictional) social possibilities and their apparent lack in the "real" world. According to Ermarth,

> the massive social and cultural re-adjustment required by industrial society prompts experiment with new forms of corporate order across the cultural range from politics to music. Economic and social versions of corporate social identity compete in nineteenth-century narrative, and the novelists tend to emphasize the limits of the economic system to show the social destructiveness of those committed exclusively to it. (136)

For example, Anthony Trollope's moral, financial, and political concerns find expression in such of his works as *The Way We Live Now* (1875) or *The Prime Minister* (1876), with the plot involving financial scandals and offering a warning against monetary and, thus, moral ruin. Likewise, numerous Dickensian characters face "the limits of the economic system." While presenting moral and financial traps in *Great Expectations*, Dickens cautions his readers against relying on the "corporate order" (Ermarth, 134).

Similarly, William Makepeace Thackeray offers an artful vision of fraud and deception in his masterly work, *Vanity Fair* (1847–1848). However, perhaps the most alarming picture of the nineteenth-century social change springs from Thomas Hardy's *Jude the Obscure* (1895), where the character's genuine efforts are marked by an ultimate social failure and moral disgrace. As it has been already mentioned, published at the end of the century, *Jude the Obscure* emerges as a horrifying comment on the Victorian class-based world. Simultaneously, Hardy's work offers no hope for the future generation. It argues that society selects individuals on the basis of their class affiliation, regardless of their skills and aspirations. Moreover, Hardy's novel carries a troubling assumption that one has no control over fate. The fear of the unavoidable and deus ex machina events hindering one's opportunities can be also traced in such works as George Eliot's *The Mill on the Floss* (1860). A similar theme imbued with anxieties echoes in Henry James's novel: *The Wings of the Dove* (1902) portrays a perplexing net of social relations and investigates an overwhelming crisis of an individual suspended between equally inevitable moral and economic choices. Similarly, in Mona Caird's *The Daughters of Danaus* (1894), one of the heroines, Hadria, seemingly endowed with the possibilities of personal development, fruitlessly seeks consolation both in the public and domestic spheres. The problems depicted in Hardy's, Eliot's, and Caird's novels appear to be astonishingly modern and relatable in the current times of the ever-present crisis of identity and moral values.

The problem of individual fate is particularly conspicuous in those Victorian works of fiction in which the characters are financially constricted, as oftentimes it hinders their possible moral development. In the nineteenth century, the definition of an "individual" paradoxically altered: it began to signify a unique and irreplaceable part of society, even though measured in terms of one's economic usefulness and success. Along with the rapid expansion of the market, society ceased to operate en masse and, to some extent, acknowledged the existence of individual contributors (Ermarth, 136). In his work *On Liberty* (1859), John Stuart Mill, the British philosopher and economist, accentuates the importance of acknowledging differences among individuals. These differences, as Mill posits, prove beneficial for the cohesion of the entire social system (Ermarth, 130):

> it is not by wearing down into uniformity all that is individual . . . but by cultivating it and calling it forth, within the limits imposed by the rights and interests of others, that human beings become a noble and beautiful object of contemplation; and as the works partake the character of those who do them, by the same process human life also becomes rich, diversified, and animating, furnishing more abundant aliment to high thoughts and elevating feelings, and strengthening the tie which binds every individual to the race, by making the race infinitely better worth belonging to. In proportion to the development of his individuality, each person becomes more valuable to himself, and is therefore capable of being more valuable to others. (*On Liberty*, 113)

According to Mill, the freedom of individual development triggers the improvement of society itself and enables further social success, as well as economic prosperity and intellectual well-being. However, as noticed by Goodlad, "for Mill the moral and intellectual consequences of individual disempowerment are devastating" (28).

Published in November 1859, Charles Darwin's evolutionary theory appeared simultaneously with Mill's *On Liberty*, introducing a bleak undertone into the so-far uplifting debate concerning individual development. Darwin's *On the Origins of Species* gave rise to the concept of Social Darwinism, the theory linking biological dispute with sociopolitical discourse. As postulated by Bernard Lightman and Bennett Zon in *Evolution and Victorian Culture*, Victorian society provided fertile ground for testing Darwin's theory:

> Social Darwinism applies Darwinian evolutionary principles to society. At its best—as an intellectual exercise—Social Darwinism tried to theorize overarching, analogical relationships between social and biological growth, but at its

worse—as the reality of socio-political policy—it was used flagrantly to justify and rationalize extermination of people drifting from evolutionarily fitness. (4)

The dissonance between Mill's uplifting notion of an individual and the politically motivated, dispiriting theory of Social Darwinism constituted one of the thought-provoking ambiguities of the Victorian age. This ambivalence is not alien to the twenty-first century society where an individual is navigating between such promoted values as selflessness and inner perfection while, oftentimes, having to fight for economic survival, social acceptance, and decent living conditions. Evolving in the second part of the nineteenth century, the notion of social Darwinism with its "survival of the fittest" slogan epitomized the proceeding cultural crisis. Elizabeth D. Ermarth quotes Benians, who states that

> certainly some end-of-the-century malaise can be associated with economic depression in the 1870s and with a new stasis in the Empire, where Britain no longer enjoyed easy industrial supremacy, where renewed war in France made peace seem less secure, and where new nationalism and tariffs in Europe gave new priority to a much older and more rapacious view of colonies. (63)

The issues of cultural depression and moral uncertainty were closely reflected in writing and counted among the concerns of the social novel, defined by Ermarth as "historical fiction" (132). The task of the Victorian social novel, Ermarth maintains, lies in "show[ing] the symbiosis of individual and social entities," therefore counteracting the actual sociocultural crisis (132). As Ermarth believes, the social novel should

> necessarily concern itself with difference. Difference in custom, wealth, language, tradition, class and experience: these constitute the basis for that mediation, that overriding common denominator of social, historical time; these provide the fractures and fault-lines that make social bridges necessary. (132–33)

However, in literature, the perfect "symbiosis" between an individual and society is often lost among the "fractures" and "fault-lines." Read as the social-problem novel, aforementioned *Jude the Obscure* discusses the issue of one's possibilities (or, rather, their lack) in the hierarchically constrained society which prevents one from obtaining happiness and success.

According to Loughlin-Chow, in the nineteenth century, the social-problem novel was also referred to as the "industrial novel" or the "condition-of-England novel" (71). The last term was coined in 1839 by Thomas Carlyle, who, in his famous *Chartism*, devoted the first chapter entitled "Condition-of-England Question" to the examination of the struggles of the working classes within the new, industrialized environment: "[a] feeling very generally exists that the condition and disposition of the Working Classes is a rather ominous matter at present; that something ought to be said and done, in regard to it" (1).

The Victorian social-problem novel was originally defined by Louis Cazamian in his 1903 work *The Social Novel in England, 1830–1850* (Nelson, 190). James G. Nelson classifies the social-problem novel as "popular in the mid-Victorian period" (199) and states that

> though none of these novels advocates either the eradication of class distinctions or placing of the classes on an equal footing (or of the sexes, for that matter), they argue for closer ties between capital and labor that hopefully will promote mutual respect and good-will, a sameness of purpose, a sense of unity. Only through community will prosperity and peace reign again in the nation. (207)

Nelson's characterization of the social-problem novel highlights the notion of "community." However, such social-problem novels as Hardy's *Jude the Obscure* reject the idea of social unity and pronounce it utterly unattainable (if not utterly unbearable, as the bleak vision in Hardy's novel implies). Charlotte Brontë's *Shirley* (1849) depicts conflicting perspectives in a class-divided society in a similar vein. Jason B. Jones sees Brontë's *Shirley* as a "paradoxical social-problem novel," pointing to the fact that the work blurs the gap between "personal intention" and "social effects," thus failing to arrive at the hypothetical unity (61, 62). As Jones asserts, "Brontë powerfully suggests that ideological explanations cannot exhaust motives in the social realm; she does not, however, assert that history is therefore void of causality" (61). Moreover, he claims that *Shirley* provides an example of an exceptional social-problem novel, as the text does not promote the demands of any particular class. Rather than that, *Shirley* offers a mature, visibly even-handed perspective on the process in which each character remains deeply preoccupied with their self-interests. According to Jones, in Brontë's text "the world is not mutually meaningful to all parties—that is, because various disputants cannot find a common language or methodology for resolving interpretative disputes—characters and groups in the novel advocate their own position regardless of their overall cost" (66). Hence, in *Shirley*, Brontë fosters discussion concerning the aim and message of the social-problem novel itself by challenging readerly expectations concerning the social classes presented in the text. Since the sociopolitical message of *Shirley* emerges as highly individualized and, thus, not unifying, it simultaneously testifies that the social-problem novel should not be concerned with "taking sides": instead, it should promote what Ermarth terms as "social bridges" (133). Yet, usually, the social-problem novel functions as a theoretical construct enabling Victorian authors to question, examine, or challenge faultless, idealistic visions of quixotic community and, oftentimes, superficial "social bridges" existing between social classes.

The idea of social centralization was emphasized not only in the literary vision of the symbiotic community, but, primarily, in the economic transformation which influenced numerous spheres of everyday life. The novelists including Trollope, James, Gaskell, or Eliot elaborated in their works on communal problems such as social insecurities or class divisions. Elizabeth Gaskell's first novel, *Mary Barton* (1848), reflects on the trials and tribulations faced by the working class in Manchester. In *North and South* (1854) Gaskell concentrates on the cruelties of the industrial revolution, whereas in *Ruth* (1853), she readily criticises the ill-treatment of the eponymous heroine, who, in society's eyes, becomes a "fallen woman." George Eliot (the pen name of Mary Ann Evans) also left a particularly important mark on the Victorian literary scene, introducing the characters who were socially excluded or trapped within social boundaries. *Middlemarch, a Study of Provincial Life* (1871–1872) is a landmark work in Eliot's artistic career dealing with such issues as the social status of women or women's expectations in Victorian (hypocritical) society. Among many of Eliot's works, the ones of key importance also include *Adam Bede* (1859) and *The Mill on the Floss* (1860), both depicting moral trials faced by nineteenth-century individuals.

As James Eli Adams posits, "class . . . entails a complex mediation between economic and social order, which depends on recognition across a wide social spectrum—a form of social exchange that the novel was especially well equipped to represent" (O'Gorman, 49). This socioeconomic order was strictly combined with the issue of morality. Charles Dickens, the writer whose works inextricably revolve around the moral issues of the era, "persistently compares the economic and the social systems of obligation," depicting the marketplace as a site of the struggle (Ermarth, 141) which can be looked at in terms of the Darwinian notion of the "survival of the fittest." Meanwhile, as Ermarth observes, Dickens abandons the idea of providence, perceiving the market as a self-regulating container (143). For instance, in Dickens's *Great Expectations* (1860–1861), Pip's flawed moral understanding of the socioeconomic order leads him to confusion until the moment when he is faced with the truth concerning the actual nature of his benefactor. Initially blinded by social hierarchism, Pip grows to eventually realize that his benefactor is the one whom society regards as an outcast, whereas those whom he supposed to be his actual benefactors from the upper classes do not care about his future. As Ermarth argues, "for social novelists the developing monetary structure of obligation is almost always a substitute for a social one" (141). In *Great Expectations*, based on an erroneous belief in his monetary obligations towards Miss Havisham, Pip strays from his path of self-development. Moreover, he does not realize the dangers of being in debt. "Debt is another locus where economic and moral, even religious meaning conflict," Ermarth admits, "in the nineteenth century, debt was a crime one went to jail for; in narrative it becomes an omnibus carrier of social cautionary tales" (143). While Pip finally recognizes his financial commitments, he still remains unable to recognize his moral debt toward the true benefactors until the day of his own economic (and moral) degradation. Thus, the actual day of the character's moral awakening arrives simultaneously with his financial downfall. This involuntary act of "breaking away" from the high social circles is an eye-opening moment for Pip, who finally begins to see the shortcomings of the social system in which morality is equalled with one's social status and financial position.

The ideas of morality, economy and community are strictly related to one another in the nineteenth-century world mirrored and reexamined in the Victorian novel. In Anne Brontë's (1820–1849) work *The Tenant of Wildfell Hall* (1848), the main protagonist, Helen, abandons her ruthless husband in order to avoid humiliation resulting from his disrespectful behaviour. In order to achieve her goal and escape poverty, she strives to make her living by means of painting. This activity provides her not only with sustenance, but also with moral consolation. Painting—as an occupation—introduces moral value into the heroine's life: it encourages self-reliance and enables personal fulfilment. It turns Helen into a full-fledged and resourceful individual who celebrates distinctive success as a Victorian woman. Thus, economy (the possibility of earning one's living) and morality ("personal uplifting") operate within similar frameworks in the Victorian social world.[1] Independence going hand in hand with financial freedom is, oftentimes, the main concern of contemporary women as well: financial freedom not only liberates, but also endows one with the feelings of self-worth and purpose, which, on the whole, introduce the key moral value into one's life. In this respect, the nineteenth-century social-problem novel carries a universal message which can be readily embraced by the twenty-first century society as well.

Anthony Trollope is another Victorian author who remained acutely sensitive to the precarious ties between economy and morality. "The competition between social and monetary motives," Ermarth states, "especially when it comes to debt, produces ironies that continually delight Trollope" (144). This "competition" appears to be especially timely in the current age, marking the neo-Victorian novels currently appearing on the literary scene as crucial components in the dialogue with, paradoxically, not-so-distant past. For instance, in Trollope's *Prime Minister* (1876), gambling is the cause of financial losses combined with moral fall (145). Trollope is also particularly sensitive to the nineteenth-century women's lives in his entire *Palliser* novel series (1864–1879).[2] He is a discerning observer of women's fates revolving around both moral and economic choices. Women marrying out of necessity for social and financial reasons, and women trespassing morally and economically sanctioned boundaries in search of personal fulfillment and happiness are filling the pages of his works. One such striking example is offered in *Can You Forgive Her?*—the novel further discussed below.

Likewise, in William Makepeace Thackeray's *Vanity Fair* (1847–1848), taking financial risks and gambling figure as economic dangers threatening male characters' lives, but, paradoxically, these dangers also pave the way for the success of one of the female characters: taking a major risk in order to gain a desired social position, Rebecca Sharp metaphorically bets on her life. At the same time, she defeats patriarchal order initially preventing her from her financial and social gains. It is singularly interesting to trace the plots involving women characters in the Victorian works preoccupied with the issues of moral and financial gains and losses. Women characters appearing in Victorian texts usually operate between two dimensions: private and public spheres. They are balancing between domestic lives—those traditionally ascribed to them—and the areas usually associated with masculine spaces, thus richly contributing to the overall picture of Victorian society at large. This picture is mirrored, reanalyzed and transformed in the present-day

Figure 5.2. Anthony Trollope c. 1870s. *Anthony Trollope, Autobiography* (William Blackwood & Sons, 1883) (Public Domain).

neo-Victorian fiction which not only seeks to reimagine the nineteenth-century past, but also to find answers related to our present. This idea will be further explored in one of the chapters of this book.

Importantly, as Victorian society became economically oriented, it gradually turned into a more "fluid" construct which enabled social shifting and metamorphosis. As already mentioned, with the emergence of the "middle-class hero," aristocracy gradually lost its significance. Consequently, the so far clear-cut idea of a gentleman as one of a noble birth became the subject of dispute as well. As Maria Pirgerou argues in *The Vicissitudes of Victorian Masculinity: The Case of the Bachelor*, "the decline of hereditary aristocracy . . . and the emergence of a new type of manhood predicated upon military valour, professional success in the world of the market and procreative potential . . . carried further implications for the construction and representation of the mid-century bachelor" (97–98). In the transforming Victorian world, the meaning of the nineteenth-century gentleman grew apparently ambiguous, as parentage no longer guaranteed social success. As Ermarth points out, "differences based on class, gender, ethnicity or nationality all submit to the new horizon and new inclusiveness of history" (169). Accordingly, the middle-class masculine hero emerged on the Victorian literary scene as the character sustained by the market and operating within its limits. In his article "Class in the Victorian Novel," James Eli Adams analyses the concept of the "self-made man" (O'Gorman, 57). The idea of the "self-made man," Adams posits, found commemoration in Samuel Smiles's *Self-Help; with Illustrations of Character and Conduct* (1859), which "celebrated the possibilities for social advancement and self-determination that awaited those with sufficient talent, initiative, and self-discipline" (57). In chapter 13, "Character—the True Gentleman," of the 1871 edition of Smiles's *Self-Help*, one can read that personal character constitutes "the noblest possession of a man" (416):

> riches and rank have no necessary connection with genuine gentlemanly qualities. The poor man may be a true gentleman,—in spirit and in daily life. He may be honest, truthful, upright, polite, temperate, courageous, self-respecting, and self-helping,—that is, be a true gentleman. (434)

As the industrial revolution proceeds with, as M. Clare Loughlin-Chow puts it, "the unprecedented urban development, the transformation of the English economy from a rural to an industrial base, and the breakdown of old relationships between employer and employee" (Baker, 71), the "new," self-made gentleman[3] is finally allowed to thrive.

Whereas in the nineteenth century the idea of a "self-made man" held sway, a "self-made woman" was far from a full-fledged concept in society where, according to Adams, "women remained 'relative creatures' who derived their status principally from their relation to man" (O'Gorman, 58). Yet, the end of the century witnessed a perceptible shift in the lives of middle-class women, as finally they "had options not readily available to their grandmothers" (Young, 2019). Young observes that, due to the "demographic imbalance" between men and women, the latter gained an opportunity to legitimately engage in work which, at last, was perceived as "professionalized, requiring a radical change in what nineteenth-century surgeon and philosopher James Hinton called the 'habit of thinking' of an entire culture" (*Victorian Spinster to New Career Woman*). The change involving professionalization of women's work and thus paving the way for their potential careers had been anticipated in Anthony Trollope's numerous works, including the aforementioned 1864–1865 *Can You Forgive Her?* The novel offers a multifaceted portrait of the Victorian woman with desires, dreams, fears, and longings reaching beyond the nineteenth-century expectations concerning her supposedly idealized, domestic life revolving around potential marriage. The protagonist of Trollope's novel, Alice Vavasor, constantly asks herself the fundamental question: "what should a woman do with her life?," at the same time musing that there must be "something over and beyond" and that "[a] woman's life is important to her" (101). Oftentimes, the nineteenth-century novels would become the mouthpiece of women's agenda of independence and self-worth, as well as the center of negotiation between gender roles. Alice Vavasor wonders whether she is destined to dedicate her entire life to marriage, or whether there is much more to her life in terms of career and possibilities—"something more" that would be readily accessible to men. "Within Victorian novels," Marisa Knox explicates,

> female characters often and unashamedly identify with male figures. *Little Women*'s Jo[4] goes so far as to call herself the "man of the family" in addition to assuming masculine roles in amateur theatricals and supporting her family through writing (Alcott 4). . . . In Charlotte Brontë's *Shirley*, the title character not only christens herself Captain Keeldar but also is referred to as her own (non-existent) brother and treated as such by the conservative Reverend Helstone without any sense of impropriety. . . . Although we see the obvious limits to this flirtation with masculinity in such heroines' traditionally feminine plot trajectories, the fact that such characters alternate between "masculine" and "feminine" attitudes—without being labeled as deviant androgynies—indicates the amount of imaginative freedom allotted to Victorian girls and women to cross and re-cross gender lines of fiction. (23)

This phenomenon also indicates that, in the nineteenth century, social and gender boundaries had been already tested in literature in relation to women's position, their lives, and their desires. Years later, the neo-Victorian novel would reach for these models, transforming them into outspoken and complex narratives no longer constrained by the nineteenth-century social decorum yet leaving them dialogically related to the Victorian texts.

If the majority of women in the nineteenth century remained confined to the domestic sphere, marriage, and imaginary, literary projections of themselves as active agents of their lives, where would be the very space granting them even temporary freedom?

The marketplace of the era, a substantial socioeconomic domain of the Victorian reality, offered women such a peculiar space—a certain degree of freedom—this time connected with the physical act of crossing boundaries from the domestic plane into the public realm.[5] Hence, the importance of the vibrant socioeconomic Victorian life enabling and influencing individual/moral choices should be stressed here once again. Initially perceived as a masculine domain, the Victorian market began to transform into a female space offering a "legitimate" and approved alternative to the domestic plane. On the one hand, the marketplace allowed women to venture out from their household while, on the other hand, the tantalizing politics of the market continued to entrap unobservant women, bringing about the threat of disastrous social consequences. Apart from the peril of becoming indebted (Ermarth, 143), the fear of temptation (excessive and thoughtless consumerism) played a paramount role in the female encounters with the market. The act of "gazing" at products, so far proclaimed as a masculine "weapon," allowed women to categorize and define marketplace commodities. Hence, women's gaze offered the power of choice. Yet, as highlighted in Christina Rossetti's (1830–1894) narrative poem *Goblin Market* (published in 1862), the marketplace also threatened to "consume" those women who lost themselves among the varieties of tempting products. Hence, in the nineteenth century, in women's case, crossing so-called "traditional" boundaries—whether social, gender or physical ones—was inherently connected with a certain level of risk. This theme will be also explored in revisionary texts, including Jean Rhys's *Wide Sargasso Sea* and John Fowles's *The French Lieutenant's Woman*. While the domestic plane offered security and relative comfort, it also propelled the feeling of entrapment and hopelessness. The marketplace and the public sphere, on the other hand, lured with freedom and the unknown, while contributing to the ruin of those who did not learn to cautiously partake of it.

Not only did the marketplace open new possibilities for those women who reasonably resisted its hidden temptations, but also it stressed the multicultural background of the Victorian world through the exuberant display of exotic products. Meanwhile, behind the notions of multiculturalism and international exchange, there lay the idea of British imperialism, intrinsically connected with money and politics. As noted by Cannon Schmitt, during the Victorian era, the British occupied Australia (claim beginning in 1770) and New Zealand (claimed 1840), seized parts of China (including Hong Kong in 1841), and expanded their holdings in Africa and Southeast Asia (annexing Burma, for instance, in 1886). Expansionist activity reached a crescendo with the "scramble for Africa" in the 1880s and 1890s, a race among European powers to establish territorial rights to those parts of the continent as yet unclaimed. (O'Gorman, 9)

While, on the one hand, imperialism triggered the supply of new products to the Victorian market, the attitude toward the market brimming with multiculturalism remained ambiguous. The issue under scrutiny is mirrored in Rossetti's *Goblin Market*, where a hostile depiction of a fairy-tale-inflected exotic market reflects common fears and prejudices towards unknown cultures.

Moreover, as Maria Pirgerou observes, "the rise of imperialism further dictated the enforcement and perception of 'the masculine ideal' and an explicit differentiation between what was conceived as 'masculine' and 'feminine' gender roles" (13–14). Bradley Deane argues in a similar vein, stating that "by the late nineteenth century" the notion of the "affectionate family man" gradually gave way to the "untamed frontiersman, the impetuous boy, and the unapologetically violent soldier" (1). The departure of the "affectionate family man" signified a further displacement of women in the domestic circle but, at the same time, offered to them a glimmer of freedom. Deane observes that "an emphasis on the competitive dimensions of manliness—as derived, for instance, from discourses of honour, gamesmanship, or military codes—provided conceptual templates through which the aggressive ideologies of the New Imperialism could be understood and valued" (15). The Victorian women in their traditionally sanctioned, domestic settings and the vulnerable inhabitants of the British colonies represented a negation of these templates. Yet, at the same time, Lesa Sholl makes an interesting claim after Inderpal Grewal, pointing out that those nineteenth-century women who were fortunate enough to travel or create travel narratives oftentimes engaged with the idea of imperialism themselves: while "mastering and rewriting the masculine discourse in travel narratives, these English women writers construct a new identity and authority for themselves" (Sholl, 130). Sholl believes that such freedom from "Victorian restraint"—the result of "their times abroad"—is discernible in Martineau's, Eliot's and Brontë's writings (130). Traveling and crossing physical borders—venturing out from the domestic sphere and going much beyond the marketplace—offered women writers a sense of validation and an opportunity to affirm themselves and rewrite their own identities as individuals. The theme of travel also dominates revisionary neo-Victorian works, with women characters traveling not only to regain their lost identities and gain knowledge about their past, but also to experience independence and assert themselves, as happens in Gail Carriger's *The Parasol Protectorate* series.

Apart from the marketplace, the "dualities" of the Victorian age were also reflected in one's inner life, especially in the form of the crisis of beliefs. According to Purchase quoted by Pirgerou, "[the Victorians] drew parallels between their outward concern with moral, physical or sexual reserve and the notion of economic saving and restraint" (224). At the same time, the idea of "self-fashioning" in the "outer" world dominated by strict economic laws contrasted with the cherished notion of domesticity associated with a secretly guarded refuge.

The Victorian idea of "self-fashioning," featured in Smiles's *Self-Help* advisory work, provided further support for the emergence of the "middle class" concept: it was reassuring that molding a "gentleman" is not merely dependent on aristocratic origins. As Pirgerou argues, the Victorian middle class "was far from fixed in character," stretching from tradesmen to scholars, thus incorporating a variety of "self-fashioned" characters who gained their position by means of work and investments (12). The economically disadvantaged yet ambitious individuals could expect to receive support from the upper classes on behalf of the paternalist ideology: "the revival of social paternalism was a dominant feature of the Victorian effort to counteract the consequences of a competitive market economy," Rosemarie Bodenheimer posits (21). As she states in *The Politics of Story in Victorian Social Fiction*, "paternalist ideology reasserted a belief that relations between employers and workers should be constituted in moral as well as economic terms and that society was properly seen as a hierarchical order in which the wealthy and powerful would protect the poor in return for their deference and duty" (21). As Goodlad acknowledges after Dandeker in her *Victorian Literature and the Victorian State*, "the system of patronage which cemented eighteenth-century British society in the absence of modern bureaucracy was not eradicated overnight" (7). Accordingly, she states, "local aristocrats continued to dominate country affairs until the 1880s" (7). Victorian society was operating within the liberalist principles. This term encompassed, as Goodlad argues,

> the high-minded cooperation sought by John Stuart Mill, Thomas Chalmers's Christian and civic community, Harriet Martineau's vision of a society fuelled by individual self-improvement, Walter Bagehot's staid confidence in the dynamism of civil society, Samuel Smiles' populist assertion of individual will, Matthew Arnold's conviction in the enlightening potential of a cultured elite, and Bernard Bosanquet's fin-de-siècle citizen ethic. (22)

The notion of the collective and unified nation did not preclude the functioning of the classes, but rather stressed the idea that each individual completed the social structure as its unique part. On the other hand, the lofty slogans of the era many a time were confronted with problems faced by the middle and working classes:

> yet even though well-to-do mid-Victorians do seem to have become extremely family-conscious and home-oriented—the ideal family unit becoming both a middle-class and working-class aspiration as the century wore on—many poor Victorian families were crowded together into dwelling houses or tenements in order to survive, particularly in inner-city and urban areas. (Purchase, 64)

Also, as mentioned before, whereas women complemented the social structure by playing meaningful roles in the functioning of their families, they did not operate within society as self-sufficient individuals. Instead, as Purchase observes, the women of the era served the needs of the patriarchal "family values":

> the economically self-sufficient family functioned to define and preserve the well-being of the working patriarch, the role of women as "angels in the house," and the successful nurture of obedient children who were born and bred to keep the whole process going. (65–66)

Yet, as the end-of-the-century literature reveals, the concept of women's presence in Victorian society had been already shifting, being questioned and transformed not only by such female writers as Charlotte Brontë, but also by such discerning male writers as Anthony Trollope and Wilkie Collins, who manifested uncommon sensitivity and knowledge related to women's lives. The women in their narratives are complex, conflicted, and protomodern in their beliefs and assumptions regarding society and life. The aforementioned shift in the perception of masculinity and the transformation of the woman from a domestic angel to a contributing member of society had already begun. The boundaries had been already tested and this process has never ceased, which is especially highlighted in the twentieth- and twenty-first-century neo-Victorian novel.

NOTES

1. In her *The Habits of Good Society: A Handbook For Ladies And Gentlemen* (1859), Jane Aster observes that bad society consists of the individuals whose "morals and manners are bad" (38). Moreover, Aster argues, "Englishmen respect nothing so much as their purses and their private affairs" (45).

2. *Prime Minister* belongs to the *Palliser* series as well.

3. Robin Gilmour argues that the "origins of the gentleman lie deep in feudal society and the qualification of birth: 'the e*ssence* of a gentleman,' Ruskin wrote, 'is what the word says, that he comes from a pure *gens*, or is perfectly bred. After that, gentleness and sympathy, or kind disposition and fine imagination'" (*Works*, volume 37, 7197). The common mistake that "gentleman" means a man with gentle disposition reflects a long-standing ambivalence in the usage of the word: as early as Chaucer "gentil" means "charming," "mild" and "tender," as well as "noble" and "well-bred." Birth was significant insofar as the man of family . . . would have greater opportunity for acquiring gentle manners and practising gentle behaviour, but every courtesy writer agreed that birth alone could not make the complete gentleman. . . . The idea of the gentleman could never have fascinated the Victorians as it did if it had been limited by caste or by a stricte science of heraldry, nor, on the other hand, if it had been a totally moralised concept, a mere synonym for the good man. It was the subtle and shifting balance between social and moral attributes. . . . By the mid-century, however, the moral element was generally acknowledged to be in the ascendant." (4).

4. Josephine March—the protagonist of Louisa May Alcott's novel (1868). The abbreviation of her name, "Jo," indicates a strong masculine point of reference.

5. In the nineteenth century, the marketplace serves as a space allowing women to physically exceed the boundaries of their houses and venture into a new place directly involved in the market economy. Therefore, I argue that it is the marketplace (instead of the "market" understood in general terms) which directly influences the Victorian women's financial and social choices.

Chapter Six

Profits, Ideals, and the "Self"

Victorian Ambiguities Rediscovered in Literature

> My experience tells me that this community, the British reading public, is upon the whole utterly averse to the teaching of bad lessons, and will not have it. They will accept a bad work, but they reject an immoral or injurious theory of life.
>
> —Anthony Trollope, *An Autobiography: And Other Writings* (246)

In order to discuss and thoroughly understand the literary projections of women in the Victorian and revisionary novel, it appears vital to dive deeper into the nineteenth-century social world with its often contradictory systems of values reflecting the "self." It seems impossible to encapsulate the nineteenth-century sociocultural world in one sentence, stating that "the Victorians were a certain way." Currently, one can find numerous contradicting statements relating to the Victorians: on the one hand, the Victorians were supposed to be prudent and abide by strict moral rules while, on the other hand, they supposedly kept dark secrets and led unprincipled lives. What is the truth? Apparently, the Victorians thrived on complexities and contradictions, closely resembling in this respect our contemporary society. These ambiguities, also defining the situation of nineteenth-century women, will be reflected not only in the literature of the era, but also in neo-Victorian novels from the twentieth- and twenty-first centuries.

A general assertion concerning men and women of the Victorian age is that women were traditionally assigned to the domestic realm, while men occupied the public sphere. Such division can be especially observed in the first part of the nineteenth century. Essentially, during the first part of the nineteenth century, the world of the middle class existed as a priori masculine, with the middle-class hero fearlessly moving through the so-far "fossilized" social hierarchy. At that time, the middle-class women could not actively influence the public sphere outside their family boundaries. However, according to Pirgerou, together with the assignment of the "separate gender roles," both middle-class men and women began to form "the social backbone of the nation" (13). Accordingly, she argues, "the emergence and formation of the middle-class was characterized by another predominantly Victorian ideal: domesticity" (12). The middle-class domestic ideal, combined with the politics of the marketplace, resulted in the ideology of "dualities," easily discernible in Victorian fiction. The public sphere allied with a predominantly aggressive masculine discourse, while the domestic plane celebrated the concept of a passive and sacrificial femininity as its domineering hallmark. In Charlotte Brontë's *Shirley* (1849), Caroline Helstone acutely suffers from the consequences of such a "private-public" dualistic arrangement. Suspended between solitude and purposelessness on the one hand and practically incapacitated by her uncle on the other, Caroline wonders:

> I have to live, perhaps, till seventy years. As far as I know I have good health; half a century of existence may lie before me. How am I to occupy it? What am I to do to fill the interval of time which spreads between me and the grave? (Brontë, *Shirley*, 133)

While the heroine strives to endow her existence with both purpose and meaning, the gloomy realization of being a dependant in her uncle's house and not having a meaningful occupation deprives her of hopes for the future. Hence, becoming a "free agent" and an acknowledged individual in the nineteenth-century social framework was intrinsically connected with economic power or, at least, with a meaningful occupation. In *Shirley*, the eponymous heroine obtains her free agency through the law of inheritance, and it is the law that relocates her from the "politics of the ballroom" to the politics of the masculine domain. Importantly, Shirley's masculine domain is not gained through what constitutes Caroline Helstone's dream—occupation or, in other words, the work of her own hands. Therefore, in Brontë's novel, there is still a vast gap between Shirley's quite passive "governance" and Caroline's ideal. Also, there is a discernible difference between Shirley's authority and Robert Moore's business dealings chiefly defined in the novel by the process of commuting between the countryside and the city—in opposition to Shirley, Moore is actively engaged in business affairs. Even though Shirley is presented as a woman readily crossing gender boundaries and confidently moving into the masculine sphere, she is still contrasted with both Robert and Caroline. Outspoken, assertive, and unashamed of her opinions, cherishing independence and knowing its value, Shirley is a strong woman who trespasses gender boundaries, yet this trespassing is still dependent on family circumstances or, in other words, on personal luck. Brontë's novel shows that circumstances greatly contribute to women's fates and, oftentimes, these are the circumstances which shape an individual, allowing women such as Shirley to bloom into their full potential, while withholding others such as Caroline from their freedom. Eventually, both heroines celebrate "victories," yet these will be also related to the domestic sphere. In Brontë's literary world, her women characters succeed while reaching a compromise between personal desires and social expectations—usually, they are allowed to thrive alongside an understanding man who becomes their *partner*—the one with whom they enter into a meaningful communion of minds.

While Caroline and Shirley represent women's desires connected with the act of crossing the supposedly "traditional" boundaries, the male character, Robert Moore, initially figures as an individual entrapped in his business routine and, at some point, insensitive toward domestic values, what may also prove disastrous to him. It seems that *Shirley* advocates a conscious balance between the private and the public, postulating that both men and women could readily partake in both spheres.

Goodlad discusses the moral "ambiguity" of the Victorians, commenting on the "two antithetical, or 'dueling,' worldviews: one moral and idealist and the other materialist" (22). The Victorians, she observes, were "syncretic thinkers drawing from two alternative worldviews, each of which" with "powerful claims to modern authenticity" (22). At the same time, Goodlad posits, Victorian antimaterialism was strictly attached to the "concept of individuality" (24), the "individuality" aiming at an extensive advancement and "boundless transformation" (25). Charlotte Brontë's novelistic "theme of success" testifies to the possibilities of such individual transformation. In her works, including *Shirley* or *Jane Eyre,* good fortune is the consequence of a morally negotiated decision and virtuous behavior. In her *Forms of Feelings in the Victorian Fiction*, Barbara Hardy suggests that "Charlotte Brontë liked to place her imagined extremes in an acceptable moral scheme, which ultimately worked towards blame and approval" (103), thus toward a moral resolution. Hence, Brontë's characters, in Hardy's view, operate within the world motivated by moral principles:

> Charlotte thrives on the polarities of violence and control, freedom and limit, passion and reason, but devises a moral structure which resolves conflict and makes extremes meet, in her strong, lamented, but morally civilized and triumphant characters, Jane Eyre, Robert Moore, and Lucy Snowe. (103)

Dualisms, the pairs of conflicting terms, worldviews or behaviors, were richly represented in the literature of the period. Ermarth believes that dualisms originated not only in order to categorize, but also to appreciate or dispraise:

> dualisms are really masked hierarchies of value that act to *sublimate difference* by implicitly depreciating or even erasing the second term. For example, in the opposition between Good or Bad—whether it is art, or persons, or food—the second, depreciated term is often little more than a negative definition, that is, often merely a container for whatever is Not-Good—in art, persons or food. . . . The slippage towards duality and hierarchy ultimately forecloses on the choice which is a pre-eminent value of historical conventions (in history it could always have been otherwise), and instead simply enthrones a prejudice. (169)

In this view, dualisms not only perpetuate social divisions, but also, while relying on conventions, provide an "abridged," simplified vision of history and society. According to Ermarth, such polarities gave rise to "male and female" or "rich and poor" distinctions accentuated and preserved in the literary discourse of the Victorian era (170). These polarities are discussed anew in neo-Victorian literature of the twentieth- and twenty-first century. In the "male and female" framework, the "male" figures as everything that the female is not. As noted by John Reed in *Victorian Conventions*, in nineteenth-century literature "characters . . . exhibit predictable combinations of attributes which result in conventional types" (5). Furthermore, Reed posits, Victorian characters "operate within equally conventional moral designs" and such construction enabled nineteenth-century writers to remain faithful to the "real" *representation* of the world (5).

While the nineteenth-century dualisms established a specific sociocultural landscape manifesting itself through divisions and oppositions which could not be analyzed otherwise than through contrast, the present-day neo-Victorian fiction strives to merge dualisms into a coherent, diversified, and dialogical whole which would represent diversified Victorian realities and our world as well. As stated initially, it seems impossible to define the Victorian age in a single sentence. Similarly, it appears improbable to encapsulate the era in a dualistic statement:

> "by gratifying the Victorian novel onto a modernist model neo-Victorian fiction produces a hybrid novelistic species with a dual system of enunciation and dual aesthetic principles resulting in an oxymoronic fusion of opposites in which coexist a sense of direction and a sense of chaos, narrative momentum and narrative disorder, a restoration of decorum and provocative breaches of decorum," states Christian Gutleben in "Hybridity as Oxymoron": "The purpose of this systematic practice of oxymoronic hybridity is to deconstruct traditional oppositions and dualities, particularly in the political and ideological sphere" (V. Guignery, ed., *Hybridity: Forms and Figures in Literature and the Visual Arts*, 59).

Gutleben aptly postulates that the neo-Victorian novel deconstructs Victorian cultural dualities while operating within a hybrid structure since "it recreates a Victorian state of affairs and simultaneously implies and encourages a contemporary interpretation" that signifies, according to him, "Bakhtin's co-presence of 'two different linguistic consciousnesses, separated from one another by an epoch' (358)" (62). In effect, the neo-Victorian novel no longer perceives Victorian society as merely operating within "poor—rich," "man—woman," "public sphere—domestic sphere" dualities but, instead, incorporates into its discourse the entire range of the so-far unheard voices and perspectives not accepted by the nineteenth-century framework, but noticed and highlighted in the twenty-first century sociocultural dimension. While clear-cut concepts relying on dualities offer a sense of hierarchy and order, blending these boundaries in the neo-Victorian novel allows for the better understanding of the past as well as the present.

Apart from such Victorian dualities as: "rich—poor," "men—women," etc., there are also dualisms embracing inconsistencies and doubts—further approximating twenty-first century society to the nineteenth-century context. Amy Woodson-Boulton enumerates such further dualities of the Victorian age as: "bombast and anxiety, pomp and doubt, confidence and self-consciousness" (110). These sound strikingly similar to the polarities of the twenty-first century as well. Hence, the revival of interest in the Victorian past is self-revealing. As Woodson-Boulton posits, "Victorian art, and the criticism it inspired, shows us yearning for absolute standards of judgement, debated in terms of the search for truth and beauty and negotiated through narrative and figurative art" (110). These dualisms and polarities are discussed still—or again—today. Yet, by elaborating on dualisms, whether moral or economic, Victorian literature replicated social inequalities as well. As recognized by Adams, the novel as a social medium was meant to provide a "guide to Victorian culture" and yet favored the representatives of the middle and upper classes (O'Gorman, 52). Similarly to Reed, Adams admits that the "narrative structure and convention" of the novel unequivocally favored a particular part of society (52). In "Class in the Victorian Novel," Adams observes that in the year 1867 "less than ½ of one percent of the population" counted themselves among the upper class gaining "more than 1000 pounds per year." On the other side of this scale figured the poor, "with incomes of 73 pounds or less" (52).

Paradoxically, it is usually the characters from upper (or middle) classes (hence, those constituting the smallest part of Victorian society) who are presented in the pages of nineteenth-century fiction. During the times supposedly celebrating one's individual potential and unique character, the diversity the poor is often obliterated and disposed of in the Victorian novel. Instead, the poor are often depicted as an anonymous crowd—a subjective, remote, and simplified experience of the upper classes. Nevertheless, Victorian literature exhibits what Adams calls "prurient fascination" with the poor, "allow[ing] the novelists to imagine forms of psychological extremity that could not be accommodated by middle-class settings" (O'Gorman, 65). Although oftentimes the poor are misrepresented in nineteenth-century fiction, there are also works faithfully portraying their individual struggles, including Benjamin Disraeli's *Sybil, or the Two Nations* (1845) and Elizabeth Gaskell's *North and South* (1854). In Disraeli's work, Charles Egremont, a Conservative Party member who desires to see the "true" life of the poor, recognizes the problem of the gap created between the two social spheres:

> I was told . . . that an impassable gulf divided the Rich and the Poor; I was told that the Privileged and the People formed Two Nations, governed by different laws, influenced by different manners, with no thoughts or sympathies in common; with an innate inability of mutual comprehension. I believed that if this were indeed the case, the ruin of our common country was at hand. (254–55)

The "urban expansion" of the 1830s and 1840s, according to Morgan, resulted in the further aggravation of discrepancies between the classes (45). The Poor Law Amendment Act (1834) did not resolve the conflict, transferring the burden of responsibility for the poor to "unions of parishes administered by boards of guardians" (O'Gorman, xv). As Morgan observes, such documents as The Poor Law Amendment Act extensively modified the perception of the lowest classes: "the poor districts became a foreign country which had to be brought to civilization by the efforts of missionaries" (87). The condition of the poor, as it was generally argued, stemmed from their individual ignorance and was ascribed to the "moral failure" (Morgan, 74). Hence, the efforts of the local unions and missionary organizations were undertaken, at least theoretically, to raise the poor from their problematic moral and financial state.

Bearing in mind the issues enumerated above, including the enduring problems of the class segregation, social divisions, and economic uncertainties of the day, the identity crisis that was soon to follow comes as no surprise. The nineteenth-century identity crisis and social divisions opened up the literary debate in the works of such authors as George Robert Gissing, Joseph Conrad, and the aforementioned Thomas Hardy (Ermarth, 63). The economic depression between 1846 and 1847 and the cultural depression at the end of the century contributed to the acute awareness that cohesion in society was, in fact, not attained.

Simultaneously, the "social" values ceased to signify the "moral" values, as is indicated in such works as Anne Brontë's *The Tenant of the Wildfell Hall* (1848) and Wilkie Collins's *The Woman in White* (1860). In both novels, the socially approved standards and modes of behavior turn out to be inadequate for the equitable development of women protagonists. Brontë's Helen and Collins's Anne Catherick struggle with social exclusion and misunderstanding. Helen's decision to abandon her husband is not socially acceptable, yet it is morally justified. Likewise, in *The Woman in White*, Anne Catherick escapes social manipulation and sticks to her private beliefs and self-created moral standards.

Importantly, Anne Catherick appears in Collins's novel as a ghostly projection rather than a material being. She is an outsider who, by adopting her own lifestyle, simultaneously loses society's favor. In the novel, Anne Catherick's uprootedness is expressed through her almost illusive presence—she is textually represented rather as a "spirit" than a living being when noticed by Hartright on the road to London. Hence, she remains ambiguous, constantly suspended between the illusory, the evanescent, and the "real," which further attests to her supposedly insignificant position as a woman in the nineteenth-century, patriarchal-oriented world. Yet, I believe that, first and foremost, Anne Catherick is a rebel at heart who subtly transforms the vision of the Victorian woman through her meaningful absences and appearances. The fact that she is such an evanescent, uprooted figure may attest to her perception as a weak individual in society's eyes, but also testifies to her unconventionality and independence, which are strong personal and moral assets. Anne's elusiveness or, in other words, the tragic beauty of this character, lies in the impossibility of defining her and thus restricting her to a given sphere. It transforms her into an outsider and an odd woman, yet it also allows her to preserve the unique, self-established notion of the self escaping all attempts at categorization. In Collins's novel, the patriarchally oriented world is troubled by Anne Catherick's undefinable presence and, thus, she is portrayed as a "mad" woman escaping from an asylum—such perception offers an easy, safe, and undemanding explanation of Anne's individuality and allows Victorian society to label her as unstable, consequently diminishing her importance. The mystery surrounding Anne Catherick can be treated as her mental instability or, instead, it can be perceived as a patriarchal problem, especially since Anne represents such an undetermined feminine presence escaping categorisation both in terms of her inner world, as well as in terms of her appearance.

On the whole, the nineteenth-century crisis of values and the growing ambiguity of moral standards contributed to the discussion concerning visual perception as well: in the world dominated by rapid social and technological changes, the quality of vision was also considered to be unreliable. "Defamiliarization"[1] initiates a debate over the issue of whether "the visual" can be "taken [for] granted," Kate Flint observes in her article "'Seeing is Believing?': Visuality and Victorian Fiction" (O'Gorman, 29). Arguing along these lines, Flint asserts after Levine that uncertainty was an intrinsic part of nineteenth-century realism, which should not be regarded as a solidly self-satisfied vision based in a misguided objectivity and faith in representation, but a highly self-conscious attempt to explore or create a new reality.... Numerous fictional scenes rely on the uncertainty of visual evidence, and on the dangers of inferring too much from what one sees. (37)

Similarly, the present-day neo-Victorian fiction relies, to a large extent, on the uncertainty concerning the Victorian past accessible to the readers through the indirect prism of literary representation. Neo-Victorian fiction can be also regarded as a "self-conscious attempt to explore or create a new reality" (37) with uncertainty and negotiation as guiding forces.

The nineteenth-century problem of visual perception signifies for Srdjan Smajić a "messy affair," while he argues that "vision is at once the most reliable and least trustworthy source of evidence for the existence of ghosts—seeing both *is* and *is not* believing" (18). In *Ghost-Seers, Detectives, and Spiritualists* . . . Smajić alleges that Victorian fiction was greatly concerned with visuality in both ghost and detective stories, with the difference that in the latter "vampires, ghosts, and similar agencies" could not appear (2). Detective stories, with Arthur Conan Doyle's leading *Sherlock Holmes* series initiated in 1887 by *A Study in Scarlet*, supported the notion of the supernatural "explained" and propounded scientific skepticism (2). The concepts of a disturbed vision of reality and deceptive senses served not only as the foundation for the creation of a new literary experience, but also as the assertion that the "self" dwells in a misleading and obscure reality additionally warped by one's fallible senses.

The notion of changing, unstable vision further influenced the concepts of "performativity" and "theatricality," envisaged both in the fiction of the era and in the daily lives of the Victorians. "Joseph Litvak explores the nineteenth-century novel as subject to these same blasphemously riotous theatrical forces," observes Lynn Voskuil: "'When theatricality surfaces in the novels of Austen and Brontë,' [Litvak] argues, 'what gets performed is a complex disruption of the patriarchal narrative enterprise in which those authors are otherwise engaged'" (9). Women's theatricality disturbs the patriarchal sociocultural arrangements in such Victorian novels as Wilkie Collins's *The Woman in White* (1860) and *No Name* (1862), Charlotte Brontë's *Villette*, (1853), and Thackeray's *Vanity Fair* (1848). During the nineteenth century, the ideas of "performativity" and "theatricality" were incorporated within the process of "self-construction," Voskuil asserts (11):

Theatricality and authenticity often functioned dynamically together to construct the symbolic typologies by which the English knew themselves as individuals, as a public, and as a nation. . . . Victorians developed *a sophisticated capacity to suspend their disbelief, to act authentically and to be theatrical at the same time.* In this way, they theatricalized the ideas and institutions they believed to be the most authentic even as they authenticated the spectacles they made of themselves. [emphasis added] (2)

Such a statement approximates the Victorians to the twenty-first century—the age in which authenticity mingles with performativity and individuality oftentimes relies on theatrical qualities. As Voskuil observes, the Victorians managed to be "authentic" and "theatrical" at the same time, reshaping the idea of performance into an actual experience of existing and living in the nineteenth-century world. Since the twenty-first-century sociocultural world relies on similar qualities of individuality and performativity, I believe that the current revival of interest in neo-Victorian fiction is fully justified. As mentioned before, neo-Victorian fiction not only allows one to reconstruct the past, but also to define the present and further understand our placement in the current sociohistorical realm. Apparently, we are not isolated from the past.

The problem of ambiguity arising from the notions of "performance" and "authenticity" is recognized in *Villette* (1853), where Brontë skilfully blots out the boundaries between the "real" and "fictitious," while allowing her drugged and hallucinating heroine to negotiate between these two planes. On the other hand, while Thackeray's *Vanity Fair* (1847) offers a "puppet show" itself, thus separating "fictitious" from the "real," it also introduces an excellent performative case of Rebecca Sharp. Becky's life is "staged" as a series of theatrical acts and behaviors leading her toward a desirable social position. Correspondingly, in one of the chapters of the novel, the actual play is being staged, drawing an analogy between Becky's ominous role of Clytemnestra and her hegemonic desires:

> Clytemnestra[2] glides swiftly into the room like an apparition—her arms are bare and white,—her tawny hair floats down her shoulders,—her face is deadly pale,—and her eyes are lighted up with a smile so ghastly, that people quake as they look at her.... Scornfully she snatches the dagger out of Aegisthus's hand, and advances to the bed. You see it shining over her head in the glimmer of the lamp, and—and the lamp goes out, with a groan, and all is dark. The darkness and the scene frightened people. Rebecca performed the part so well, and with such ghastly truth, that the spectators were all dumb, until, with a burst, all the lamps of the hall blazed out again, when everybody began to shout applause. (Thackeray, *Vanity Fair*, 502)

Thackeray's social world in *Vanity Fair* proves to be a mere puppet show, as the narrator eventually states: "Ah! *Vanitas Vanitatum!* Which of us is happy in this world? . . . Come, children, let us shut up the box and the puppets, for our play is played out" (680). Thackeray's novel mirrors the Shakespearian assertion that "all the world's a stage." However, when looked at as a parody, *Vanity Fair* also corresponds with Oscar Wilde's affirmation that "the world is a stage, but the play is badly cast"—Thackeray's world is dominated by appearances and "pawns" rather than by authentic characters.[3] Such textual construction points to the problem of the social world resembling a theater; the world in which one paves their way toward success through the act of performance. Collins's *No Name* (1862) presents such a strenuous road toward succeeding on the actual stage. Yet, the protagonist, Magdalen Vanstone, performs numerous theatrical roles and dons disfiguring disguises not to attain fame, but in order to get her revenge on a greedy uncle.

As mentioned above, Victorian identity was carefully structured on the one hand and equally unsettled on the other. The ambivalent messages sent by the nineteenth-century sociocultural discourse included the insistence on being both theatrical and authentic, with the demand to adhere to one's moral and economic standards at the same time. Arguing along these lines, even though it might not be always possible to unequivocally judge the Victorians by twenty-first-century standards, it is necessary to acknowledge historical continuity between the past and our present, especially since the problems of identity and authenticity emerge in the present-day era as well and dualisms are still proliferating in our contemporary world. Hence, I argue that contemporaneity is dialogically structured by the Victorian past, together with its historical and cultural "baggage." Consequently, modern society remains, to a large extent, "Victorian." It struggles with similar "Victorian issues," yet presented under divergent names and entangled within an altered (neo-Victorian) discourse. In the next chapter, we shall examine the "molding" of the woman within the Victorian sociocultural context.

NOTES

1. In Collins's novel *The Woman in White* Anne Catherick is constructed as an almost intangible presence who resembles a ghost, because, figuratively speaking, she remains socially undefinable. Depicted through Hartright's gaze, Anne Catherick becomes defamiliarized. Victor Shklovsky used the term "defamiliarization" in 1917. According to Striedter, he "singled out the 'device of defamiliarization' (*priem ostraneniya*) as the characteristic device of literature. Therewith he invented a term whose importance would extend far beyond Russian Formalism to work its effect on modern art and aesthetics. . . . First, defamiliarization impedes the kind of perception automatized by linguistic and social conventions, forcing the beholder to see things anew, correcting his relationship to the world around him. Second, in a kind of countermovement, by impeding perception, defamiliarization directs perception to the estranging and impending form of self" (23–24).

2. In Greek mythology, Clytemnestra murdered her husband Agamemnon on his return from the Trojan war while, at the same time, engaging in a relationship with her lover Aegisthus.

3. Thackeray's characters are "pawns" wearing masks. Hence, Thackeray distances himself from his own characters, endowing them with theatrical qualities.

Chapter Seven

The Woman Question or Women Questions?

The Victorian age painted the vision of a woman which became deeply rooted in the present-day consciousness and discourse as well. "A woman who meets the world with intensity is a woman who endures lashes of shame and disapproval, from within as well as without," Cote asserts ("Wonderland: An Introduction"). Apparently, even nowadays, when a woman reaches beyond the so-called conventional framework, she still might be perceived as touching upon the discourse of impropriety. She is supposed to be attractive yet modest, natural yet theatrical, successful yet not daring, unassuming yet beaming with wit and intelligence and, on top of that, she dons the "angel in the house" domestic role while supposedly pursuing an interesting career. Analyzing women characters against the Victorian and modern sociocultural backgrounds is an especially fascinating task, as women are situated at the center of socially constructed realities, including numerous domestic and public realms.

"What is a Woman?," inquires Jeanette King in her work *The Victorian Women Question in Contemporary Feminist Fiction* (8). When applied to the Victorian discourse, the question becomes intricate: it is the inquiry into *what* a woman is and not *who* she is, highlighting the fact that the status of the nineteenth-century woman as a full-fledged, developed figure requires validation.[1] "The Woman Question really was a question, a debate rather than a series of pronouncements, conducted by the middle class primarily in print, and richly explored in fiction" (Matthews, ed., 71). Accordingly, the woman has to be looked at from the historical, scientific, and cultural perspectives. In the Victorian era, the general discourse concerning women gradually turned into the rhetoric of science, since women were described in terms of their biological functioning. However, the nineteenth-century medical discourse cannot be fully acknowledged as "scientific" or "objective," since it relied too firmly on assumptions and imagination.[2] Similarly, the Victorian reality was often described in terms of *what it should ideally look like* rather than *how it functioned*. Since one cannot gain direct access to the past, it is possible to rely on literary sources while identifying a substantial gap between the two models: the model of the idealized Victorian world versus its "actual" functioning in the nineteenth-century reality. As indicated in the previous chapter, the prevalent literary discourse of the Victorian era presented the world in its idealized version by means of "dualisms." Along with the development of the reading culture, literature began to represent literary characters as "emblematic types." Victorian fiction, Reed posits, substantially relies on conventional character types (22):

> In Victorian literature, what we would call realistic motivation is often incorporate with type fulfilment. Characters do not act according to a system of humors or ruling passions, nor are they moved by the complexes and neuroses of the twentieth-century man; instead, they exhibit predictable combinations of attributes which result in conventional types. These types, moreover, often operate within equally conventional moral designs. (5)

Consequently, in the sociocultural discourse of the era, the notion of "*who the woman is*" coincided with a particular "type fulfilment."[3] In Brontë's *Jane Eyre*, Reed observes, the eponymous heroine "paints pictures of morally emblematic significance," and in Kingsley's *Yeast* (1848) "Lancelot Smith . . . produces a drawing entitled 'The Triumph of Woman,' which symbolically describes woman's ennobling purpose" (23). The woman was meant to be noble yet, supposedly, not as noble as the man. Thereupon, the "man-woman" distinction was traditionally supported by such dualisms as: "intellect-nature," "intellect-feelings," "mind-body," "active-passive," "public-private," "public-domestic," "justice-sympathy," or "reason-emotions" (King, 14–23). Paradoxically, strong dichotomies existed in representations of women characters themselves, including such contrary images as "angels" and "fallen women" or "madonnas" and "magdalenas." King offers an idealized vision of the woman in the following passage:

> Images of the Madonna and of angels therefore contribute to the formation of the Victorian feminine ideal, in both visual and literary representation. What emerges out of this iconography is a highly idealised picture of a woman as *disembodied, spiritual, and, above all, chaste.* [emphasis added] (King, 10)

The case of the "fallen woman" appears more intricate since, as Lyn Pykett notes in *The 'Improper Feminine*,' in the nineteenth-century discourse the "fallen women" figured both as predators and victims (64). A striking portrayal of the "fallen woman" can be found in Elizabeth Barrett Browning's epic poem *Aurora Leigh* (1853) and in *Ruth* (1853), the novel written by Elizabeth Gaskell. Deborah A. Logan observes that

> In a variety of ways, Gaskell's Ruth and Elizabeth Barrett Browning's Marian Erle in *Aurora Leigh* provide the basis for the fallen woman archetype. Both characters are sexually exploited while young, ignorant, and vulnerable; both are working class yet drawn with an "inherent" moral purity not acquired through birth or marriage; both bear illegitimate children in whom they delight and through whom their social "sin" finds redemption; both are apprenticed seamstresses and thus vulnerable to exploitation on several levels; both refuse marital legitimation; and finally, neither achieves social integration. (47)

The "fallen woman" plays a meaningful role in the Victorian literary discourse, since the term not only allows for the "demonization" of the "immoral" female protagonists, but also enables their "purification" through the unmasking of the Victorian social hypocrisy which led them astray. Both Ruth and Marian Erle, the supposed "fallen women" are, in fact, noble and honorable individuals who simply do not fit into the socially sanctioned pattern and who were used and abandoned by the patriarchal world. Despite the assumed "falling," they appear to be the strongholds of sacrifice and endurance.

Another interesting case of "fallenness" can be found in Charles Kingsley's *Hypathia: Or, New Foes with an Old Face* (1853). Although the novel mainly concentrates on religious dilemmas and the plot is set in ancient times, the eponymous Hypathia epitomizes unconventionality and stubbornness which turn her in society's eyes into an "odd," "fallen" woman and contribute to her future doom. Hypathia, a twenty-five-year-old Greek and a pagan philosopher in her quest for the ideal Platonic state, becomes the prey of a prejudiced religious crowd, thus turning into "the first victim of the misogynist witch hunts that would plague future centuries" (Watts, 144). Incorporating the figure of Hypatia into the Victorian literary discourse is a symbolic act which not only manifests Kingsley's religious concerns, but also perceives the so-called "fallen" women as victims of senseless enmity. Analyzing the notion of "fallen women" in Victorian discourse, Logan observes that a distinction should have been drawn between "fallenness" and "falling" (13). Referring to Beth Kalikoff's "The Falling Women in Three Victorian Novels," she notices that the concept of fallenness is applied "to heroines who do not technically fall—Jane Eyre, Mary Barton, and Maggie Tulliver" (13). As she argues, attributing the concept of fallenness to such heroines "demonstrates the power of the stereotype to construct deviant behaviour even where none exists" (14). Yet, the "moral dualisms" of the era strictly divided women into the "fallen" and "morally correct" ones.

Victorian narratives portrayed the "ideal" women as selfless, spiritual "givers" who, while devoid of any expectations themselves, followed their disinterested "natures" in order to provide domestic comfort and moral salvation to their husbands and families. Coventry Patmore's poem *The Angel in the House* (1854–1863), dedicated to his wife, prizes the attributes of the ideal female companion—the perfect angelic spouse whose task lies in offering moral comfort and domestic bliss. While developing an image of the woman as an angelic creature whose desire is to "please" others (Patmore, 257), the poem encapsulated the philosophy of the Victorian epoch. The overall image of the woman emerging from the poem forms, in Elizabeth Langland's words, "a convenient shorthand for a type generally celebrated in tracts and novels, the selfless, virtuous, pure, and spiritualized deity, who presided over hearth and home and whose presence was a refuge from the storms of a commercial strife" (69). At the same time, Langland aptly notices Patmore's inconsistency: while asserting that women remain excluded from the public sphere, he simultaneously approves of Queen Victoria—the most recognizable female in the public space, an independent and robust politician (70). Hence, Langland argues, Patmore's poem is not convincing. While he strives to "justify women's exclusion from public life as a personal privilege, [he] runs into contradiction, a very prominent public woman: Victoria" (Langland, 70).

Patmore's poem encourages one to inquire why the Victorian social discourse excluded women from the public sphere. According to Simon Morgan, it was the acknowledgment that the exclusion from the public sphere signified a privilege for women, thus allowing them to protect their moral purity: "a distance needed to be maintained from the public sphere, in order that they [women] could exercise a beneficial and calming influence" (41). Such discourse, constructed as an attempt at restraining women's self-will and independence, offered a blissful vision of women as "the 'spiritual guardians' of men" (Morgan, 40).

As "spiritual guardians," women were essentially depicted through the prism of others' needs. Hence, women were supposed to nurture their virtues *for others*. They were depicted as *wives and mothers* whose duty was to bring up their children *for the benefit of the nation* [emphasis added]. Essentially, women appeared in the idealized domestic discourse as a part of the greater, collective entity (family, nation) whom they devotedly served. Yet, as already indicated, several writers of the Victorian era, including Charlotte Brontë, Thomas Hardy, Charles Dickens, Anthony Trollope, and Wilkie Collins, carefully examined women's position in their writing, already consciously transgressing the boundaries portraying them either as fallen villains or domestic angels while taking an independent and transformative stance. Analyzing Hardy's novels, Rita Öztürk explicates that "while *Tess of the d'Urbervilles* mainly concentrates on the issue of woman's individuality, *Jude the Obscure* focuses on both male and female individuality, universalizing the issues of individuality against society and its institutions (69). As she states after Draper, in Hardy's *Jude the Obscure*

> Sue and Jude are particularly "at odds" with the marriage code and its formalities. They believe that a marriage contract would kill the freshness of their love, and so Jude's tragedy pivots on the theme of formal marriage laws. . . . Hardy uses marriage to attack society at large. For him, marriage summarizes or accounts for the many of the social institutions which he seems to criticize. . . . The social conventions and institutions should aim to create harmony between the society and the individual. (70)

In Hardy's novel, marriage is projected as a limiting framework which deprives one of the self. It incorporates an individual into a larger, depersonalized project with no space to reflect upon one's desires and convictions.

The notion of the selfless[4] rejection of one's individuality can be contrasted with the modern perception of women characters in neo-Victorian texts in which individuality becomes the major celebrated feature. In the nineteenth century women were treated as subjects necessarily connected to others, also in the field of personal education which was meant to benefit their domestic environments. For instance, according to Morgan, while "many writers, particularly before the 1840s and 1850s, believed that the majority of women would spend their lives in a domestic environment," they simultaneously encouraged the idea of female education (37). The purpose of such an undertaking was quintessentially utilitarian, since it was believed that educated women could indirectly influence the well-being of the nation by exerting a healing influence on their husbands (Morgan, 41). To substantiate, Morgan quotes J. D. Mille's idea of women engaging in the study of economy: "by participating actively in the economy, women would be better able to educate their sons to face the public world" (42). Women could also benefit from education "in order to prevent the misdirection of their energies and to maximize their usefulness" (42). The principle of Bentham's utilitarianism states that one's morality is measured in terms of the benefits it brought to others. Consequently, female development aimed at the prosperity of other recipients, including husbands, sons, or the entire nation.[5]

Such "selfless education" claims found support among the women of the era as well. Morgan provides an example of Emily Shirreff, a pioneering supporter of higher education for women. As he observes, Shirreff "encouraged women to take a role in their husbands' or fathers' businesses, but felt that women should not try to support themselves by work unless it was absolutely necessary" (42). Shirreff asserted that engaging in the economic sphere would deprive women of the perfect tie with the other sex (42). Additionally, men figured as "physical guardians" of women and it was women's task to influence men's morality in a subtle, indirect way (40). As King posits, "women were expected to fill the vacuum left by the death of religious certainty, revered not only as the embodiment of virtue themselves, but as the guardians of male virtue" associated with the domestic region (11).

According to Morgan, "the general assumption was that women would have husbands to support them" (42). Hence, the concept of a "single woman" did not gain approval within the Victorian discourse. Admittedly, there were women who were not married or even lived in seclusion, however, their independent lifestyle did not agree with the sanctioned social order. The attitudes toward the "odd women"[6]—single females at the marriageable age—remained ambivalent. The most famous complaint against an alleged uselessness of such women can be found in William Rathbone Greg's essay *Why Are Women Redundant?* (1862). "A state of society so mature, so elaborate, so highly organized as ours cannot fail to abound in painful and complicated problems," Greg deplores (3). Furthermore, Greg argues with disapproval:

> there are hundreds of thousands of women—not to speak more largely still—scattered through ranks, but proportionally numerous in the middle and upper classes—who have to earn their own living, instead of spending and husbanding the earnings of men; who, not having the natural duties and labours of wives and mothers, have to carve out artificial and painfully-sought occupations for themselves; who, in place of completing, sweetening, and embellishing the existence of others, are compelled to lead an independent and incomplete existence of their own. (5)

In Greg's argumentation, the idea of "incompleteness" is linked to the notion of "independence," equally threatening to his vision of society. Unmarried women are "redundant," Greg asserts, because they are devoid of "natural duties and labours of wives and mothers." The term "natural" enters the Victorian discourse as yet another normative indicator of one's place and obligations. Female "nature" turns into a pseudoscientific idea shaping the female figure endowed with such "natural" traits as selflessness, affectionateness, and an innate need to serve others. As Barbara T. Gates argues in *Kindred Nature: Victorian and Edwardian Women Embrace the Living World*,

> thinking in essences was at the bottom of mythologies about women and earthiness when Victorian scientists and social scientist joined ranks with men of letters to characterize women in terms of their own "nature," which to most of these men meant female sexuality and reproductive functions. This landed women squarely in (or as) the lap of nature. (12)

The women who remained socially idle and, thus, "redundant," were often looked upon with suspicion. The category of "redundant" women included widows and spinsters, with the latter turning into the most "troublesome" case (since their status was the most questionable and lamentable, according to such authors as William R. Greg). In contrast to a spinster, a middle-class or an upper-class widow's social position was both dignified and secure: she had been already married and the marriage was terminated due to natural causes not dependent on her actions. Moreover, a widow's reputation was intact, and her future was financially secure. She had already performed the essential "duties" of a wife and she had been respectfully planted in Victorian society. Such is the case of Arabella Greenow—the widow appearing in Anthony Trollope's *Can You Forgive Her?* (1864). While marrying a rich, older man, she secures her distinguished status in society's eyes. After her husband's death, she metaphorically becomes "free again," indulging in subtle flirtations with younger men, taking care of her physical appearance and actively plotting to marry off her younger female relatives while, at the same time, securing her financial independence on remarrying herself. Even though one might look critically at Greenow's initial decision to marry a much older men for reasons apparently not connected with love, her kind disposition, assertiveness, honesty, kindness, and sympathy toward other women make her one of the most likeable characters in Trollope's novel.

Never married before, spinsters were perceived as dangerous: as King asserts, the "angel in the house" model embraced the approved "figure of the sexless angel" (11). While spinsters, according to King, should have been praised for their chastity, they were "pathologised, and represented as an object of pity or disgust" (32). At the same time, "passionlessness" was sanctioned as a "physiological norm" and "any evidence of sexuality in a woman could be deemed deviant" (21).[7] The ambivalence of this line of reasoning contributed to further social divisions between Victorian men and women. On the one hand, "spinsters" were perceived as social benefactresses and selfless contributors to the national welfare. On the other hand, they were criticised for not adhering to their "female nature." Jennifer Phegley inquires: "who was a spinster and when might she become an old maid?" (151). "Technically," Phegley observes, "a spinster was a woman young enough to still expect to find a husband and an old maid was a woman presumed to be beyond marriageable age" (151).

Comparing and contrasting the concepts of an "old maid" and a "bachelor" adds yet another puzzling aspect to the debate concerning nineteenth-century standards. As Maria Pirgerou observes, the bachelor signified "an in-between kind of male subjectivity occupying both the private and public spheres which Victorians were so keen on keeping distinctly apart" (224). In contrast, the spinster was restricted to the private domain and usually appeared in public only in order to perform charitable acts. While the bachelor's status was transitory and led toward the future realization of the masculine ideal, the spinster lived as a stagnant figure, both praised and shunned. Shella Jeffreys observes in *The Spinster and Her Enemies: Feminism and Sexuality, 1880–1930* that individuals such as W. R. Greg deplored the fate of single women, since they posed a substantial threat to masculine integrity. Jeffreys challenges Greg's argument since it "gives an idea of the total contempt for women who failed to perform their life's work of servicing men" (87). Jeffreys highlights, in turn, that "spinsterhood . . . was associated with sterility, destructiveness and anti-life values" (142). As mentioned before, Charlotte Brontë was one of the novelists who would be subtly crossing and testing the boundaries of the conventional nineteenth-century discourse: as she readily shows in her novel, *Shirley*, the "old maids" cannot easily escape social scrutiny. In chapter 10, Brontë aptly unmasks masculine attitudes toward spinsters encapsulated in Robert Moore's thoughts:

> Moore was not habitually given to sarcasm, especially on anything humbler or weaker than himself; but he had once or twice happened to be in the room when Miss Mann had made a call on his sister, and after listening to her conversation and viewing her features for a time, he had gone out into the garden where his little cousin was tending some of his favourite flowers, and while standing near and watching her he had amused himself with comparing fair youth, delicate and attractive, with shrivelled eld, livid and loveless, and in jestingly repeating to a smiling girl the vinegar discourse of a cankered old maid. (135)

The spinster was portrayed as dauntingly "shrivelled," "livid," and "loveless" and, what is more, she remained "livid" because of being "loveless." Apparently, her presence was pushed to the border of society. As Jeffreys posits, one of the "fronts" battling against spinsters maintained that they "suffered from thwarted desire which turned them into vicious and destructive creatures" (97). The Victorian spinster was discredited, as she did not appear *in relation* to the man, which proved dangerous for a conventional dualistic structure. "If anti-spinster feeling is declining a little at present," Jeffreys observes, "this could be because there are so few spinsters today that they are not seen to constitute so serious a threat" (87).

Yet, at the same time, together with her solitude, the spinster could potentially receive independence and prominence as an individual, actively participating in social life, for instance, in the above mentioned charity events. Defamed and yet, at the same time, freed from marital bonds, the spinster was involved in her private life much more easily than any other woman of the epoch—apart from the widow. Morgan offers an example of Ellen Heaton from Leeds:

> Ellen Heaton never married and was a woman of independent means. She travelled widely on the continent and attended meetings of the British Association for the Advancement of Science whenever possible. She also did her best to gain entry to the Victorian literary and art world, maintaining correspondences with John Ruskin, Dante Gabrielle Rossetti, and Elizabeth Barrett Browning. It was on Ruskin's advice that she purchased eight paintings by J. M. W. Turner, and commissioned eight by Rossetti and two by Arthur Hughes, as well as a chalk drawing of E. B. Browning by Field Talfourd. (63)

While "female collectors like Ellen seem to have been a rarity," Morgan observes, the single women of the era still travelled and developed their tastes for art and education (64). This was necessarily the privilege of the middle- and upper-class women, even though "when the plight of the middle-class spinster is written about in the history books, it is generally posed as the excruciating difficulty felt by women who were desperate for husbands" (Jeffreys, 88). According to Jeffreys, the working-class spinsters had yet another choice—they were "absorbed in the domestic servant industry which relied almost entirely on unmarried women" (87).

Another possible choice for a spinster was an engagement with education—she could work as a tutor or mentor. It was already argued that nineteenth-century women were educated for the sake of their husbands and families. Yet, in Brontë's *Shirley*, Caroline Helstone dreams about becoming a governess in order to fill her time with a meaningful activity. Mrs. Pryor, who eventually turns out to be Caroline's mother, is a governess as well, escaping into the reality built upon the work ethics in order to obliterate the past involving her violent husband. Once again, Charlotte Brontë ventures out beyond the boundaries of the conventional discourse while showing those women for whom work and occupation offer emotional and mental escape.

Mary Wollstonecraft (1759–1797) commented on the importance of women's education even before the Victorian era officially began. In her *A Vindication of the Rights of Women* (1792), she emphasized the importance of "the family and the environment in which good citizens were formed" (Morgan, 38). Even though it advocated women's education for the sake of men's betterment, *A Vindication* marked a starting point in the struggle for women's rights.[8] As Morgan maintains, by acknowledging their "responsibilities" included in *A Vindication*, middle-class women managed to obtain greater independence:

> Despite their uneven access to the levers of social power, middle-class women were able to develop a lively sense of their civic responsibilities and duties. Although they were mostly excluded by law from exercising direct political rights, women were able to mobilize contemporary discourses of femininity, such as the evangelical language of "woman's mission," or the extension of their

domestic roles as wives, mothers and household managers, in order to broaden their sphere of competence. (195)

The rhetoric of female independence was, thus, disguised among other discourses of the era, including the religious and moral ones. In her *Vindication* Mary Wollstonecraft asserts: "let men become more chaste and modest, and if women do not grow wiser in the same ratio, it will be clear that they have weaker understanding" (10). Importantly, this argumentation adheres not only to women and their supposed goals in society, but also to men and their responsibilities.

One can read in the "Introduction" to *Wollstonecraft . . .* that the authoress of *Vindication* hopes to reach middle-class women "first and foremost" (x). While Wollstonecraft indicates that education plays a paramount role in the betterment of women's lives, she refuses to acknowledge that it is absolutely necessary for the healthy social life (11). What one discovers in *A Vindication* is primarily "a more fundamental attack on the mores of her day and the institutions which she thought sustained them" (xi). The "ideal woman" arising from the pages of Wollstonecraft's work is

> A mother who, having exerted herself to develop her mind and acquire an education before marriage, devotes her life to the upbringing of her children and attends to the needs of those in her household and community, [who] is an interesting, trustworthy, and life-long companion to her husband, but would also be able to survive as a widow and provide for her children by exercising a honourable trade or skill. (xi)

Apparently, Wollstonecraft anticipates a shift in men's behavior toward women and insists on the acknowledgment of women as rational beings.

However, "The Woman Question" posited in the pamphlet is still far from the expectations of the fin-de-siècle "New Woman." In Wollstonecraft's 1792 work women still figure as men's companions who must be interesting and educated for men's sake.

A Vindication of the Rights of Women constructs an individual who cultivates her best qualities for *the benefit of others*. Such a perception of femininity is not remote from John Ruskin's (1819–1900) notion of womanhood contained in his *Sesame and Lilies* (1865). Ruskin, art critic, social thinker, and philosopher, draws an idealistic vision of the woman tirelessly caring for the hearth and home. "And wherever a true wife comes, this home is always round her," he asserts (78). Furthermore, it is interesting to observe how Ruskin, similarly to Wollstonecraft, connects the notion of domesticity with education:

I have been trying, thus far, to show you what should be the place, and what the power of woman. Now, secondly, we ask, what kind of education is to fit her for those? And if you indeed think this a true conception of her office and dignity, it will not be difficult to trace the course of education which would fit her for the one, and raise her to the other.

The first of our duties to her—no thoughtful persons now doubt this—is to secure for her such physical training and exercise as may confirm her health, and perfect her beauty. . . . Thus, then, you have first to mould her physical frame, and then, as the strength she gains will permit you, to fill and temper her mind with all knowledge and thoughts which tend to confirm its natural instincts of justice, and refine its natural tact of love.

All such knowledge should be given her as may enable her to understand, and even to aid, the work of men. (78–79, 81)

In Ruskin's work, the woman figures as a passive being who needs to be "filled" with knowledge and "trained" in order to perform the expected social role. Ruskin perpetuates the nineteenth-century rhetoric and combines the notion of female education with the idea of domestic duty. However, to do justice to Ruskin's well-meant claim, it is indispensable to notice that, just as Mary Wollstonecraft does, he finds fault with men's behavior as well. Hence, he aptly states that "we hear of the mission and of the rights of Women, as if these could ever be separate from the mission and the rights of Man" (66). Furthermore, Ruskin advocates women's rights by indicating that

and not less wrong—perhaps even more foolishly wrong . . . is the idea that woman is only the shadow and attendant image of her lord, owing him a thoughtless and servile obedience, and supported altogether in her weakness by the pre-eminence of his fortitude. (66)

In his work, Ruskin supports women's rights and, simultaneously, remains restrained by the nineteenth-century philosophical framework while articulating his ideas concerning domestic life. Jeanette King states that Ruskin offers "a Romantic idealisation of woman's role as guardian of the 'sacred place,' home" (9). Yet, in his work, Ruskin also strives to cross the "private-public" boundary while still remaining entrapped by the common discourse of the era:

Generally, we are under impression that a man's duties are public, and a woman's private. But this is not altogether so. A man has a personal work or duty, relating to his own home, and a public work or duty, which is the expansion of the other, relating to the state. So a woman has a personal work or duty, relating to her own home, and a public work and duty, which is also the expansion of that, Ruskin observes. (92)

Ruskin defines women's public duty as the assistance "in the ordering, in the comforting, and in the beautiful adornment of the state" (66). While these obligations are strictly in favor of the patriarchal order, they also recognize the female subject as a participant who contributes to the commonwealth.

John Stuart Mill (1806–1873), perhaps the most zealous defender of women's rights, offered another perspective on women's social entrapment in his *The Subjection of Women* (1869). Mill straightforwardly draws parallels between a married woman and a slave:

> civilisation and Christianity have restored to the woman her just rights. Meanwhile the wife is the actual bond-servant of her husband: no less so, as far as legal obligation goes, than slaves commonly so called. She vows a lifelong obedience to him at the altar, and is held to it all through her life by law. . . . She can do no act whatever but by his permission, at least tacit. She can acquire no property but for him; the instant it becomes hers, even if by inheritance, it becomes *ipso facto* his. In this respect the wife's position under the common law of England is worse than that of slaves in the laws of many countries. (55)

In the above-presented passage, Mill refers to the issue of inheritance, which proved particularly unfavourable for the Victorian women. While getting married, women would lose their independence, becoming symbolically converted into their husbands' slaves.[9] Deprived of equal possibilities of education, they were often left hopelessly impoverished. The 1870 Married Women's Property Act initiated a gradual social change, positioning female subjects as legal owners of their individually earned money. It allowed women "to keep earnings, property acquired after marriage and [to] open a separate savings account" (O'Gorman, xix). The Married Women's Property Act from 1882 paved the way for those married women who strove to obtain rights to their property. Paradoxically, it was difficult to combine legal restrictions constantly faced by Victorian women with the fact that Queen Victoria was also a woman and, in 1887, celebrated her Golden Jubilee (xxi). While until that time women managed to become "visible" and "heard," their situation had not altered dramatically: the hopes placed in Queen Victoria—the female monarch—were acutely disappointed.

"The Woman Question" debate was repeatedly undertaken by such Victorian feminists as Emily Davies, Josephine Butler, Barbara Bodichon, or Millicent Garrett Fawcett. In 1894, Sarah Grand coined the term the "New Woman," opening a new chapter in women's history. As Langland observes, while Grand hoped "to celebrate the emergence of the domestic woman into the new woman as a rather simple affirmation of change through ideological conflict," she had to acknowledge that "such an uncomplicated genealogy would be to reintroduce . . . the idealist historical narrative" (247). According to Sally Ledger, (*The New Woman: Fiction and Feminism at the Fin de Siècle*), the eponymous "New Woman . . . had a multiple identity. She was, variously, a feminist activist, a social reformer, a popular novelist, a suffragette playwright, a woman poet; she was also a fictional construct, a discursive response to the activities of the late nineteenth-century women's movement" (1). Importantly, Ledger divides the concept of the "New Woman" into a historical figure and a fictional construct. The latter paved the way for the neo-Victorian literary heroine.

Hence, the "New Woman" evolved as a character with "numerous faces," varying from an independent heroine breaking free from the patriarchal norms to a sexually liberated femme fatale. Essentially, the "New Woman" emerged as the concept which initially ridiculed the claims of feminist circles: in 1891–1892, having in mind the "New Woman," Eliza Lynn Linton depicted a raging creature—the "Wild Woman" (12). According to Ledger, the "Wild Woman" was "a creature who opposed marriage, who vociferously demanded political rights, and who sought 'absolute personal independence coupled with supreme power over men'" (12). On the other hand, in modern neo-Victorian fiction, the term "New Woman" indicates a character advocating her right to individuality. Hence, the term evolved and, simultaneously, became endowed with multiple meanings. However, first and foremost, the "New Woman" introduced a change in the literary discourse, enabling new voices to enter the scene.

Moreover, the concept of the "New Woman" challenged the validity of the "angel in the house" model, as it questioned the angelic, domestic qualities of the female character. "Mental breakdown and subjugation to social convention were the common fate of pioneering fictional New Women," Ledger observes, offering the example of Thomas Hardy's heroine, Sue Bridehead, who reshapes from an independent scholar into a lunatic and miserable character (182). However, novels such as Amy Levy's *The Romance of a Shop* (1888) portray a more positive aspect of the New Woman's struggle for independence. In Levy's work, the Lorimer sisters escape poverty while opening their private photography business. The novel features bittersweet events from the sisters' lives, but also offers a tinge of hope for the New Woman's future. On the other hand, there is also a constant tension between the traditional female boundaries and the new, independent spaces into which the New Women venture in Levy's text. The heroines are constantly subjected to social scrutiny:

> Levy intensifies this narrative gaze upon women in the public sphere of modern London by giving the Lorimers a profession that insists that they travel through the streets and into homes and studios, and that requires that they record and sell the products of this gaze. In this way Levy allows her central characters to be

> both subjects and objects of scopic power. With our early twenty-first-century literary attention to in-betweenness and border-crossing, Levy's exploration of the transitional status of young urban women on the verge of the twentieth century finds contemporary resonance as well. (Bernstein, *Introduction*, *The Romance of a Shop*, 41)

At the fin de siècle, the literary Victorian woman was an unstable character, balancing between domestic bliss and her impending lunacy caused by the sense of entrapment, as well as conflicting desires and expectations. As observed by Alex Owen, "there was another Victorian discourse of 'the feminine,' a discourse concerned with a supposed female depravity, bestiality, and rampant sexuality, and one which displaced these elements on to the very poor and insane" (7). Such discourse, Owen posits, finds its source in the class system (8). It stems from the prejudice of the upper classes against the lower spheres of society. For instance, the figure of the governess signified both the notions of the domestic ideal and the danger of subversion, as she was unmarried and stayed away from home. At the same time, the governess was meant to bridge the gap between the morality of the middle class and the working-class standards (Poovey, 128). On the other hand, the "angel in the house" concept remained exclusively attached to the middle-class rhetoric. Yet, as Owen argues, it is essential to recognize that the nineteenth-century discourse hosted numerous women belonging not only to the middle, but also to the upper and working classes. Thus, particular instances of femininity cannot be sufficiently named and defined by the unified patriarchal discourse since, as Owen posits, "class and sexual meanings were interdependent" (8). Owen proposes spiritualism as the concept binding diversified notions of femininity. "Spiritualist literature was full of references to its women as gentle maidens or loving wives and mothers, women who mutedly radiated grace, charm, and beauty, whilst embodying the highest moral and domestic virtues," he asserts (8).[10]

> Spiritualist women became the embodiment of the Evangelical ideal. . . . Spiritualists assumed that it was innate femininity, in particular, female passivity, which facilitated this renunciation of self and cultivation of mediumistic powers. Passivity, or the lack of masculine will-power, might have been constructed as that which made women the gentle, retiring creatures of prescriptive literature—but it was also, for spiritualists, the very quality which facilitated spirit communication. They therefore privileged passivity and sought to develop it. Passivity became, in the spiritual vocabulary, synonymous with power. (Owen, 10)

Writing about female passivity, Owen also concentrates on the notion of a "medium"—the female figure inscribed in the Victorian culture, known for "mediating" between her audience and the spiritual world during spiritual seances, thus enabling spirits to materialise and communicate with the crowd. "Spiritualists believed that a materialisation medium drew on her own energy, and often also that of her sitters, to produce the spirit form. ... Materialisation was said to require *total 'mind-passivity'* on the part of the medium" [emphasis added], Owen explicates (63). The idea of the spiritual, passive woman provides a substitute for the "angel in the house" model. Moreover, spiritualism potentially embraced all Victorian women and did not favor the middle class.

However, together with the idea of spiritualism, there further spread the already mentioned notion of the unpredictability of women's nature.[11] Once glorified in Patmore's poem as a domestic angel, the Victorian woman turned into a weak and irrational person when scrutinized in the light of the alleged biological sciences. In the nineteenth century, science, religion and politics conspired together in order to endow the woman with "female nature" that promoted a sacrificial desire to serve others. This benevolent "nature" was also, according to the nineteenth-century discourse, incorporated in women's irrationality. The supposed irrationality required a specific medical discourse. As believed by King, in the Victorian era,

> only woman required a separately defined area of medical knowledge, since only she deviated from the "human" norm represented by man. "The Sex Question" usually meant "the Woman Question," since only women were perceived as being defined by their sex. Man, in contrast, literally signified mankind as the focus of analysis in areas such as history, philosophy and anthropology. (30)

Meanwhile, Darwinism encouraged physical and mental discrepancy between men and women. Close to the Darwinian sciences was phrenology, a pseudo-science estimating one's intellectual capacity and personal characteristics on the basis of the size of one's skull. Both these approaches degraded women to the level of less significant species, pronouncing them entirely dependent on men and forcefully secluded "in the safety of home." This "safety" was meant to preserve their innocence and ignorance of the uncompromising (masculine) world:

> In the safety of her own home the Victorian lady was protected from the sexual and material dangers or primitive life, so had been able to evolve to her highest form. Not only her own interests, but those of her children demanded that she remain in such seclusion. As the weaker partner, moreover, woman had developed secondary sexual characteristics which increased the chance of survival, and which were passed on to her daughters. (King, 28–29)

A much more optimistic account of the middle-class women's lives and their possibilities can be found in Simon Morgan's *A Victorian Woman's Place: Public Culture in the Nineteenth Century*. As Morgan's work proves, nineteenth-century women played a substantial role in the formation of the middle class:

> Although contemporary gender ideologies justified the exclusion of women from full citizenship on such grounds as lack of financial and emotional independence or inferiority of intellect, women made a substantial contribution to associations and projects that historians have seen as key to the construction of middle-class identity. (5)

Morgan highlights the indirect role of middle-class women in the development of the public sphere, stresses vitality of their philanthropist activities among the poor and the role of the gradually emerging political movement against patriarchal limitations. As he upholds, Victorian women performed a collective task that contributed to the twenty-first-century perception of womanhood as well.

While Victorian writers often adhere to conventional types, they are conscious of the nineteenth-century stereotypes as well and, thus, challenge emblematic representations of literary characters in order to expose cracks in the imperfect social system. The heroines of the Victorian novels further explored in my work (Brontë's Jane Eyre or Collins's Anne Catherick included) are suspended between social classes, possess no clear origins, act independently, and face the consequences of their actions and desires. Simultaneously, they challenge the "angel in the house" model, they turn into "fallen women," preserve emotional independence, cherish intelligence, negotiate social possibilities, but also fall into the trap of vulnerability. Hence, they expose the imperfections and predominant ambivalences of the Victorian era and, decidedly, pave the way for the highly individualized and self-conscious neo-Victorian woman.

NOTES

1. "What is a Woman?"—such statement recalls Michel Foucault's lecture entitled *What is an author?*—according to Foucault, the author is an ideological figure which halts the process of literary interpretation. However, whereas Foucault depreciates the status of the author, King does not treat "a Woman" as a mere ideological fabrication. Importantly, in King's statement, the word "Woman" begins with the capital letter. The common ground between Foucault and King can be found in the assertion that both the author and woman are created by discourse.

2. "Cott argues that what began as ideology became medical 'knowledge' in mid-century, so that later in the century doctors could take over the role of ministers, advising on sexual and 'moral' problems among women. . . . So-called knowledge about women's physiology and pathology was applied to the regulation of social life," observes King (23–24).

3. This "type fulfilment" is perfectly illustrated in John Ruskin's *Sesame and Lilies: The Three Lectures*, where he states: "What the man is at his own gate, defending it, if need be, against insult and spoil, that also, not in a less, but in a more devoted measure, he is to be at the gate of his country, leaving his home, if need be, even to the spoiler, to do his more incumbent work. And, in like manner, what the woman is to be within her gates, as the centre of order, the balm of distress, and the mirror of beauty: that she is also to be without gates, where order is more difficult, distress more imminent, loveliness more rare" (111).

4. The concept of female selflessness was readily embraced by the Victorian discourse on female morality. It found expression not only in Patmore's famous poem, but also in Lord Alfred Tennyson's (1809–1892) works. To substantiate, Tennyson's *The Lady of Shalott* (1833), drawing on the Arthurian legend, relates the story of the Lady, who spends her life peacefully weaving a web in the interior of her house (under the influence of the magic spell). Forbidden to look outside, she observes the "reality" as a reflection in her mirror. On seeing Sir Lancelot in the mirror, the Lady leaves her shelter and, aware of her impending doom, follows Sir Lancelot to Camelot. She drifts on the river in her boat and dies before reaching her destination. Significantly, the lady writes her name on the boat before her first and last travel. "The poem's popularity rests . . . on its embodiment of the highly complex Victorian conception of woman and the correlative Victorian attitude toward the home," Elizabeth Nelson posits, "the tension Tennyson establishes between the interior room and the exterior world, between the natural, material world and the shadow of that world reflected in the Lady's magic mirror, gives expression to the Victorian preoccupation with the contrast between the exterior and the interior worlds" (web). The Lady's selflessness lies in the fact that, using Nelson's word, she remains "unattainable": "Tennyson's Lady of Shalott, who could not be more unattainable, perfectly embodies the Victorian image of the ideal woman: virginal, embowered, spiritual and mysterious, dedicated to her womanly tasks" (web). Therefore, when governed by self-interests contrasting with the female ideal, the Lady of Shalott meets her unavoidable doom.

5. Victorian women were supposed to be socially "useful." Each sphere of their lives was theoretically subordinated to the utilitarian aim of benefiting others. The debate over women's role included the aforementioned issue of education. While there existed a claim that "the middle-classes were educating their daughters as decorative toys," still "most reformers believed that girls' education should enable them to cope better with what would be expected of them in life" (Morgan, 36). Thus, women had "a particular role to play in the encouragement of public virtue" (39). According to Morgan, this role was directed at exerting a positive influence on husbands and children and, especially, on sons "who were to be the future citizens" (38). Women's education was, primarily, to make a "domestic impact" on the masculine world and thus the "citizens" of the Victorian world were brought up in the domestic sphere.

6. The term "odd women," applying to the uneven number of women at the marriageable age living in England (as compared to the number of men), inspired George Gissing to analyse this theme in his novel. *The Odd Women* (1893) portrays the lives of the eponymous "odd" heroines, showing how criticism and unbending moral "standards" inevitably lead to the ruin of the unconventional female characters who are not only "uneven" in number but also "at odds" with general expectations. Hence, being unconventional ("odd") implied strangeness as well.

7. See also: Agnieszka Gromkowska-Melosik, *Kobieta Epoki Wiktoriańskiej: Tożsamość, Ciało i Medykalizacja.*

8. While Wollstonecraft argued for "a radical restructuring of power relations *within* the household, ... it is significant that [her] ideal of educated female citizens would produce 'more observant daughters, more affectionate sisters, more faithful wives, more reasonable mothers'" (Morgan, 38). Hence, Wollstonecraft's postulate highlights social benefits of women's education: in the nineteenth century, the change in the feminine sphere was directed toward a contribution to society. Apparently, the change was encouraged not for the sake of women but, rather, for the benefit of society—such assumption contradicts the modern understanding of "individuality," cherished in numerous neo-Victorian texts.

9. The anxiety of losing personal integrity after marriage and the possible dire consequences of marrying an unworthy (and dangerous) man are portrayed in George Eliot's *Romola* (1862–1863): The eponymous heroine discovers her husband's false character after their marriage and strives to free herself from his legal influence. Although set in fifteenth-century Florence, the novel responds to the concerns of the Victorian era, as both the fifteenth century and the Victorian age were filled with social and intellectual turmoil. *Romola* dwells on the constraints imposed on (Victorian) women in terms of their intellectual and financial incapaciation. The eponymous heroine struggles with her husband's treachery, seeking consolation in spiritualism. Her fifteenth-century struggles correspond with the Victorian dilemmas.

10. The topics of spiritualist literature covered, among many others, "temperance, dietary reform, phrenology, and the 'related' sciences of mesmerism and psychology, as well as publications dealing with social and political reform" (Owen, 24). Such topics were included in a "vast array" of spiritualist literature as distributed by Burns, who, in 1863, established the Progressive Library and Spiritual Institution in Southampton Row, Holborn (Owen, 24).

11. Hysteria was regarded as the female infirmity. "The feelings most likely to give rise to hysteria were sexual feelings, and it is here that the complexity of Victorian attitudes towards female sexuality becomes most apparent. While female insanity was associated with the illicit expression of sexual feelings, hysteria was associated with their repression" (King, 22).

Chapter Eight

The Ethics of the Past and the Present

The Nineteenth Century Reimagined in the Modern World

The post-Victorian era is a term often applied to the times following the year of Queen Victoria's death—1901. In his *Post-Victorian Britain 1902–1951*, L. C. B. Seaman highlights the importance of Victoria's hegemony while stating that

> the Queen had linked the England of 1900 with the still largely rural England of the age before the Railway Mania; she had also linked England with the continent of Europe in a more personal way than has since been possible. . . . [She] in a symbolic way bound England. (7)

Queen Victoria's tremendous impact on the development of England led to her enduring idolization. Currently, the abiding presence of her nineteenth-century legacy in the contemporary, digital age also accounts for the modern interest in the Victorian revision.

Beginning from the 1950s, postmodernism paved the way for the new understanding of society and its historical indebtedness. The prefix "post" indicates a temporal detachment from what is gone and directly unattainable. Simultaneously, it raises questions concerning the present attitude towards the relations with the past. Postmodernism, as defined by Kevin O'Donnell, "is the name given to a range of philosophical positions and aesthetic styles that has developed since the 1950s" (6). Rather than being defined by a single theoretical framework, postmodernism questions the notions of universalism, centrality, and unified historical narratives. While introducing discourses ranging from historical skepticism to the constructive questioning of the nature of "truth," postmodernism strives to fill in cultural gaps remaining after the embittering postwar social landscape.

In the postmodern era, O'Donnell posits, "life and society become decentered; there is a marketplace of values, reasons and lifestyles on offer" (20). Furthermore, as he aptly observes, "our generation is more ironically self-aware than any previous one. We realize that we are children of our time, and we play with ideas and styles from other eras quite deliberately" (29). Consequently, the nineteenth-century discourse finds its place among modern writers, readers, and scholars who experiment with the past, striving to find the link between the Victorian lifestyle and the modern commodified society. In this interplay between *now* and *then*, reaching for the Victorian experience turns into the process of learning about oneself: "to explore the postmodern is to explore ourselves again and to link up with a partially forgotten past" (O'Donnell, 6).

According to McHale, "postmodernism is a discursive construct" (5). McHale's "POSTmodernISM" addresses the issues highlighted by the prefix and suffix of the term:

> The ISM (to begin at the end) does double duty. It announces that the referent here is not merely a chronological division but an organized system—a poetics, in fact—while at the same time properly identifying what exactly it is that postmodernism is *post*. Postmodernism is not post modern, whatever that might mean, but post modernism; it does not come *after the present* (a solecism), but after the *modernist movement*. Thus the term "postmodernism," if we take it literally enough, *á la lettre*, signifies a poetics of early twentieth-century modernism, and not some hypothetical writing of the future. As for the prefix POST, here I want to emphasize the element of logical and historical *consequence* rather than sheer temporal *posteriority*. Postmodernism follows *from* modernism, in some sense, more than it follows *after* modernism. (5)

Apparently, McHale stresses the importance of historical continuity between modernism and postmodernism.

Postmodernism challenges the idea of a single, central historical narrative and, instead, it celebrates "non-linear, expressive and supra-rational discourses that have been marginalized and atrophied under the influence of Enlightenment," (O'Donnell, 6) also embracing the notion of neo-Victorianism with its multifaceted forms and voices. The previously disregarded voices from the past residing in the marginalized and obliterated nineteenth-century narratives begin to flourish in the socio-cultural environment conscious of its historical heritage. The postwar relativity, the rapidly growing market of diverse products and the progressive "commodification" of the so-called "truths" and "values" propelled the cultural quest for the supposedly "better" bygone. The nostalgia for the "secure past," epitomized in Bakhtin's statement that "the dead are loved in a different way," constitutes one of the factors in the modern investigation of the nineteenth century (*Dialogic Imagination*, 20). On the other hand, there is a concurrent anxiety dominated by the feeling of "belatedness" which, according to Ann Heilmann and Mark Llewellyn, "implies creative impotence" (3). The impossibility of recapturing the past *as it was* thus turns into the possibility of re-narrating it in numerous *potential* ways which, however, do not guarantee arriving at the "ultimate truth."[1] While postmodernism restored the interest in the so-far marginalized voices, the neo-Victorian literature of the twenty-first century further expanded the search for these so-far disregarded Victorian narratives, exploring the past through the eyes of the society living in the present-day era.

Interestingly enough, while the current "Victorian nostalgia" tries to detach itself from the notion of "consumerist lifestyle," it was the nineteenth century that introduced the notions of the market and marketplace into daily discourse. Thus, the question that arises is whether neo-Victorian literature is an endeavor to restore the "Victorian values" or whether it testifies to the fact that the Victorians are not remote from modern society in terms of its consumerist approach to life. Contemporary writers, scholars and readers test and adapt the nineteenth-century "boundaries," approximating them to the modern framework of standards and expectations. Figuratively speaking, in the postmodern cacophony of discourses, the past "dons" multiple "attires" depending on historical and cultural points of reference. The summoning of the past ab extra, "the disease of looking backwards," as humorously pointed out by Simon Joyce in his *The Victorians in the Rearview Mirror* (2), serves numerous purposes, including those involving marketing and politics.

The Victorian past, as it seems, can be appropriated by anyone, yet such appropriation frequently carries the dangers of misinterpretation or simplification. Arguing along these lines, Heilmann and Llewellyn instance Margaret Thatcher's idea of "Victorian values" reduced merely to the notion of conservative beliefs (5). Hence, it is crucial to perceive the task of re-narrating the Victorian past not only as a creative process, but also as an ethical decision.

In *A Theory of Adaptation* Linda Hutcheon states that "when we call a work an adaptation, we openly announce its overt relationship to another work or works" (6). At the same time, Hutcheon argues, the value of adaptations as individual works separated from the source text should not be disregarded (6), since "adaptation is repetition, but repetition without replication" (7). To "adapt," she observes, means to "adjust," to "alter" or "to make suitable" (7). This involves treating an adaptation as a "transposition of particular work or works"—a "process of creation" or a "process of reception" (7–8). Adaptation, she goes on to say, is necessarily a form of intertextuality. Hence, readers respond to adaptations in individualized ways, drawing on their memories of the previous source texts (8). Therefore, adaptation seeks to engage in an interactive, dynamic exchange of narratives, memories and possibilities, where each source text reveals different connotations for various readers. Paradoxically, as observed by Heilmann and Llewellyn, "adaptation is by its nature an evolving form, and one which we inherited from the nineteenth century" (244). Likewise, while approximating the literary past to the modern perspective, one reaches for Victorian "literary devices."

In her work *Adaptation and Appropriation*, Sanders also links the notion of adaptation with intertextuality, recognizing that "the impulse towards intertextuality and the narrative and architectural *bricolage* that can result from that impulse, is regarded by many as a central tenet of postmodernism" (17). Approached from the postmodern perspective, culture and history are transformed into a "patchwork" or a collage, where a priori ideas are adapted and appropriated by means of "variation, interpretation, continuation, transformation, imitation, pastiche, parody, forgery, travesty, transposition, revaluation, revision, rewriting, echo" (Sanders, 18). Incorporated into the list, the term "forgery" has the most negative connotation and suggests that the quality of adaptation depends on ethical decisions as much as on the degree of "faithfulness" to the original text.

Sanders makes a distinction between adaptation and appropriation, claiming that the latter "frequently affects a more decisive journey away from the informing source into a wholly new cultural product and domain" (26). In contrast, for Hutcheon, appropriation carries a multifaceted meaning: while appropriation can serve as a creative adaptation, "(re-)interpretation" and ("re)creation," it may abuse the source text as well (8). However, as she points out, "for every aggressive appropriator . . . there is a patient salvager" (8). This claim fully applies to neo-Victorian revisionary fiction, where the line between a playful yet ethical re-creation of the original work and its commercial exploitation appears to be rather thin.

As Heilmann and Llewellyn highlight, an unprofessional and uncritical appropriation of the Victorian past carries numerous risks: "What contemporary adaptations of the Victorian text do . . . is utilize the precursor text as a means to reflect the ideology of the present as divorced from the past" (235). Furthermore, they argue that "adaptation of history, the media moguls suggest, is fair game in the interests of audience attraction" (237). Hence, Heilmann and Llewellyn believe that the essence of appropriation lies in the issue of historical indebtedness and in ethical treatment of the source text. As they maintain, Victorians adapted the past in order to gain knowledge about themselves rather than to rob the bygone of its substance and quality for the sake of shocking or amusing the audience. Victorians were "anxious about their own position in the historical continuum," posits Llewellyn in his article "What Is Neo-Victorian Studies?" (173). "The thinkers of the nineteenth century frequently turned to history," he observes, "to provide sustenance to their own stability and potential" (173).

Heilmann and Llewellyn call into question the present-day focus on entertainment and catering for an undemanding audience, both leading to literary and historical relativism. What follows, they discuss the works of two authors, D. J. Taylor (*Kept: A Victorian Mystery* 2006) and Michel Faber (*The Crimson Petal and the White* 2002), who stretch the boundaries of ethical writing:

> Adaptation can also constitute a simpler attempt to make texts 'relevant' or easily comprehensible to new audiences and readerships via the processes of proximation and updating. In the case of neither Faber nor Taylor are things as clear-cut as this statement might suggest, unless we take their making the Victorian (or Victorian texts) "easily comprehensible" as part of an ironic comment on the notion of appropriation as an aesthetic mode. Taylor's use of Victoriana in his novel is excessive to the extreme and almost promotes the text as literally devouring the literature from which it is born on and on which it feeds. This consuming approach to the Victorian intertext posits the way in which the narrative ethics of the neo-Victorian are complicated via the "theft" (read appropriation) of the structural fabric and textual characteristics from the "original" nineteenth-century novel. (17)

While "updating" the Victorian age, one can also distort its "primary qualities": modern appropriations affect the perception of nineteenth-century literary characters and the portrayals of nineteenth-century historical figures. In this context, Heilmann and Llewellyn refer to James Wilson's *The Dark Clue: A Novel of Suspense* (2001):

> Wilson's novel confounds the distinctions between real and fictional individuals and in so doing takes biographical speculation about the lives of individuals from beyond the Victorian period and moves beyond it. . . . The fact that the "sexually aggressive element" [in Wilson's text] is portrayed in relation to a character adopted from a Victorian narrative (Walter Hartright from Wilkie Collins's *The Woman in White*, 1860), who commits a sexual attack on a character from the same story (Marian Halcombe), is but an example of how contemporary writers use nineteenth-century texts as an imaginative repository. What is more ethically questionable is the fact that Wilson's novel speculates on this sexual attack as a result of the influence of J. W. M. Turner, the subject of the biography Hartright has been commissioned to write. The gradual descent into madness of the central protagonist of the novel is thus drawn into an analogous relationship with the "insanity" of the real-life Turner. This does raise ethical questions, and also aesthetic issues concerning the relationship between text and reality, and the appropriation of a historical identity for the purpose of blurring the boundaries between fiction and fact, literature and life. (21–22)

Adaptation can greatly affect the reception of previously written Victorian works while presenting them in a distorted way. Neo-Victorian texts, treated as adaptations, are bound to be analyzed in ethical terms. Therefore, apart from moral doubts concerning the representation of historical figures in neo-Victorian fiction, another ethical question touches upon our modern rights to the Victorian texts. Are neo-Victorian texts written to offer intellectual fulfilment or are they supposed to cater for a superfluous delight in crime and violence?

While emphasizing and bringing to the surface the so-far omitted and marginalized voices, taking an ethical stance is still a vital component of neo-Victorian narratives—otherwise, they might be transformed exactly into what they wish to criticize. I believe that ethics and empathy are integral parts of the reading process and so is appreciation of literary characters created by other writers. Empathetic reworkings of Victorian texts not only offer a step forward toward uplifting marginalized nineteenth-century voices, but also toward appreciating the readers' "relationship" with literary characters portrayed in the nineteenth-century novel. Neo-Victorian fiction is not merely a task of transforming and shifting the text into whatever might fit into the modern context while incorporating historical figures into new narratives in a questionable manner but, rather, it is a thoughtful, ethical, responsible and empathetic engagement with the past. Only then, I believe, will the so-far omitted, marginalized voices be truly highlighted, heard, and appreciated on the neo-Victorian literary scene. Neo-Victorian fiction might build upon Victorian texts and criticize them in a constructive way, yet still it is vital to remember that without Victorian source texts, there would be nothing to transform, bring to the surface, or enhance. Unquestionably, source texts are the starting point of the modern discussion concerning the past and the present. Adaptations and appropriations of Victorian literature can dangerously warp the meaning of nineteenth-century texts. However, the process of adaptation is also capable of introducing a constructive dialogue of voices which can be discussed in Bakhtinian terms. Adaptation should necessarily be based on a dialogue involving the idea of ethics perceived by Emmanuel Levinas as "the pre-systematic, original language 'before words' . . . in general" (Eskin, 34). Thus, while appropriation has a wide range of meanings, as the above-presented examples indicate, the term *domestication*,[2] as I believe, seems to be more adequate (in contrast to appropriation) in the discussion concerning neo-Victorian literature. The term *domestication* implies a conscious cognition and acknowledgment of the bygone in the modern cultural framework. *Domestication* suggests that nineteenth-century fiction becomes gradually "accommodated" in modern reality in the process which stretches throughout the epochs. Through *domestication*, Victorian texts become familiar to modern readers and are incorporated into their cultural experience. In this sense, the current age recognizes the presence of the nineteenth-century literary discourse and strives to accommodate it in the contemporary environment, yet not necessarily through appropriation or "warping."

NOTES

1. By the "ultimate truth" I understand the final and complete narrative of the past which, from the above-presented perspective, cannot be obtained.

2. *Oxford Dictionary of English* defines the verb "domesticate" as "tam[ing] an animal and keep[ing] it as a pet or on a farm" but also "mak[ing] (someone) fond of and good at home life and the tasks that it involves" (Stevenson, ed., 519). In a metaphorical sense, when "domesticated" within the pages of neo-Victorian texts, the Victorian past becomes "tamed": intentionally modified and readjusted to the "new life." Yet, it is not forcefully appropriated but rather incorporated in the modern literary framework.

Chapter Nine

Beyond Nostalgia

Filling the Modern Culture with Victorianism[1]

According to Cora Kaplan, the author of *Victoriana: Histories, Fictions, Criticism*, the "new age" began to view the Victorians

> not simply as that always selective and unreliable thing, historical memory, so easily cloyed with nostalgia or soured into persecution of the dead, but as what we might call history out of place, something atemporal and almost spooky in its effects, yet busily at work continuing this time—yours and mine—of late Capitalism. (56)

Moreover, while depicting the recurring interest in the nineteenth-century world, Kaplan recognizes the significance of historical continuity when she asserts that "the modernist period may have increasingly replaced the Victorian as a still coercive antecedent" (6). The "pleasures and dangers" of the interest in what Kaplan terms as "Victoriana" stem from the persistent presence of nineteenth-century objects in the postmodern environment (6). Alongside the nostalgia-awakening items and Victorian pieces of architecture, Kaplan recognizes the subsistence of Victoriana in "a film, a pastiche, fiction, a retro style, even a biography" (3). Therefore, Victoriana has become a breeding ground for postmodern arts and media. Llewellyn and Heilmann refer to the numerous examples of "Victorianising" our "presence," including the expansion of "theme parks" such as "the Great Victorian Theme Park" or "Dickens World" theme park (213–14). They also refer to the figure of Andrew Davies, a Welsh screenplay writer, whose "identity as an adaptor of nineteenth-century, particularly Victorian contexts has made him a cultural authority on the Victorian and neo-Victorian literary spheres" (237). Visually appealing theme parks and state-of-the-art cinematic adaptations bear witness to the development of what Allen names as "technological society" (181), which is predominantly interested in reproduced, visual arts and objects rather than in literary media of communication. Hence, we define ourselves and our culture anew by reintroducing Victorian reproductions into our technologically dominated landscape.

"Technological society," Allen observes, "is dominated by reproductions of original works" (181–82). The mass production of videos and movies, the expansion of photography, books, e-books, paintings, drawings, and semi-original objects enhances the experience of the Victorian past and, at the same time, makes one ignorant of the nineteenth century, as the replicas often offer an incomplete and fabricated experience. Postmodernism, as Allen posits, defines itself as the age of reproduction, reenactment, mimicry, and renewal. Hence, while filling the cultural vacuum[2] with nineteenth-century replicas and artifacts, postmodernism embarks on the quest for its own identity. Yet, it must be observed that postmodern reproductions often allow one to access the past in its highly "abridged," simplified version, as I will attempt to present in the next part of this chapter on the examples of the selected literary works.

Paradoxically, the postmodern interest in revisiting the Victorian era results from the temporal detachment from this period and the concurrent desire to bring it closer to the present. "At the height of our (post)modernity, why do we continually mark and stage a return to a period that was caught between two 'bigger' notions [Romanticism and Modernism]?," inquires Llewellyn in his "Neo-Victorianism: An Introduction" (167).

Louisa Hadley tries to account for the significance of this "resurgence" of the nineteenth century in our modern culture: she observes that the Victorians appear attractive to the postmodern audience as they are removed from the direct sphere of influence, and yet they are still located within historical vicinity. In *Neo-Victorian Fiction and Historical Narrative: The Victorians and Us*, Hadley explicates that "the appeal of the Victorians is a result of the complex combination of their historical proximity and distance from the contemporary era" (14). Llewellyn holds a similar opinion, suggesting that

> the approaches required to reading the neo-Victorian and do it critical justice are exactly the same mix of contextual and textual awareness required to address the multiplicity of the Victorians themselves. . . . The Victorian and neo-Victorian offer the simultaneous possibilities of proximity and distance. ("Neo-Victorianism: An Introduction," 175)

Arguing along these lines, it seems that the temporal distance from the Victorian era increases the chances of a multifaceted modern revision of the past. According to Kaplan, we are enchanted by the Victorians because the "distant" signifies a fascinating "antique" and "exotic":

for while the high literary modernism and the popular culture in the first half of the twentieth century defined itself through an explicit or tacit rejection of the cultural preferences and social mores of the Victorian world, distance from the period had not only produced detailed—and controversial—historical analyses of its customs, practices and influence, but has gradually lent it over time the charm of antiquity and the exotic, so that increasingly, in the new millennium, even its worst abuses seem to fascinate rather than appall. Genealogically speaking, the Victorian is no longer seen as a disapproving parent of the louche modernity of the opening of the last century." (6)

The plurality of terms defining revisionary Victorian fiction deserves consideration as well. The authors of *Neo-Victorianism* enumerate the most popular prefixes: "neo-," "faux-," "retro-," and "post-" (Heilmann, Llewellyn 23). These diversified terms highlight different qualities of the revisionary process. Kirchknopf accounts for these terminological discrepancies in her article "(Re)workings of Nineteenth-Century Fiction: Definitions, Terminology, Context" while referring to Sally Shuttleworth's term "retro-Victorian" novel:

> she identifies *retro-Victorian fiction* as a type of historical novel, and explains that the category of historical novel is broadly understood and thus inclusive of historiographic metafiction (Shuttleworth 1998:254). The author [Shuttleworth] delimits her analysis to a specific subset of *retro-Victorian novels*—explicitly nostalgic texts that engage with the discourse of natural history—but does not provide any further definition (Shuttleworth 1998:253). (Kirchknopf, 62)

The term "retro-Victorian" seems to entirely locate its interests in the past. Similarly, it emphasizes a sentimental longing for the bygone. Thus, it appears that "retro-Victorian" overlooks the actual interplay between the past and the present.

"Post-Victorian" is yet another option discussed by Kirchknopf in her article. Coined by Georges Letissier, the term "post-Victorian" connects postmodernism with Victorianism, primarily stressing the vitality of modern historical settings (64).

Another perspective on postmodern revisionary literature is provided by Kaplan's "Victoriana," the term initially assigned to the material objects from the era, but gradually broadened to include "postmodern rewritings of Victorian texts" (65). Finally, as Kirchknopf highlights, the term embraces all Victorian "representations and reproductions" (65). Furthermore, Kirchknopf offers the term "Postmodern Victoriana" in order to "add a qualifier" to Kaplan's terminology and enable the new perspectives of interpretation (66).

The growing commitment to the literary revision resulted in the introduction of such other terms as: "Victoriography," or the previously mentioned "historical novel" and "historiographic metafiction" (66). The latter terms,

Kirchknopf notes, "prove necessary in a generic sense, but they do not specify the age that is being refashioned" (66). Likewise, the term "contemporary historical fiction" is too remote from its object of interest while terms such as: "pseudo-historical fiction" or "pseudo-Victorian fiction" imply a potential lack of veracity.

The last term Kirchknopf discusses in her article, the "neo-Victorian novel," is of paramount importance in this book. Kirchknopf introduces Dana Shiller's paper "The Redemptive Past in the Neo-Victorian Novel" (1997), which defines the "neo-Victorian" novel as simultaneously merged in the present and concerned with the past: "at once characteristic of postmodernism and imbued with a historicity reminiscent of the nineteenth-century novel (1997: 538)" (Kirchknopf, 62). Alongside with Shiller's definition of the neo-Victorian novel, Kirchknopf introduces Daniel Bormann's interpretation of the neo-Victorian work as

> a fictional text which creates meaning from the background of awareness of time as flowing and as poised uneasily between *the Victorian* past and the present; which secondly deals dominantly with topics which belong to the field of history, historiography and/or the philosophy of history *in dialogue with a Victorian past*; and which thirdly can do so at all narrative levels and in any possible discursive form, be it through narration of action, through static description, argumentative exposition or stream-of-consciousness techniques (Bormann 2002:62). (Kirchknopf, 63)

Shiller's and Bormann's definitions reveal different shades of meaning of neo-Victorian texts. Yet, both Shiller's and Bormann's choices of terminology seem to be convincing since, first and foremost, the proposed prefix "neo-" escapes nostalgic notions of loss and anxiety, remaining open to creativity and narrative challenges. Shiller's definition offers the basis for the perception of neo-Victorian texts as those works which bridge the gap between the present and the bygone. Bormann is much more specific in his investigation, as he places neo-Victorian texts in a historical context remaining in a dialogue with the past. According to Bormann, neo-Victorian texts emerge influenced by "the background of awareness of time" (Kirchknopf, 63), shaped by contemporary narrative modes often uncommon back in the nineteenth century. "Neo-Victorian fiction," Louisa Hadley indicates, signifies bi-directionality: it "attempt[s] to narrate the Victorian past" and "explore[s] the ways in which the past has been narrated in the present" (26–27). Furthermore, neo-Victorian fiction embraces "the possibility of establishing an empathic connection to the past without resulting in presentism" (26). This "empathic connection," together with an ethical approach to the literary "resurgence," appears paramount in the study of the neo-Victorian genre that seeks to revisit the past from a dialogical perspective. Hence, in this book, I solely adhere to the term "neo-Victorian," as it offers a sense of bi-directionality and connectedness between the past and the present.

At the same time, other terms—including "faux," "retro," and "post"—signal different forms of engagement with the Victorian past, attesting to its complexity and multilayered structure. The term "neo-Victorian" appears to be especially vital in the process of restoring to the literary scene the unheard nineteenth-century voices, as it implies the newness and freshness of this enterprise without necessarily looking in a single, isolated direction, be it the past or the present. "Neo-Victorian" is all-embracing, implying dialogical coexistence of narratives and intertextual engagement with the sociohistorical discourse. Yet, "the neo-Victorian," as stipulated by Heilmann and Llewellyn, "is *more than* historical fiction set in the nineteenth century. To be part of the neo-Victorianism . . . , texts . . . must in some respect be *self-consciously engaged with the act of (re)interpretation, (re-discovery and (re)vision concerning the Victorians*" [emphasis original] (4). Such definition entails the belief in bridging the gap between the past and the present by means of rewritten (hence, "experimental") narratives, as the prefix "re" implies the concept of an experiment. Neo-Victorian literature escapes the label of "historical fiction," as it challenges the authority of an unquestionable "historical truth" and introduces a dialogue of voices (sensu Bakhtin). As observed by Gutleben, neo-Victorian fiction unleashes the "private voices" that can be heard exclusively by the modern readers. Commenting on Sarah Waters's *Affinity* (1999), Gutleben argues that "public Victorian voices differ radically from their private improper voices and the truth of their stories is never known by their Victorian counterparts: only the twentieth-century reader hears these voices, as if the addressee of such a discourse were necessarily modern" (37). Consequently, neo-Victorian literature offers a binary approach towards the so-called historical "truth" and thus proves that not every neo-Victorian novel can be labeled precisely as "historical fiction."[3] In Hadley's view, neo-Victorian fiction "is not only concerned with reinserting the Victorians into historical narrative, but also with exploring the ways in which historical narratives affect modern responses to the past" (6). Hence, while referring to neo-Victorian writings, I advocate the term "historiographic metafiction" instead of "historical fiction." Historiographic metafiction, the term used in Linda Hutcheon's *A Poetics of Postmodernism* (1988),

> is a characteristic genre of postmodern literature, not only because of its proliferation but also because it encapsulates the very contradictions at work in postmodern itself. . . . The metafictional aspects of neo-Victorian texts are inflected with a self-conscious questioning of the possibilities of narrating the past, read in relation to Victorian forms of historical narrative. (Hadley, 18, 19)

Perceived as historiographic metafiction, neo-Victorian works restage the past in its "unofficial" version. The reintroduction of previously omitted voices into the literary discourse opens up the possibility of reviving the Victorians as those who are similar, at least to some extent, to *us*. Consequently, such possibility allows for the domestication of nineteenth-century discourses in our present-day consciousness. As Hutcheon argues, "postmodern fiction suggests that to re-write or to re-present the past in fiction and in history is, in both cases, to open it up to the present, to prevent it from being conclusive and teleological" (110). Hutcheon defines historiographic metafiction as "play[ing] upon the truth and lies of the historical record" (114). She points to the difference between the aforementioned historical fiction and historiographic metafiction, stating that it

> lies in the way in which postmodern fiction actually uses detail or historical data. Historical fiction (*pace* Lukács) usually incorporates and assimilates these data in order to lend a feeling of veritability (or an air of dense specificity and particularity) to the fictional world. Historiographic metafiction incorporates, but rarely assimilates such data. More often, the process of *attempting* to assimilate is what is foregrounded: we watch the narrators of Ondaatje's *Running in the Family* or Findley's *The Wars* trying to make sense of the historical facts they have collected. As readers, we see both the collecting and the attempts to make narrative order. Historiographic metafiction acknowledges the paradox of the *reality* of the past but its *textualized accessibility* to us today. [emphasis in the original] (114)

According to Hutcheon, historiographic metafiction introduces historical figures not to "legitimize" the fictional world but, rather, to pose fundamental questions concerning our current knowledge of the past:

> In many historical novels, the real figures of the past are deployed to validate or authenticate the fictional world by their presence, as if to hide the joins between fiction and history in a formal and ontological sleight of hand. The metafictional self-reflexivity of postmodern novels prevents any such subterfuge, and poses that ontological join as a problem: how do we know the past? What do (what can) we know of it now? (114–15)

Thus, as it seems, historiographic metafiction highlights its own textual construction and, instead of searching for the conclusive, ultimate narratives, it experiments with both history and fiction. Moreover, as Gutleben observes, the introduction of a priori disregarded voices enables a literary paradigm shift:

These choices of mouthpieces constitute by their very existence a departure from and a renewal of the Victorian prototype. To regenerate the tradition they fictively continue, the retro-Victorian novels invert its priorities: the excluded becomes included, the unheard becomes voiced, the hidden becomes foregrounded, the marginal becomes central. To retrieve the forgotten of history and lend them a voice is the very principle of postmodern revisionism. (124)

Gutleben expresses a similar view as Llewellyn, who claims that "neo-Victorianism . . . blurs the distinctions between criticism and creativity, with each becoming a reflection of self and other" ("What is Neo-Victorian Studies?," 170). It is "the desire to reach beyond," "write back" and to "refresh and re-vitalise the importance of that earlier text to here and now" that prompts the current Victorian resurrection (Llewellyn, 170–71). Referring to the notion of palimpsest[4]—a document on which the initial writing was replaced with a new record—Llewellyn discusses neo-Victorian fiction as "palimpsestuous"—occupied with "the obscured and the unseen" (171). At the same time, he recognizes that neo-Victorian fiction serves as a narrative proposal rather than historical evidence:

> this is not to say that we take these texts as the evidence that we cannot find in the archives; nor does it propose that we ignore the evidence which *is* obscurely there in favour of these neater, rounder, and more clearly *(t)here* narratives. But it does mean opening up aspects of our present to a relationship with the Victorian past in ways that offer new possibilities for simultaneously thinking through where we come from. (171)

Hence, in my view, neo-Victorian fiction implies rethinking of our current sociohistorical placement and relationship in society. It implies a considerate looking back at the historical past through the prism of literature while being aware that the literary tools for looking back are only a proposal—a single aspect or a vision in the sea of narrative possibilities proliferating in the current age. Neo-Victorian fiction works against dualisms and clear-cut statements embraced during the Victorian age as, instead of gathering evidence, it gathers dialogical perspectives which help one to find out where we are at present. In fact, in many ways, especially while trying to transform the nineteenth-century muffled voices into fully audible narratives, we glance at the Victorian past as if it was a mirror reflection of our present—sometimes warped, sometimes remodeled, but always related to the current time and age. If it was not so, the Victorian past would not play such a paramount role in our consciousness.

In this book, neo-Victorian works are perceived as texts either fully or partially located in the Victorian setting and exhibiting "a form of ventriloquism":

> Ventriloquism involves both 'speaking like' and 'speaking as' a Victorian. ... Thus, while "speaking like" a Victorian could result in a surface imitation of Victorian narrative forms, "speaking as" a Victorian requires an understanding of the historical conditions to which those forms are responding. (Hadley, 160)

I understand ventriloquism as a self-aware, revisionary voice which, while hiding in the Victorian past, offers a narrative of the present. While Hadley mentions the "surface imitation of Victorian narrative forms," Andrea Kirchknopf elaborates on the issue of writerly mimicry, enumerating the qualities that make the text "neo-Victorian":

> The postmodern rewrites of Victorian texts keep the average length and structure of Victorian novels: the bulky 500 pages ... are usually divided into books or chapters, sometimes preceded by chapter summaries or epigraphs. They imitate prevalent genres of nineteenth century, such as Bildungsroman, or the social, industrial and sensation novels, creatively intermingled with conventions of the (auto)biographical and (pseudo)historical novels, thus creating a hybridity of genres abundant in parody and pastiche so characteristic of postmodern novelistic discourse. The narrative design of those novels tends to be like that of their Victorian predecessors' and they typically employ narrative voices of the types dominant in nineteenth-century texts, i.e., the first person character narrator or the third person omniscient one. (54)

Importantly, Kirchknopf's definition employs the notion of "parody and pastiche." However, based on Frederick Jameson's thought, Hadley argues that pastiche is disengaged from historical commitment and, thus, incongruent with the task of the neo-Victorian genre. "For Jameson," she posits,

> pastiche is parody dislocated from any political or satirical intent, leaving only a "linguistic mask" that is divorced from its historical referent. In light of neo-Victorian fiction's commitment to the historical referent of the Victorian era, the concept of pastiche is clearly inadequate for understanding the approach of its authors writing *as* Victorians. (159)

Heilmann and Llewellyn also unanimously agree that the concept of pastiche is divergent from the notion of neo-Victorian literary revision. As they state,

> it would be false to suggest that texts which merely rewrite Victorian novels in contemporary ways are doing anything other than a straightforward pastiche: meeting a market demand but not necessarily adding anything new to our understanding of how fiction works, what that fiction can do, or possibly what it cannot do. (23)

Eventually, Hadley rejects both concepts of pastiche and parody in favor of ventriloquism (160), the term adopted by Kate Mitchell in *History and Cultural Memory in Neo-Victorian Fiction*. Referring to Sarah Waters's revisionary novels, Mitchell indicates that they "ventriloquise Victorian gothic and sensation fiction" (141–42). In Helen Davies's work, *Gender and Ventriloquism in Victorian and neo-Victorian Fiction: Passionate Puppets*, the term constitutes "a focal point for negotiating the politics of neo-Victorian literature" (6). It is the focal point that introduces the postmodern self-awareness defined from the current historical standpoint.

At present, the most enthusiastically revived nineteenth-century works include such diverse genres as biographies and detective novels. While experimenting with the Victorian "Life and Letters" mode of writing (Hadley, 36), modern authors address the issue of "biographical truth." Such is the context of Syrie James's *The Secret Diaries of Charlotte Brontë* (2009)—a fictional autobiography of the nineteenth-century authoress. In James's preface to Brontë's fictionalized biography, one reads:

Dear Reader,

Imagine, if you will, that a great discovery has been made, which sparked enormous excitement in the literary world: a series of journals, which have lain buried and forgotten for more than a century in the cellar of a remote farmhouse in Britain Isles, have been officially authenticated as the private diaries of Charlotte Brontë. What would those diaries reveal? (vi)

James' preface can be perceived as Genette's intended paratext or, in other words, the "frame" of the text: it prepares the reader for the encounter with a fictional autobiography of the actual Victorian writer. Besides, it builds expectations towards the text while employing the idea of discovery and revelation. The preface alludes to Brontë's writing mode as well, intimately addressing the "Dear Reader" in Brontë's manner characteristic of her novels and thus setting the scene for secrecy. The implication that the novel contains an enigmatic record from Charlotte Brontë's diary not only challenges the "Life and Letters" biographical mode, but also explores the possibility of alternative narratives of the past. The aim of James's experiment with the text lies in developing a vision of Brontë's life that departs from the dominant biographical discourse. Therefore, *The Secret Diaries* stands in the shadow of such texts as Elizabeth Gaskell's *The Life of Charlotte Brontë* (1857), Winifred Gérin's *Charlotte Brontë: The Evolution of Genius* (1967), and Rebecca Fraser's *Charlotte Brontë: A Writer's Life* (2003). At the same time, James's work instigates a complex polemic with the past, since the first-person narration "approximates" the past to the reader's zone. Reading

Brontë's supposed "mysterious diary" allows one not only to recognize in Brontë a writer, but also a "real" woman. Hence, James's text fulfills the desire to picture the Victorians as individuals who are similar to modern readers in their hopes, dreams, and perspectives on life. At the same time, James's work does not alter Brontë's biography and adheres to literary ethics. It works as a "possibility" enriching one's vision of Charlotte's life as a woman writer. James's empirical writing encourages an empathetic reflection over history and historical figures as it *domesticates* the past in the twenty-first century consciousness.

Apart from Syrie James, other modern writers eagerly pursue the idea of "fictionalizing" Charlotte Brontë's biography, treating her life as the repository for ideas. For instance, Laura Joh Rowland revives Charlotte Brontë's narratives in her *The Secret Adventures of Charlotte Brontë* (2008) and *Bedlam* (2010). In Rowland's works, Brontë appears suspended between "reality" and fiction, witnessing crime, murder, and conspiracy. As a semi-fictional character, she is able to relate her "own" story. While Roland's work experiments with historical narratives, it also raises questions regarding Brontë as a historical figure: to what extent is it justified to alter one's biography and what is the purpose of such a revision? Moreover, how does Roland's novel enrich the general cultural understanding of the Victorian past? Both James's and Rowland's novels have mystery at their core. In James's text, it is the revelation of the diary that triggers the plot, while in Rowland's work Brontë witnesses a crime. The "new dimension" of neo-Victorian detective fiction is highlighted by Louisa Hadley, who argues that "it [neo-Victorian fiction] engages in the process of historical recovery" (60). As Hadley explicates, the plot of detective fiction follows the pattern of neo-Victorian "reconstruction": "like the crime story, the past is characterized by an 'absence'; it can never wholly be recovered in the present" (61). Nevertheless, according to Hadley, "a confident assertion to knowledge is only possible in a fictional world; in the real world, knowledge has its limits" (78). Consequently, neo-Victorian texts trace the lost and hidden elements of the Victorian past and inscribe them into new literary contexts as if they were puzzle pieces. Clare Boylan's *Emma Brown* (2003) provides another example of the neo-Victorian detective novel portraying an enigmatic case of an orphaned child. While the eponymous Emma embarks on the quest for her lost identity, she also develops as a self-conscious individual.

Boylan's work can be treated as a "postmodern romance" (the term used in Heidi Hansson's work). The features further approximating Boylan's work to the "postmodern romance" are: a "happy ending" sealed by marriage and a strenuous path to go through beforehand, with the unbending protagonist—Emma—struggling with challenging twists of fate. In the postmodern romance, the reader can find universal, familiar characteristics termed by

Hansson as "common ground" enabling the understanding of the text: "an important problem which is shared by many writers of fiction today is how to make it possible to create meaning when there are neither common value systems not common cultural beliefs to lean on," Hansson postulates,

> there is an urgent need for both writers and readers to find common ground, otherwise communication through literature runs the risk of becoming impossible and obsolete. Postmodern romances capitalize on the popularity and familiarity of the romance to create this common ground, which means that the works have to be recognisable as romances. Like medieval and Renaissance romances, postmodern ones frequently bring in a miraculous dimension, like the historical ones they are acutely aware of the importance of the past, and like women's popular romances they tell love stories. Intertextual references establish the connections. (3)

In Boylan's novel, Emma's quest, the "miraculous dimension" of her story and the intertextual references to Charlotte Brontë's *Jane Eyre* all contribute to the story that strives to rebuild the past from the available literary and historical "building blocks." The revived romance incorporates the themes of loss, obliteration, and the journey for reassessment of Emma's integrity. The qualifier "postmodern" adheres also to the self-reflexive nature of the text. Thus, even though Boylan's heroine is placed in the Victorian environment, her quest is essentially postmodern as it challenges nineteenth-century bildungsroman narratives. Emma's metamorphosis from an orphaned girl to a self-aware woman challenges Brontë's "Cinderella plot" from *Jane Eyre*: what Jane owes to her unwavering virtue and marvelous coincidences, Emma attains mostly by effort and excessively hard work. Emma's quest is filled with "lucky coincidences" (such as meeting the characters who "complete" her knowledge about the past), but it is primarily Emma's hard work and independence which greatly contribute to her future success. As a child, Emma is confronted with bleak prospects of homelessness. Unlike Jane Eyre, who looks after a doll, Emma responsibly nurtures an abandoned child. Boylan's heroine prematurely dons the role of an adult and struggles with financial difficulties. In this sense, Boylan's novel fills the gaps in the nineteenth-century literary discourse, offering a story in which Emma's voice asserts that it is not only one's virtue that contributes to a potential success in the Victorian world but also, unfortunately, one's financial security as well.

Emma Brown draws parallels between nineteenth-century and postmodern notions of commodification, while simultaneously questioning contemporary Victorian nostalgia. There is a strong sense of bitterness in Boylan's picture of the Victorian world, where the plain Jane Eyre, although virtuous and modest, has no right to survive. The world presented in *Emma Brown* is the world relying on the concept of the "survival of the fittest": when Emma decides to visit the Great Exhibition, she is denied admission, and her money mysteriously disappears:

> "My job is to take money and nothing else," the ticket-seller responded. "I can admit no one who cannot pay."
>
> "Those girls behind me had no money," Emma said. "You let them in because they were cheerful and pretty."
>
> "I did no such thing!" he protested. "They had a purse of money and they paid me from it."
>
> "Oh, it was them," Emma said dejectedly. "They must have taken my purse when they danced around with me." (392)

Similarly, in chapter 35, Emma is "gripped by a sense of remembered dread so wrong that all the gay spring scene around her seemed to vanish. *They had no money*" [emphasis added] (391–92). In Boylan's novel, the economically oriented concerns are highlighted and "resurrected" in the Victorian setting. In this sense, Boylan's modern work offers an alternative narrative to Brontë's miraculous moral victory from *Jane Eyre*: Emma wins because she works hard and does not merely rely on fortunate twists of fate. Hence, even though she initially suffers, she remains in control of her life.

There is no sentiment in Boylan's literary representation of nineteenth-century London, where wealth and beauty prevail over righteousness. While the feeling of nostalgia for the past is obliterated in the text, the modern longing for the sentimental "Victoriana" is undermined as well. Boylan offers a conscious reflection on the past rather than a meaningless idealization of the period. Llewellyn recognizes the risk of the thoughtless Victorian nostalgia, labeling it as "period fetishism":

> this is a fact of our contemporary culture; that in bookstores and TV guides all around us what we see is the "nostalgic tug" that the (quasi-)Victorian exerts on the mainstream identification of our own time as a period in search of its past. (167)

The search for the past, Llewellyn posits, should be based on a constructive, multi-perspective approach to the bygone rather than on a "nostalgic tug" and wishful thinking about the nineteenth century. In Boylan's novel, there is a thin line between "reality" and nostalgia: Emma and the ill, abandoned girl Jenny long for a homelike and peaceful place. On seeing the Great Exhibition, they wishfully imagine that it is heaven. However, there is an omnipresent danger resulting from the lack of financial stability which disturbs the "heavenly" vision. Clare Boylan's "Victorian heaven" is open only for the privileged ones. Although Emma and Jenny emerge victorious from their dramatic quest, the novel contains a warning against thoughtless glorification of the Victorian past. Since the neo-Victorian novel is concerned with both the past and the present, it is also a reminder that, in our contemporaneity, morally attained victories too often compete with materialism. It seems that even though our historical placement is changing, the problems of the past are still reappearing.

NOTES

1. A part of this chapter was published in *Athens Journal of Humanities and Arts*, volume 5, issue 4, October 2018, 469–82.
2. I perceive the modern age as suspended in the "cultural vacuum" filled with replicas from the past. Present-day culture is highly reliant on reproductions and revived discourses accommodated in the twenty-first-century context. There is little if any cultural novelty which could be offered by and fully produced in the modern age.
3. As mentioned before, the neo-Victorian fiction "restages" history and "rewrites" it from numerous, often contrasting perspectives. In effect, neo-Victorian fiction offers a number of parallel narratives instead of a unified historical message.
4. "Palimpsests" have been already mentioned as the notion incorporated into Genette's study.

Chapter Ten

Women and Spiritual Revival

According to Heilmann and Llewellyn, "loss, mourning and regeneration" as well as "a retracing and piecing together of the protagonist's roots" are characteristic themes of neo-Victorian fiction (34). They especially emphasize the process of "anamnesis," which indicates learning through recollection (34). Hence, retrospective reading serves as a paramount element in understanding neo-Victorian texts.

While nineteenth-century discourses established a narrative connection between women's vulnerability and their supposed spiritual "natures," neo-Victorianism embraces spiritualism as a means of "establish[ing] a more active engagement with the Victorian past" (Hadley, 85). Contemporary writers, such as Sarah Waters and Michèle Roberts, devote considerable attention to the notion of spiritualism, which allows them to enrich nineteenth-century discourses with previously marginalized or obliterated voices. For instance, Waters's *Affinity* (1999) portrays Selina Dawes—a medium who propels the action of the novel. Through the character of Selina, Waters explores the concepts of deception and "blurred reality." The novel questions a stable idea of "reality" and investigates alternative ways of accessing the past. Balancing between the storyline and metaphysical occurrences which serve as "possible narrative options," *Affinity* gains a metafictional dimension, turning into the neo-Victorian text about the possibilities of reviving the bygone: while Waters presents a world surrounded by mystery and deceit, it is only the narrative that "puts the pieces together," reconstructs the plot and "re-orders" the initially hostile world so that it becomes more comprehensible. Hence, the plot construction in Waters's work is typical of the neo-Victorian novel.

In Jean Rhys's *Wide Sargasso Sea* (1966) there is no direct reference to spiritualism apart from the introduction of the "obeah" magic. Nevertheless, the text is filled with a spectral presence. The heroine of Creole heritage, Antoinette, uses magic as a defense against her self-interested husband and as a means of gaining his love. Gradually, Antoinette plunges into the world suspended between reality and magic in order to defend herself against desperation and madness. Paradoxically, the spiritual atmosphere surrounding the heroine triggers her husband's hostility and accusations. Removed from her Caribbean home, Antoinette is deprived of her name, possessions, and history. Hence, to survive, she chooses the world of imagination as a last resort. The longing for safety is expressed through Antoinette's childhood yearning for a magic wand. Similarly, imagination enables Antoinette to construct her own reality while she is locked in the attic by her ruthless husband. As the prisoner of the attic, Antoinette strives to preserve her past and identity by means of her favorite dress removed from the wardrobe. The heroine "re-imagines" her past while looking at the dress which turns into a "spiritual gate" to the bygone. In this sense, removing the dress from the wardrobe turns into a spiritual experience where the past becomes almost tangible for the imprisoned heroine:

> as soon as I turned the key I saw it hanging, the colour of fire and sunset. The colour of flamboyant flowers. "If you are buried under a flamboyant tree," I said, "your soul is lifted up when it flowers. Everyone wants that." . . . The scent that came from the dress was very faint at first, then it grew stronger. The smell of vetiver and frangipani, of cinnamon and dust and lime trees when they are flowering. The smell of the sun and the smell of the rain. (119–20)

Antoinette's story is a profound example of the neo-Victorian narrative concerned with reimagining, rewriting, and rediscovering the fate of nineteenth-century women—especially those women who found themselves on the margin of the dominant Victorian discourse. "An imaginative approach to the past is necessary to recuperate the narratives of women who have been written out of official accounts of the past," Louisa Hadley reiterates (116).

Importantly, Rhys's account of Antoinette's life challenges the original story of Charlotte Brontë's Bertha in *Jane Eyre*. Rhys's postcolonial neo-Victorian narrative endows Bertha with a voice and encourages the reader to reflect upon the multifaceted nature of the literary past. In effect, *Wide Sargasso Sea* provides an indirect commentary on the modern revision of the nineteenth-century literary past in which spirituality and spiritual perception of women play a significant role. Antoinette possesses a rich spiritual life and imagination which help her to survive and create her own, relatively safe inward world. It is precisely the inward world of the heroine which gains prominence in Rhys's novel and offers redemption to Rhys's Antoinette. *Wide Sargasso Sea* abounds in descriptions of magic and magical rituals associated with Antoinette and her nurse, Christophine. Whereas for Antoinette magic signifies safety and her ability to turn the vision of reality into a safer environment, it creates the notion of danger in Rochester's eyes. For him, Antoinette is not a delicate, genuine, spiritual figure, but a dangerous and inwardly unstable outsider. What for Antoinette is her saving grace supposedly reveals her unbridled and dangerous nature in Rochester's eyes. What allows Antoinette to deal with her loveless reality and look upon herself as an individual is treated by Rochester as a threat. In *Wide Sargasso Sea*, Antoinette's reviving spirituality is demonized through the patriarchal gaze. Correspondingly, in *Jane Eyre*, Bertha Mason, with her inscrutable inner life and behavior, is the epitome of Mr. Rochester's patriarchal fears as, essentially, he cannot control her beyond locking her up in the attic. Bertha's supposed unpredictability adds to her perception as a spiritual figure verging on a possessed femininity. In *Wide Sargasso Sea*, Rhys skillfully re-narrates Bertha's story, posing a question whether, in fact, Bertha's image in *Jane Eyre* is not filtered through patriarchal perspectives of the Victorian age and whether, in fact, her perception is not warped out of proportion in order to conform to the patriarchal idea of female madness. In *Wide Sargasso Sea*, turning Antoinette's spirituality into madness becomes a convenient tool for labeling her as worthless and dangerous in Rochester's eyes. Thus, in the neo-Victorian novel, women's spiritual life is presented both as a redeeming power and a threat to patriarchal stability. Neo-Victorian fiction engages in what Graham Allen presupposes to be the postmodern "playful registering of culture's current saturation of signs and sign-systems" (190). Although submerged in the Victorian world, Rhys's heroine responds to the current inquiries that alter and profile the vision of Victorian women and their relationship with spiritualism. In *Nostalgic Postmodernism*, Christian Gutleben posits that

> for ideological, ethical and perhaps commercial reasons the foregrounding of the discarded society was impossible for the Victorian novel, essentially written for the middle-classes, but today, at the time of the politically correct, these voices correspond precisely to readerly expectations. (37)

In this light, I argue once again that the task of neo-Victorian fiction lies not only in an experimental play with the bygone, but also in a conscious reflection on the past, in its previously omitted and hidden narratives and, finally, in its enduring influence on our current historical placement.

Chapter Eleven

Women and Family in the Neo-Victorian Novel

In order to properly introduce the literary figure of the neo-Victorian woman it is indispensable to discuss her origin and, thus, pay a visit to the neo-Victorian family. It is a rather gloomy visit, as Marie-Luise Kohlke and Christian Gutleben observe in *Neo-Victorian Families: Gender, Sexual and Cultural Politics* that the neo-Victorian family not only aspires to abolish the Victorian myth of the perfect household, but also alludes to the modern breakdown in human relations:

> On the one hand, the neo-Victorian family offers a more nuanced understanding of the advent and structural stresses of the modern-day Western capitalist system, nation states and the bigger "human family" of globalised society, reflecting emergent conflicts between the growth of self-interested individualism and altruistic collaboration for the common good. On the other, the family trope enables a quasi-genealogical exploration of cultural legacy. (5)

However, as they highlight, the family myth is revised in the "twentieth- and twenty-first century social organisation, with its seemingly rootless and fragmented kinship patterns, careerist singledom, childless coupledom, quickie divorces, patchwork families and failing inter-generational contract" (5). The neo-Victorian family is portrayed as dysfunctional and rootless. The flawed state of the neo-Victorian household contributes to the crisis of an individual, as well as to the feelings of seclusion and identity dilemmas. The notion of uprootedness inherent in the neo-Victorian novel triggers the development of the character who initiates the quest for the self. Literary characters, initially likened to a "blank page" without a stable past and origin (since they descend from a "broken" neo-Victorian family without its history or traditions), gradually construct self-created identities and histories.

While the Victorian novel incorporates into the bildungsroman the theme of a broken home, one-parent family, or orphanhood in order to present the final victory of virtue over earthly trials, the neo-Victorian genre offers uprootedness as a potential for personal growth. Thus, it alludes to the postmodern social disruption, but also subverts the "immaculate Victorian family" myth, placing one's individuality in the center of the new discourse.

The trope of self-awareness and victorious self-development is perpetuated in such neo-Victorian works as Jean Rhys's *Wide Sargasso Sea*, Clare Boylan's *Emma Brown*, Syrie James's *The Secret Diaries of Charlotte Brontë*, and Gail Carriger's *Soulless*. While Rhys's heroine, Antoinette, loses the battle for the self in an uncompromising and merciless world, she still leaves her mark in the form of her narrative. Self-creativity and self-reflexivity are the dominant features of the neo-Victorian heroine, who strives to detach herself from her roots in order to be transformed into an (at least mentally) independent, full-fledged figure.

In Boylan's, James's, and Carriger's works, women characters either overcome struggles with their dysfunctional families, remain plagued by family problems, or do not possess the place of origin. For example, as a character in James's novel, Charlotte Brontë deals with persistent family problems involving her violent brother and ill sisters. Alexia Tarabotti in Carriger's work unceasingly escapes the hypocrisy of her conceited sisters and narrow-minded parents. On the other hand, Boylan's Emma Brown seeks to establish her place of origin and struggles victoriously to retrieve her lost name.

In contrast to their nineteenth-century predecessors, neo-Victorian women characters seek their own happiness and do not define themselves against their families and husbands. As I have argued in one of the previous chapters, the Victorian woman was encouraged to learn as long as her knowledge proved profitable for her homeland, husband or family. When it comes to neo-Victorian women characters, the modern preoccupation with individuality prevails over their assumed sacrificial identity.

King addresses this issue from the feminist standpoint and acknowledges that the way in which they are represented accounts for the dominant "experience of gender" (178). Hence, the literary debate over the "woman question" continues in the modern world. While discussing the selected works in the next chapter, I hope to prove that neo-Victorian literary women possess complex histories and identities which account for the multifaceted nature of the so-called "woman question." Consequently, it appears impossible to analyze "femininity" as a universal and unequivocal concept. Instead, I present the plurality of literary "women" as submerged in a heterogeneous experience of the postmodern Victorian encounter. Genette's intertextual theory and Bakhtinian dialogism both allow for profound analyses of interconnectedness between nineteenth-century works and the neo-Victorian novel.

PART II

Diving into the Neo-Victorian Novel

Women Characters Reintroduced in Intertextual Dialogue

Dear Reader, as we have already visited neo-Victorian household, it is the time to encounter neo-Victorian women in the selected texts. This chapter revisits the notion of nineteenth-century women characters in a contemporary vein, drawing on the intertextual dialogue between nineteenth-century and modern texts. As mentioned previously, the literary works introduced in this book include: Gail Carriger's *Soulless* (2009), Syrie James's *The Secret Diaries of Charlotte Brontë* (2009), Clare Boylan's *Emma Brown* (coauthored with Charlotte Brontë, published in 2003), Jean Rhys's *Wide Sargasso Sea* (1966), Wilkie Collins's *The Woman in White* (1859), and Charlotte Brontë's *Jane Eyre* (1847).

The women characters appearing in this chapter can be divided into three categories based on different representational aspects as introduced by James Phelan in his *Reading People, Reading Plot*. These are: the "mimetic," "thematic," and "synthetic" aspects. As Phelan argues, the *mimetic* component of the character describes a specific situation when a "person is not really a person" but mirrors somebody (2). When it comes to the *thematic* component of the character, Phelan posits that it is highlighted when the character is "taken as a representative figure" although "this component may not always be developed" (3). Finally, Phelan notices, "part of being a fictional character ... is being artificial in this sense, and part of knowing a character is knowing that he/she/(it) is a construct. I will hereafter call the 'artificial' component of the character the *synthetic*" (2).

The "mimetic" aspect "refers to that component of the character directed to its imitation of a possible person" (Clanton, 47). It is realized in Syrie James's aforementioned biofictional work, where Charlotte Brontë figures as the eponymous heroine of her own life re-narrated in the first person in the form of a diary. The "thematic" aspect reveals "the character as a representative of some larger group or idea" (Clanton, 47), as in the case of such figures as Boylan's Emma Brown, Rhys's Antoinette, Brontë's Jane Eyre, and Collins's Anne Catherick. These literary figures turn into the spokeswomen of nineteenth-century uprooted women, embodying the universal idea of the Victorian woman's struggle for acknowledgment and recognition. Finally, the "synthetic" aspect is "aimed at the character as an artificial construct" (Clanton, 47). It is discernible in Gail Carriger's novel, where the protagonist, Alexia Tarabotti, possesses characteristics of both the Victorian and modern woman. Presented as an imaginary construct suspended between the semi-modern, high-tech reality, and the traditional Victorian world, Alexia offers the reader a unique experience of rediscovering the nineteenth century from an "ultramodern" angle. Moreover, she reexamines and redefines the notion of the New Woman, engaging thereby in a dialogical debate concerning the understanding of this much-used term.

The literary discussion offered in this chapter is, for the sake of clarity, divided into four parts. The first part concentrates on the notion of the New Woman as presented in Gail Carriger's *Soulless*. Hence, it offers analysis of the "synthetic" aspect of the character. It also introduces a fundamental debate concerning the notion of the New Woman and its changing status. The second part engages in the examination of interdependencies between textually represented society and textually re-created female garments on the pages of both Victorian and neo-Victorian texts. The third part pertains to the issues of women's voicelessness and uprootedness as re-narrated in the neo-Victorian novel. This part offers a study of the "thematic" characters. Finally, the fourth part presents a study in Boylan's neo-Victorian biography of Charlotte Brontë which not only restages Brontë's life in the form of a diary, but also engages the reader in an empathetic "interaction" with the text through the "mimetic" character of Brontë. Dear Reader, let us proceed!

Chapter Twelve

The New Woman Restaged

The Madwoman in the Library and the Man in Ruskin's Garden in Gail Carriger's Soulless

The concept of the New Woman is dialogical, historical, modern, and notoriously ambiguous at the same time. Numerous conceptualizations of the literary New Woman suggest that there is an ongoing search for what Elaine Showalter terms as a "coherent moral code" (*The Odd Women*, Gissing, viii). Yet, as already observed, the search for the New Woman reveals the deep complexity of the term itself. The notion of the New Woman appeared for the first time as early as 1865 (Heilmann, 22). According to Heilmann, the New Woman marks her inaugural appearance in the *Westminster Review* as "the subversive heroine of the new sensation novels," simultaneously labeled as "the Devil in the House" (Heilmann, 22). The 1865 issue of the *Westminster Review* highlights the rebellious potential of the New Woman and fashions her as an "anti-heroine"—the negation of Coventry Patmore's "angel" and a threat to domestic bliss.

However, Heilmann observes, the concept of the New Woman was officially absorbed by the Victorian discourse no sooner than in 1894. Nevertheless, it has to be highlighted that Heilmann presents Michelle E. Tusan's claim that "the New Woman was invented by feminist periodicals . . . such as the *Woman's Harold*" dating as early as 1893. It was actually Sarah Grand's article, "The New Aspect of the Woman Question" (1894), published in *The North American Review* (vol. 158, no. 448, 1894) that triggered a fundamental debate concerning the notion of the New Woman and, in particular, the endangered state of chivalric masculinity. "Manliness is at a premium now," observes Grand, and she deplores: "man in his manners becomes more and more wanting until we seem to be near the time when there will be nothing left of him but the old Adam who said, 'it wasn't me'" (275). Grand emphasizes the idea that women's actions are inseparably connected with men's behavior. Consequently, she hopes that "the man of the future will be better while the woman will be stronger and wiser" (272).

The feminine-masculine interdependency (highlighted in Grand's observations) emphasizes a dialogical potential of the New Woman—not only does she represent a permanently reconstructed idea, but also she remains in a dialogue with the figure of the man. The literary New Woman cannot exist in isolation: instead, her existence in literature is essentially verified in relation to and through masculine characters.

As mentioned above, the New Woman evolved as an ever-altering, dialogical concept. Heilmann notices that in 1865 the New Woman fulfilled the role of a "subversive heroine" (22), while in 1893 she turned into "the fin-de-siècle" female (23). Only a year later, in 1894, did the conservative press of the period reshape the New Woman into "a dystopian figure of degeneration," while 1895 brought yet another change, placing the New Woman on the altar of domestic ideal (23).

> From 1897 the terms of the debate shifted yet again. As the New Woman ceased to signify the British feminist and became a term of reference for continental women's movements, she began to disappear from the pages of feminist periodicals; in 1898 the mainstream press followed suit. It was only after the turn of the century, in the wake of suffragette activism, that the concept underwent a revival. (Heilmann after Tusan, 23)

Consequently, the New Woman turned into a fictional, legendary character, or into what Talia Schaffer simply terms as "fiction" (Richardson, ed., 42). As she asserts, "fictionalizing" allowed the critics to reshape the New Woman into a subjective construct. Accordingly, Schaffer notices that, through her emotional proclamation, Grand "constructs a meta-history which conveys her own psychological sense of the real enormity of the change. . . . Grand *wants* the New Woman to be a fiction; she's much more impressive that way" (42). During the process of fictionalization, Grand's New Woman becomes a universal figure representing a generic female ideal.

In response to Grand's remarks, Quida (Maria Louise Ramé) wrote an article entitled "The New Woman" also included in *The North American Review* (May 1894). Importantly, while constructing a fictional, whimsical figure of the New Woman, Quida also draws on the contrast between men and women. It further confirms the claim concerning a dialogical nature of the New Woman as a construct: the New Woman cannot exist without her (masculine) counterpart. In her article, Quida is highly concerned with the alleged shortcomings of the New Woman, as she proclaims that "the error of the New

Woman (as of many an old one) lies in speaking of women as the victims of men, and entirely ignoring the frequency with which men are the victims of women" (615). Accordingly, Quida claims that "in nine cases out of ten also she [the woman] becomes corrupt herself because she likes it" and accuses the New Woman of "fierce vanity, . . . undigested knowledge, . . . over-weening of her own value and her fatal want of all sense of the ridiculous" (615). For her, the New Woman is an absurd, flamboyant construct, wearing

> an inverted plate on her head tied on with strings under her double-chin; she has balloon-sleeves, a bodice tight to bursting, a waist of ludicrous dimensions in proportion to her portly person; she is gesticulating with one hand, of which all the fingers are stuck out in ungraceful defiance of all artistic laws of gesture. (613)

Figure 12.1. "Bloomer" dress of the 1850s. "The Bloomer Costume," by Nathaniel Currier (1851) (Public Domain).

The above-presented description—a caricature portraying warped femininity—is derived from "an illustrated journal of a woman's meeting" which, Quida believes, gives justice to the depiction of the fallacious New Woman (612). The heaviest charge against the New Woman is, according to Quida, the waste of her inner, "womanly" potential:

> woman, whether new or old, has immense fields of culture untilled, immense areas of influence wholly neglected. She does almost nothing with the resources she possesses, because her whole energy is concentrated on desiring and demanding those she has not. She can write and print anything she chooses; and she scarcely ever takes the pains to acquire correct grammar or elegance of style before wasting ink and paper. She can paint and model any subjects she chooses, but she imprisons herself in men's *at'eliers* to endeavor to steal their technique and their methods, and thus loses any originality she might possess. (Quida, 613)

While Quida's argument against women wasting their individual potential for the sake of unfounded mimicry appears accurate, the portrayal of the New Woman as ridiculous and vain seems highly subjective and serves a particular purpose. As Talia Schaffer posits, Quida fictionalizes the New Woman in her own way in order to create an alternative meaning of this figure:

> by inventing and then attacking a demonic New Woman, Quida creates a straw (wo)man, and thereby constructs herself as its opposite. If Quida can see that the New Woman is extremist and outrageous, why then, Quida herself must be moderate and reasonable. In fact, the "New Woman" functions as a demonic double of the writer. It serves the psychological and rhetorical function of evacuating unpleasant characteristics and thereby leaving behind a residually purified authorial self. (Richardson, ed., 45–46)

Quida uses the figure of the New Woman in order to distance herself from the negative characteristics of this literary character. On the other hand, Sarah Grand introduces the New Woman as a part of the "nineteenth-century female legend" in order to construct the basis for the community of women. The dialogue between Grand and Quida highlights the freedom of expression in literature, but also emphasizes the arbitrariness of writerly purposes. However, first and foremost, it attests to the fact that literature serves as the means to create diversified sociocultural narratives.

Freedom of expression, Talia Schaffer observes, allowed Grand and Quida to place their conflicting New Women in the same "Ruskinian garden." Paradoxically, both the "demonic" New Woman and the "angelic" one find their places in Ruskin's narrative.

The idea of the "garden" as the starting point for the discussion concerning female domesticity stems from Ruskin's essay "Of Queen's Gardens," published in 1865 in the collection *Sesame and Lilies*. As Ruskin observes, it is the woman's task to nourish and nurture the loved ones in a protected space of the metaphorical "garden":

> You have heard it said . . . that flowers only flourish rightly in the garden of some one who loves them. . . . And do you think it not a greater thing, that all this, (and how much more than this!) you *can* do, for fairer flowers than these—flowers that could bless you for having blessed them, and will love you for having loved them;—flowers that have eyes like yours, and thoughts like yours, and lives like yours; which, once saved, you save forever? (98)

Ruskin emphasizes the domestic potential residing in women. Moreover, he stresses their ability to revitalize others. Hence, in their households, women don the roles of gardeners who nurture their families—the "most precious flowers." Simultaneously, in his essay, Ruskin disapproves of those women who reside behind garden gates, ignoring the actual world around them.

Three decades later, both Grand's and Quida's New Women approach the gates of Ruskin's garden in order to argue their cases. Interestingly enough, Grand and Quida support their conflicting arguments by means of the same imagery. For example, Grand postulates that women should bring men out of ignorance and, therefore, the New Woman cannot "shut herself up" in the symbolic garden:

> we have been reproached by Ruskin for shutting ourselves up behind park palings and garden walls, regardless of the waste world that moans in misery without, and that has been too much our attitude; but the day of our acquiescence is over. (274)

Paradoxically, Quida's argument is the equivalent of Grand's claim. In "The New Woman," she adheres to a practical comparison, scrutinizing the New Woman as a negligent planter: "The New Woman reminds me of an agriculturalist who, discarding a fine farm of his own, and leaving it to nettles, stones, thistles, and wire-worms, should spend his whole time in demanding neighboring fields which are not his," concludes Quida, thus asserting that nineteenth-century New Women voluntarily relinquish their inherent, revitalizing potential (618).

For Quida, Ruskin's garden is the desired place of return, while for Grand, it signifies the starting point for social revision. Nonetheless, for both of them, Ruskin's garden embraces the notions of mythical purity and healing domesticity indisputably associated with women. The perplexing use of Ruskin's imagery in the two conflicting articles prompts Schaffer to acknowledge that as the New Woman becomes a literary construct, Quida and Grand appropriate the rhetorical lessons of their predecessors, placing Ruskinian metaphors . . . in the service of their own notions of womanhood. . . . By treating the New Woman as a purely imaginary caricature, Quida and Grand were able to stretch, distort, and duplicate this figure for whatever rhetorical or psychological purpose they wanted. . . . In her brief career, she [the New Woman] was ascribed more opinions, positions, and beliefs than any real woman could have absorbed in a lifetime; she was used as a public relations technique. (Richardson, ed., 47, 50)

As argued before, the notion of the New Woman could not exist in isolation and was constantly gauged against the fluctuating concept of masculinity. The use of the male-female analogy brought about in 1890s, as McDonald notices, the appearance of the "New Man"—the New Woman's counterpart. The image of the New Man was as contradictory and multilayered as that of his female companion, McDonald argues. The New Man was once "effeminate and ridiculous," while, at other times, he would become a "romantic partner" of the New Woman and a "new father" of her children (web). Such ambivalence, as argued by Schaffer, places the New Man and the New Woman as "the twin extremes of ordinary gender identity" (*The Forgotten Female Aesthetes*, 19). The New Man represents the opposite of the New Woman, while he also stands in a moral opposition to his conservative masculine predecessors.

Defined through the prism of the Victorian man (or: the New Man), the literary New Woman is hardly ever capable of forming a successful, romantic relationship, Chris Willis observes. "The New Woman is thus portrayed as attractive, intelligent and honourable, but she ultimately loses out to the 'womanly' woman," Willis asserts: "The message recurs throughout popular New Woman fiction: if the New Woman is to find a mate she must become as 'womanly' as her less politicized sisters" (Richardson, ed., 57–58). However, Willis also depicts Dagmar—a sophisticated character from L. T. Meade's[1] novel *The Cleverest Woman in England* (1898), who represents both the domestic and intellectual ideal of femininity (58). Written in 1898, the novel targets readers of popular fiction. Hence, Willis highlights the impact of nineteenth-century commercial fiction on the perception of the New Woman. Commercial fiction, he claims, molded the figure of the New Woman as it "reached a wider and more varied audience. People who would not normally buy New Woman fiction bought detective and romantic novels which featured New Woman protagonists" (64). The conclusion in Willis's article is that "by marketing the New Woman for mass consumption, the writers of commercial fiction ensured her a prominent and lasting place in popular culture" (64). In the twentieth and twenty-first century, "the New Woman legend" is revised in the neo-Victorian vein, as I present in the subsequent part of the chapter dedicated to Gail Carriger's intriguing novel *Soulless* (2009).

Whereas literature served as the primary record of the processes going on in Victorian society, it remained in dialogue with the theater, which eagerly embraced the concept of the New Woman, attesting to her presence in high culture as well. Henrik Ibsen, the nineteenth-century Norwegian playwright, successfully divided the English audience over the notion of liberated women. Hence, although of Norwegian origin, Ibsen inscribed himself in the history of the Victorian theater. As Sally Ledger observes, Victorian bohemians and intellectuals ardently received Ibsen's "dramatic representation of women and womanhood" (79). Ibsen moved the English audience with his disquieting yet realistic play *A Doll's House* staged at London Novelty Theater in June 1889 (Ledger, 79). Yet, introducing Ibsen's play in London was a challenging undertaking:

> In 1884 two playwrights, Arthur Jones and Henry Herman, took the basic situation of *A Doll's House* and adapted it to fit current taste under a new title *Breaking a Butterfly*. It was a start, though a depressively timid encounter with Ibsen's profound searches into human nature. In fact, when *A Doll's House* was properly presented in 1889 and later in the 1890s when the Ibsen controversy was at its height, most audiences were engaged and receptive. It was critics (at least, some of them) who vented most of the sound and fury at what they perceived to be immoral. They believed that Ibsen was poisoning the London stage and using the theatre to subvert established taste and values. (Siddall, 60)

A Doll's House, a three-act play, features Nora Helmer, a dramatic character who fulfills the "angel in the house" domestic scenario, yet, deep inside, feels "deprived of herself." Although Nora Helmer cannot be perceived as an example of a "full-fledged," liberated New Woman, she decidedly "paves the way" for the appearance of this construct. Although not as strong, decisive or demanding as the present-day New Woman, Nora is also capable of finally "standing her ground" and making a choice: ultimately, she abandons her husband and children, as she cannot exist without her "true" self. Hence, she transforms from a "domestic servant" into a self-conscious individual. Ibsen's *A Doll's House* accentuates a ghastly discrepancy between the masculine vision of woman's happiness and her hopeless efforts to adjust to the masculine idea of femininity. The social world, Ibsen pessimistically suggests, is built on the masculine thought. Since the traditional domestic pattern projected by men remains "widely socially accepted," women strive to persuade themselves that it is their only way toward happiness and fulfillment. Similarly, Nora Helmer struggles to accept her "happy fate," but her efforts remain futile.

There are two contradicting personas disguised in Nora's character. One of them is the voice of social reason, while the other represents Nora's suppressed desires, ambitions, and feelings. Nora apprehensively tries to persuade herself into believing that she is lucky:

> My goodness, it's delightful to think of . . . ! Free from care! To be able to be free from care, quite free from care; to be able to play and romp with the children; to be able to keep the house beautifully and have everything just as Torvald [the husband] likes it! (Ibsen, *A Doll's House*, 13)

On the other hand, what Nora primarily portrays as a happy "fairy tale," hides cracks and scars that cannot be obliterated from her consciousness. She is aware of the fact that her husband perceives her as a child or the eponymous doll shut in a dollhouse—the caricature of Ruskin's excellent garden.

Nora's husband is not her partner, because he does not accept his wife's equality. Instead, Nora is turned into a commodity, while Torvald claims that she is "thoughtless and that it [is] his duty as [her] husband not to indulge [her] in . . . whims and caprices" (12). At the same time, he disposes of Nora's disguised independence and her skillful ways of dealing with household economic problems. What is more, he is unaware of Nora's material and spiritual sacrifices, as well as of her deep concern for his health. Joan Templeton observes that Ibsen's play constitutes

> the greatest literary argument against the notion of the 'two spheres,' the neat centuries-old division of the world into his and hers that the nineteenth century made a doctrine for living. The home, the woman's place, is a make-believe world fit for dolls; the chivalric ideal, the old credo of male *noblesse oblige* the bourgeois century resurrected to justify the cloistering of the female, proves, when put to test, pure humbug. . . . And she [Nora], who has secretly saved his [husband's] life and paid for it through years of hard work, all the while playing the silly doll to his wise man, recognizes the enormous significance of her folly born from love. (137–38)

While Nora's husband is convinced of his generous conduct, he remains unaware of his numerous shortcomings. In the play, the "two spheres" are reversed, and, finally, it is Nora who actively chooses her life while leaving home. Hence, it is the woman who makes a decision, although the choice carries an inconceivable amount of suffering.

Performed in the Novelty Theater, Ibsen's play foreshadowed the onset of the new era beginning with the advent of the Victorian New Woman. "Ibsen's challenging and subversive female character roles were, then, immensely influential in the formation of the identity of the New Woman in 1890s London," Ledger observes (81). Moreover, she believes that "Ibsenism sounded the death knell for those 'Victorian Values' which had been so pervasive in Britain throughout the second half of the nineteenth century" (81). Accordingly, as the "Victorian values" became passé, the New Woman began to be associated with the age of decadence and feminism. For instance, Heilmann notices that the notion of the New Woman began embracing the concept of suffragists as well:

> It can hardly be a coincidence that the term "feminism," coined in the early nineteenth century by Charles Fourier, entered the English language at the same time as that of the "New Woman" (1894/1895), and was then applied to suffragists. (*New Woman Fiction*, 4–5)

Heilmann also emphasizes the inconsistency of the term, pointing out that the New Woman "stood at once for the degeneration of society and for that society's moral regeneration" (1). These destructive and revitalizing powers of the New Woman are the reflection of conflicts faced by Victorian society at the fin de siècle. However, the New Woman cannot be perceived as an equivalent of a feminist or a decadent per se. Rather than that, the invention of the New Woman sheds light on "a wider discourse on decadence, degeneration and the crisis of masculinity in society, art and literature" (Heilmann, *New Woman Fiction*, 46).

In the twentieth and twenty-first century, the New Woman "returns": her prevalent presence in neo-Victorian revisionary fiction attests to the claim that the sociocultural issues related to her figure remain unsolved or, at least, are open to discussion and reassessment. The return of the New Woman reasserts the notion of historical continuity, as she remains in a dialogue with her Victorian literary alter egos, which can be interpreted as a Bakhtinian conversation between the equally privileged voices or as a dialogue of ideas, termed by Holquist as "a meditation on how we know" (16). Ann Heilmann argues in the following way:

> New Woman was ever-present. The many terms with which the *fin de siècle* sought to capture the phenomenon of the New Woman are an indication of how firmly forty years of feminist activism had established the notion of the 'Modern Woman' in the public consciousness. Some terms—"Novissima," "the advanced woman of to-day" and "the Woman of the Period"—stressed her avant-gardist and trend-setting effect, and could connote praise or censure. Those sympathetic to the New Woman saw her as a positive force for social change. Her opponents stressed her superficiality and love of sensation; the term "Woman of the Period" was a belated attempt to revive the one-time furore over the "Girl of the Period," whom in 1868 Eliza Lynn Linton had berated as selfish, fun-loving, "fast" and immoral. Associated with the social and political problems of the day, the New Woman conjured up an army of unmarried "Odd Women," or married

but unoccupied "Superfluous Wom[e]n," her synonyms reflecting the anxieties aroused by her political demands (the "Wild Woman") and her strictures on male sexual conduct (the "Modern Man-Hater"). By her very "oddness" she raised the spectre of sexual deviance, her difference from other ("normal") women, her "odd" rejection *of* men, her own rejection *by* men (hence her redundancy) all pointing to her transgressive potential. (*New Woman Fiction*, 16)

Highlighting the presence of numerous and often contradictory terms used for delineating the figure of the New Woman, Heilmann's definition testifies to the fact that the New Woman is a (politicized) multipurpose concept stemming from a subjective perception rather than a universal notion of the construct. Once again, the vast terminology surrounding the New Woman proves that the Victorian era is not as consistent and unitary as it is often perceived by the twenty-first-century readers. On the contrary, it is filled with paradoxes, such as the New Woman herself.

In the twentieth and twenty-first century, writers revisit the literary images of Victorian women in their modern works. A very interesting example of the neo-Victorian woman is offered by John Fowles in his seminal novel *The French Lieutenant's Woman* (1969). Fowles introduces Sarah Woodruff, a foreign-looking, enigmatic character whose past and identity are fully veiled in mystery. Sarah spins her own narrative, thus deliberately creating her own *fictional* identity on the pages of a *fictional, consciously postmodern* text [emphasis added]. It is the male character (the French foreigner) around whom Sarah builds her own narrative, thus "warping" and "using" his image for her own narrative self-creation. The fictitious story of her supposed abuse imparts Sarah her longed-for independence as a social outsider and, therefore, grants her freedom from all social constraints. Yet, paradoxically, as aptly noticed by Aleksandra Kędzierska, the heroine "is not really free; she can rewrite the grammar of love, transferring the power to her sex, but, ironically, she will remain enslaved, if no longer to the French connection, then to the Saxon Genitive which is the true determiner of who she is and why" (217).

Gail Carriger's *Soulless* (2009), the first novel in the *Parasol Protectorate* series, differs from the above-introduced example, as it depicts a well-read Victorian female character from a middle-class family who does not seem to struggle with worldly trials and, unlike such characters as Sarah Woodruff, does not rely on a fictitious narrative in order to gain independence and construct her own identity. Carriger's work belongs to the steampunk genre—a literary trend which accentuates the expansion of the new modern genres and their revisionary potential in the twenty-first century. In the *The Steampunk Bible: An Illustrated Guide to the World of Imaginary Airships, Corsets and Goggles, Mad Scientists, and Strange Literature*, one can find a definition of steampunk fiction as "colonial and empire-based . . . , with steam technology" (9). Jeff VanderMeer, the author of *The Steampunk Bible*, uses Czesław Milosz's statement in order to discuss the importance of the revisionary approach to the past: "the past takes its meaning from whatever we do right now" (13). Hence, steampunk revisionary fiction reshapes the past in an experimental, technologically-based way, endowing it with a new meaning corresponding with modern sociocultural concerns: "steampunk's key lessons are not about the past. They are about the instability and obsolescence of our own times. We are a technological society," posits VanderMeer, and

> when we trifle, in our sly, Gothic, grave-robbing fashion, with archaic and eclipsed technologies, we are secretly preparing ourselves for the death of our own tech. Steampunk is popular now because people are unconsciously realizing that the way we live has already died. We are sleepwalking. We are ruled by rapacious, dogmatic, heavily-armed fossil-moguls who rob us and force us to live like corpses. Steampunk is a pretty way of coping with this truth. (13)

In this sense, the nostalgia associated with steampunk and the crisis inherent in the twenty-first-century world are dialogically correlated with the feeling of disbelief haunting the Victorians, who were also "sleepwalking" at the end of the nineteenth century, overwhelmed by their own dramatic technological changes and a gradual disappearance of "traditional," stable moral codes. Technological progress, thriving urban life, and the resulting abrupt social change evoked fears of loneliness and isolation. As noted by Walter E. Houghton in *The Victorian Frame of Mind, 1830–1870*,

> the feeling of loneliness and isolation, so characteristic of modern man, first appeared in the nineteenth century. With the breakup of a long-established order and the resulting fragmentation of both society and thought, the old ties were snapped, and men became acutely conscious of separation. They felt isolated by dividing barriers; lonely for a lost companionship, human and divine; nostalgic for an earlier world of country peace and unifying belief. . . . In the new liberal theory all men were free, politically and economically, owing no one any service beyond the fulfillment of legal contracts. (77)

The Victorian New Woman supported the concept of lonesome individuality: she was free, self-conscious and independent, "owing no one . . . beyond the fulfillment of legal contracts" (77). On the other hand, she also represented a dissolution of social bonds and an isolated, self-absorbed lifestyle. Thus, the nineteenth-century New Woman embodied a cultural change both welcomed and feared by many Victorians. The New Woman presented in Gail Carriger's twenty-first century experimental novel responds dialogically to the nineteenth-century "revolting" female counterpart. Carriger's heroine, Alexia Tarabotti, constitutes a mirror reflection of the nineteenth-century

"Woman of the Period" in terms of her struggle for independence and individuality. However, her mentality is strictly modern as she makes an active and fearless use of steampunk technology, provokingly placed in the center of the fictional Victorian landscape. Hence, in Carriger's *Soulless*, Alexia—the New Woman of the twenty-first century—is a representative of the lonely, technologically dominated, modern world which blends experimentally with the Victorian environment, its etiquette, manners, and dress code. Apart from binding the nineteenth century with the modern world, Carriger introduces into her work science fiction and spiritual themes, including those involving ghosts, werewolves, and vampires.[2] Read dialogically, *Soulless* offers a world of paradoxes, where the "Victorian" coexists with the "contemporary" and the "fantastical." Moreover, *Soulless* interestingly challenges the modern absurdities of twenty-first-century popular fiction with its experimental, postmodern narratives and contemporary heyday of "cheap" vampire stories.

Alexia Tarabotti, the protagonist of Carriger's novel, is a twenty-seven-year old spinster of Italian origin living with her grumpy and spoiled family in nineteenth-century London. Alexia "had been a spinster for as long as she could remember" and, even worse, "had been born that way, full of logic and reason and sharp words" (*Soulless*, 26). Being an "odd woman" and deprived of marriage prospects due to her prominent Italian nose and "unfeminine" scholarly inclinations, Alexia creates her own world dominated by books, libraries, and never-ending cups of tea. Her social position appears to be more complicated, as Alexa is deprived of a soul and, therefore, as suggested in the novel, lacks the manners of a well-bred Victorian lady.[3] This leads to numerous unforeseen events, including Alexia's involvement in the plot of vanishing vampires. The events trigger a love affair between Alexia and a werewolf of high social standing—Lord Conan Maccon, who, "relatively new to the London area . . . , gave young ladies heart palpitations . . . with a favourable combination of mystery, pre-eminence, and danger" (14).

Gail Carriger's Victorian England is taken over by science, technology, medicine, and modernity. As a result, the literary vision appears greatly altered from the "original" nineteenth-century landscape: it includes a lady traveling in a carriage and a dirigible floating in the skies. The society presented in *Soulless* exemplifies the most baffling and engaging part of the overall textual picture. Essentially, it is built upon a certain hierarchy. In her novels, Carriger establishes a double-edged hierarchy gradation: the first is based on the social status of the individuals, while the other, as indicated by Mike Perschon in his internet blog *Steampunk Scholar*, rests upon *the hierarchy of soul*. This interesting maneuver incorporates into the novel a set of expressive supernatural characters: werewolves, vampires, and ghosts. While werewolves' "social circles" are based upon "pack dynamics," vampires are governed by the "hive Queens." Moreover, these extraordinary creatures possess a "surplus" of soul. In this sense, the concept of "soul" gains quantitative meaning, and the body can be perceived as a container for one's soul. The fictionalized Victorian England hosts ordinary humans too who can boast an average "quantity" of soul. Moreover, the hierarchy includes few preternaturals—the individuals who are in a soulless state. To these belongs Alexia Tarabotti.

As already mentioned, she appears in the social order under the label of a "spinster." As observed by Elaine Showalter in her Introduction to Gissing's *The Odd Women*, "traditionally ridiculed in the pages of *Punch* and in the operettas of Gilbert and Sullivan, the spinster was seen by the Victorians as a comic figure, a sexual reject, and a failure" (viii). Precisely as a spinster, Alexia is a distinctive and odd figure among her contemporaries. "The eccentric spinster, desiccated, domineering, and laughable, signified both the perils of not being incorporated into a family and the embodiment of qualities that women, at least, *should* not bring into the family," observes Claudia Nelson in *Family Ties in Victorian England* (133). Aged twenty-seven, of foreign (Italian) origin and with low marriage prospects, Alexia is considered to be a burden. However, she does not believe that her social status is inconvenient:

> under ordinary circumstances, walks in Hyde Park were the kind of thing a single young lady of good breeding was not supposed to do without her mama and possibly an elderly female relation or two in attendance. Miss Tarabotti felt such rules did not entirely apply to her, as she was a spinster. Had been a spinster for as long as she could remember. In her more acerbic moments, she felt she had been born a spinster. (Carriger, 26)

In the course of events, Alexia eventually marries Lord Conall Maccon—the earl of Woolsey and a well-prospering werewolf, hence proving that the impossibility of finding a "proper" partner is no longer a malady of the twenty-first-century New Woman. In *Soulless*, the desired Victorian "happy ending" is interwoven into the theme of the triumphant, twenty-first-century woman. Alexia's wedding is necessarily "a masterpiece of social engineering," yet, first and foremost, it serves as the means of attaining her true personal happiness (284).

As Chris Willis indicates, Victorian "authors were left with the problem of finding a man to match the New Woman" (56). The nineteenth-century New Woman was usually too smart or too independent to fit in the constraints of the Victorian marriage and peacefully inhabit the Ruskinian garden. Decidedly, she was an individuality. Henrik Ibsen's Nora from *A Doll's House* speaks for the entire group of women restrained physically and intellectually by nineteenth-century marriage. On the other hand, heroines such as Charlotte Brontë's Lucy Snowe are overpowered by inner isolation, unable to fully share their lives with the men who pose a potential threat of a lifelong confinement. In *Soulless*, a fairytale marriage between Alexia and her intellectual match, Lord Maccon, not only fulfills the traditionally expected pattern of the Victorian novel, but also emphasizes a universal desire for an ideal love story based on mutual feelings and understanding. *Soulless* concentrates on the self-awareness of contemporary women who no longer get married because of responsibilities toward their families and nation, but rather because they find an intellectual and spiritual match. Unconcerned with strict moralities of the Victorian marriage, Alexia attributes her successful wedding to love rather than to convenience: while being "soulless," she does not feel obliged to follow the Victorian canon of social norms. Hence, Alexia's "soullessness" is an excuse for her "selfish" ("selfish" from the nineteenth-century perspective) quest for personal happiness in the Victorian world.

Alexia's physical appearance also challenges the Victorian canon of beauty. By creating her heroine as both mentally and physically distinctive, Carriger highlights the twenty-first-century celebration of individualism. As the New (twenty-first century) Woman, Alexia Tarbotti is no longer defined through the prism of her conservative and self-conceited family (as depicted in *Soulless*). Rather than that, she is presented as a full-fledged, self-sufficient individual who consciously draws a line between herself and the world.

As already stated, Alexia's appearance departs from the canonical notion of Victorian beauty: Carriger's heroine possesses a dark, olive complexion and a prominent nose, while her head is adorned with a shock of frizzy hair. The author of *Soulless* parodies the Victorian canon of beauty in chapter 2, as Alexia's mother complains about her daughter's appearance:

> "Really, darling," Alexia's mother had said at the time in tones of the deepest condescension, "with that nose and that skin, there is simply no point in us going to the expense. I have got your sisters to think of." So Alexia, whose nose really wasn't that big and whose skin really wasn't that tan, had gone on the shelf at fifteen. Not that she had ever actually coveted the burden of a husband, but it would have been nice to know she could get one if she ever changed her mind. Alexia did enjoy dancing, so she would have liked to attend at least one ball as an available young lady rather than always ending up skulking in libraries. (Carriger, 26)

While estimating her daughter's social usefulness, Mrs. Loontwill advocates the nineteenth-century postulate concerning woman's domestic vocation. Interestingly enough, it is a woman (Alexia's mother) judging another woman (her daughter). Thereby, it is the female gaze (and not the male one, as usually proclaimed) that determines Alexia's supposed social prospects. Hence, patriarchal claims referring to women are paradoxically sustained and proliferated by motherly figures.

Since Alexia obviously does not fit into the role of "the angel in the house," both in terms of her complexion and mental constitution, she is eventually rejected as a family burden. Hence, her identity is not defined against her family background or in relation to the potential husband—she is not "an available young lady." "Skulking in libraries," Alexia does not intend to perform a utilitarian social function of a married woman or that of a charitable spinster (26). On the contrary, Carriger's heroine reflects on the idea of a husband as that of an optional commodity. According to Alexia, it is men who eventually become appropriated by women.

In *Soulless*, Miss Tarabotti is surrounded by women fulfilling "the angel in the house" model. These are necessarily parodied figures, such as Alexia's friend—Miss Ivy Hisselpenny or Alexia's stepsisters Evelyn and Felicity. Ignorant and shallow inside, on the surface the Misses Loontwill precisely impersonate Victorian female "angels":

> Both Felicity and Evelyn were markedly different from their older half sister. No one upon meeting the three together would have thought Alexia related to the other two at all. Aside from an obvious lack of Italian blood and completely soul-ridden states, Felicity and Evelyn were both quite beautiful: pale insipid blondes with wide blue eyes and small rosebud mouths. (22)

Miss Hisselpenny is portrayed as a caricatured vision of a young Victorian lady: "She was the unfortunate victim of circumstances that dictated she be only-just-pretty only-just-wealthy, and possessed of a terrible propensity for wearing extremely silly hats" (27). However, from the perspective of Victorian society presented in the novel, it is Alexia who is "the unfortunate victim of circumstances." Alexia, the daughter of Mrs. Loontwill's former husband, inherited after her father not only his Italian surname, but also a seemingly "unfeminine" character. As Mrs. Loontwill reflects on her eldest daughter, she wonders:

> Really, what *had* she been thinking, marrying an Italian? Well, she had been young and Alessandro Tarabotti so very handsome. But there was something else about Alexia, something . . . revoltingly independent, that Mrs. Loontwill could not blame entirely on her first husband. And, of course, she refused to take the blame herself. Whatever it was, Alexia had been born that way, full of logic and reason and sharp words. Not for the first time, Mrs. Loontwill lamented the fact that her eldest had not been a male child; it would have made life very much easier for them all. (26)

Mrs. Loontwill's reasoning adheres to the Victorian belief in the superiority of masculine reason. Alexia's social exclusion is the result of her abnormal "revolting independen[cy]" and her "sharp words," conventionally ascribed to men. As mentioned before, the heroine's alienation is justified by the state of her "soullessness." The soul, as a spiritual medium, was widely associated with the ideal Victorian femininity. Talairach-Vielmas observes that "by downplaying their carnal appetites, [Victorian] women hushed their own physicality, and this behavioural management testified to their own spirituality" (36). Hence, the nineteenth-century feminine ideal is based on a spiritual scaffolding of which Carriger's heroine is deprived due to her "preternatural" nature. In the eyes of the morally rigid London society, Alexia's "soulless" state turns her not only into an "odd" woman, but also into an "unfeminine" woman.

On the other hand, the metaphysical state of "soullessness" remains in dialogue with the frame of mind of the literary New Woman. As one reads in Carriger's novel, "Miss Tarabotti generally kept her soulless state quite hush-hush, even from her own family. She was not undead, mind you; she was a living, breathing human but simply . . . lacking" (21). In this sense, Alexia's "soullessness" can be likened to a state of inner restlessness, already articulated in the nineteenth century by such female characters as, for example, the Ibsenian heroine who is imprisoned in her domestic role. Nora abandons the domestic sphere because she cannot keep her "soulless state quite hush-hush" anymore. Entrapped in "the angel in the house" model, confined to passivity in the Ruskinian garden, Victorian women were, nevertheless, "living" and "breathing" humans and not merely decorative commodities.

The threatening lack of occupation, the reduction of women's intellectual potential and the detrimental results of enforced passivity are widely demonstrated in such texts as Charlotte Brontë's novel *Shirley*, where Caroline Helstone struggles to find the meaning of her desolate life while sewing and engaging in charity works.

Unlike Caroline, Alexia Tarabotti possesses a considerable amount of self-will and independence paradoxically resulting from her social exclusion. Mrs. Loontwill, Alexia's mother, acknowledges that "she had thought that putting Alexia on the shelf would keep the exasperating girl out of trouble. Instead, she had inadvertently managed to give Alexia an ever-increasing degree of freedom" (24). Thus, in the text, social rejection works as the beginning of personal liberation. Consequently, Alexia "dangerously" cultivates her mind, revealing her scholarly tendencies during a dinner party given by Lord Blingchester:

> Miss Tarabotti, never one to pass up an opportunity to display her bluestocking tendencies, matched wits with the young scientist on a wide range of subjects.

Leaving the weighing of souls for another occasion, the salad course moved them on to recent innovations in various engine designs. Over fruit and bonbons, they broached the psychological correlation between mental and behavioural phenomena and how this might affect vampire hive dynamics. (106)

Library turns into Alexia's favorite refuge where she fulfills her intellectual ambitions but, primarily, attains peace of mind. Reading serves as both a liberating and dangerous activity for a young Victorian woman: "On the one hand, regulated and supervised reading was a vital part of a woman's education, improving knowledge, confidence, social grace, as well as intellect and imagination," states Catherine Golden.

> On the other hand, some feared reading could have damning effects. Critics presented a range of arguments against women's reading that tapped into biology, medicine, and morality. From an antifiction vantage point, a book of romance, sensation fiction, or sentimental fiction could arouse a female's sexual impulses, drain her vital energies, damage her mental and reproductive health, divorce her attention from her maternal and domestic duties, undermine her self-control, and rot her mind, leading to ruination. (21–22)

Offering Alexia the freedom to explore libraries, Mrs. Loontwill unknowingly contributes to her daughter's further "ruination," as understood in conventional, nineteenth-century terms.

Furthermore, as Elaine Showalter observes in *A Literature of Their Own*, "denied participation in public life, women were forced to cultivate their feelings and to overvalue romance. In the novels, emotion rushed in to fill the vacuum of experience, and critics found this intensity, this obsession with personal relationships, unrealistic and even oppressive" (79–80). In her treatment of the library as a peaceful refuge, Alexia resembles the eponymous heroine of Brontë's *Jane Eyre*: Jane, escaping from a painful realization that she is an unwanted outsider in the Reeds' household, indulges in reading Bewick's *History of British Birds*. When the tyrannizing John Reed enters the room, Jane draws the curtain in order to create her private space: "'it is well I drew the curtain,' thought I; and I wished fervently he might not discover my hiding place" (8). The independent act of drawing the curtain and marking her privacy ranks Jane Eyre into the community of the budding literary New Women, even though in the Reeds' house she is still a girl.

Similarly as in the case of Jane Eyre, from an early childhood, books provide Alexia with a form of escapism and reassurance. Hence, reading allows Carriger's heroine to come to terms with her "abnormal" identity:

> the fact that she was preternatural had been explained to *her* at age six by a nice gentleman from the Civil Service. . . . Miss Alexia, age six, had nodded politely

at the nice silver-haired gentleman. Then she had made certain to read oodles of ancient Greek philosophy dealing with reason, logic, and ethics. *If she had no soul, she had also no morals*, so she reckoned she had best develop some kind of alternative. Her mama thought her a bluestocking, which was soulless enough as far as Mrs. Loontwill was concerned, and was terribly upset by her eldest daughter's propensity for libraries. It would be too bothersome to have to face her mama in one just now. [emphasis added] (12)

It is interesting to observe how Alexia's soulless state is combined with the idea of "no morals," what further justifies her "dangerous" reading passion. For Alexia, independent reading is synonymous with the creation of her private sphere. Catherine Golden argues that independent reading opened up new intellectual possibilities for nineteenth-century women:

> Independent reading outside the family circle, which opponents of women's reading labeled isolated and solitary, gave women an opportunity not only to learn but to think and imagine. . . . Reading on her own, a woman could experience a life free from duties and rigid gender expectations. (28)

Hence, while reading, Alexia gains space, knowledge and independence, very much in the manner of her Victorian predecessors. Moreover, together with her scholarly training, she attains self-awareness that allows her to accept her distinctiveness as an individual.

Gail Carriger's *Soulless* offers an engaging literary experiment where the heroine endowed with the twenty-first century mentality (or: the condition of "soullessness") faces a rigorous Victorian world. Scholarly inclinations, "unfeminine" temper, uncompromising nature and undesirable outer characteristics (olive complexion and a prominent nose) push Miss Tarabotti to the margin of stereotypical Victorian womanhood. Before her (indecently) happy marriage, Alexia figures as an *outsider*—an *odd woman*: single, unmarried and thus strange. The term *odd women*, referring to the unequal number of single women at marriageable age living in Victorian England, acquired a special meaning after the publication of William Rathbone Greg's essay "Why Are Women Redundant?" (1862). In his work, Greg deplores that England possesses two classes of women, both essentially wretched: the governesses and the old maids, who, unmarried and left to "useless" occupations, equally waste their lives. Greg describes them in the following words:

> As we go a few steps higher in the social scale, we find two classes of similar abnormal existences; women, more or less well educated, spending youth and middle life as governesses, living laboriously, yet perhaps not uncomfortably, but laying by nothing, and retiring to a lonely and destitute old age: and old maids, with just enough income to live upon, but wretched and deteriorating,

their minds narrowing, and their hearts withering, because they have nothing to do, and none to love, cherish and obey. (6)

Greg implies that women, in order to endow their lives with a purpose, should undeniably be of service to men. Additionally, he argues that women are naturally "attached to others and connected with other existences, which they embellish, facilitate and serve" (26). Hence, Greg's words support my argument that in the patriarchal world Victorian women are perceived as givers, disinterested and selfless, existing only *with* and *for* the sake of others, functioning as decorative commodities *through* and *for* somebody's presence.

In *Soulless*, one can find an indirect answer to Greg's assumptions. Alexia courageously defends her independence while opposing Lord Maccon's first marriage proposal. In chapter 9, "A Problem of Werewolf Proportions," Mrs. Loontwill enters the parlor only to discover her unchaperoned eldest daughter in the suspicious company of Lord Maccon. The outrageous discovery is followed by Mrs. Loontwill's "decorous . . . hysterics" and her insistence on Alexia's immediate marriage (169). When Squire Loontwill appears in the parlor, his wife exclaims: "Oh, Herbert, . . . you must *make* him [Lord Maccon] marry her! Call the parson immediately!" (170).

Carriger wittingly parodies Victorian engagement ceremonies, exposing and ridiculing family pressure, as well as the incapacitation of a potential "marriage victim." Jennifer Phegley's informative work, *Courtship and Marriage in Victorian England,* emphasizes the importance of parental influence in the nineteenth-century marriage:

> To assist their judgment in matters of the heart, ladies were advised to consult the more objective opinions of their parents. Since a lady "has probably first met the gentleman at a ball, or other festive occasion, where the excitement of the scene has reflected on every object a roseate tint," she is most in need of "the very best advice accompanied with a considerate regard for her overwrought feelings" that only a mother can provide. Parents or paid chaperones were charged with assessing an admirer's rank and character, hopefully prior to the formation of an attachment. (36)

Mrs. Loontwill's inability to provide her daughter with "the very best advice" based on reason and experience is satirized throughout the entire novel. With the opening pages, Mrs. Loontwill dismisses her eldest daughter as "unmarriageable," whereas on discovering Alexia's encounter with the earl of Woolsey, she shows inability to act as a reasonable adviser. Although Alexia is in love with Lord Maccon, she opposes her family's pressure, thus demonstrating that independence is an integral part of preserving her selfhood. Alexia's conduct contrasts with sacrificial, family-governed arrangements underlying Victorian marriages:

"Mama," she [Alexia] said, gesturing expansively, "I will not have you manipulating this situation. No one need know what has occurred in this room. . . . My reputation will remain intact, and Lord Maccon will remain a free man. And now I have a headache; please excuse me." (175)

While refusing to be treated as a commodity, Alexia highlights her personal integrity. Thus, she gains the status of a physically and intellectually distinctive individual endowed with a liberated mind. Accordingly, in *Soulless*, one gets acquainted with Alexia's protomodern thoughts on marriage: *"reputation be damned,* thought she. *It is not as though I have any significant prospects to ruin"* (168). Carriger's heroine treats reputation—the primary ingredient of the Victorian woman's integrity—as a subsidiary issue. Instead, she advocates twenty-first-century philosophy with one's feelings and highly individualized interests prevailing over the normative standards of reputation.

In *The Victorian Novel in Context*, Grace Moore discusses at length the concept of reputation as recognized in the nineteenth-century novel. "In a world where young girls were raised to net the best possible husband, a woman's reputation was her most valuable asset and many Victorian novels explore the consequences of compromising a woman's good name," she observes (80). According to Moore, Charlotte Brontë's *Jane Eyre* engages in a debate concerning her potentially dangerous moral position:

> Jane Eyre shows her awareness of the social and moral danger she is placed in by Mr Rochester's attempt to ensnare her in a bigamous marriage when she leaves the temptations of Thornfield Hall, fearing that she will yield to Mr Rochester if she remains. Having heard Rochester speak contemptuously of his former mistresses, she understands that if she succumbs to his entreaties she will not enjoy the safety afforded by marriage and runs the risk of being cast aside once her novelty value has diminished. . . . Jane is ultimately rewarded for her strength of character when she is reunited with the recently widowed Rochester and able to become his wife. (81–82)

Jane's cautious behavior is rewarded because, as Moore argues, she is "too moral and too prudent to gamble with Rochester as his previous mistresses had done" and because she is aware that "without a legal contract of marriage to support her claim, she will be unprotected" (82). Jane opposes Rochester, thus preserving her respectability, which is, according to Sally Mitchell's *Daily Life in Victorian England*, a term "closely associated with the concept of independence" (262). On the contrary, Alexia emerges victorious from her romantic entanglement with Lord Maccon because she ultimately dispenses with morality as framed by nineteenth-century standards.[4] Paradoxically, it offers her independence, that is: respectability. By postponing her marriage, Alexia affirms her autonomy in decision-making. Her victory is prompted by

Figure 12.2. "And have you a pale blue dress on?" by F. H. Townsend (from the second edition of Jane Eyre, 1847) (Public Domain).

social exclusion, while personal freedom paradoxically follows that exclusion. Thus, paradoxically, Alexia wins because she is an odd woman. At the same time, she does not dispose of her "womanliness." In Carriger's novel, oddness signifies opportunities and social isolation involves benefits and liberating decisions.

Nevertheless, while in the twenty-first century *Soulless* praises female independence and individuality in an effortless and plausible way, *Jane Eyre*, published in 1847, remains confined to the Victorian moral framework. Although Brontë's work offers a relatively revolutionary vision of the self-conscious and mentally emancipated heroine, Jane is aware that acting in accordance with her feelings will bring about her moral fall. Brontë's heroines, such as Jane Eyre, Lucy Snowe in *Villette*, and Caroline Helstone in *Shirley*, invariably experience conflicts between their feelings and the worldly expectations imposed on them by society and they all push back in various ways. Jane overcomes her feelings toward Mr. Rochester as she perceives an impending moral danger just in time. Lucy Snowe is too introverted and apprehensive to acknowledge her need for affection, and Caroline Helstone remains incapable of articulating her feelings, as it is unbecoming for a woman to reveal her sentiments.

The possible loss of conventionally understood reputation haunts Anne Brontë's heroine as well. In *The Tenant of Wildfell Hall*, Helen Graham has to atone only because she escapes her husband's cruelty. While abandoning her persecutor, Helen bravely withstands unjust social opinions and, similarly to Carriger's heroine, finds comfort in living in seclusion. Although the novel provides a Victorian "happy ending" (Helen eventually marries happily), it offers a bitter reflection on the warped meaning of reputation as well. Helen opposes cruelty and chooses the welfare of her son, Arthur, yet she is condemned for abandoning her husband and living independently. In chapter 37, Helen reflects on her state:

> Another year is past; and I am weary of this life. And yet I cannot wish to leave it: whatever afflictions assail me here, I cannot wish to go and leave my darling [Arthur] in this dark and wicked world alone, without a friend to guide him through its weary mazes, to warn him of its thousand snares, and guard him from the perils that beset him on every hand. (255)

Hence, while Helen is accused of breaking family ties, she asserts that her courageous decision is undertaken for the sake of her son. What constitutes positive, moral behavior for Anne Brontë's character appears to be a form of corruption in the eyes of Victorian society. This reflection attests to the split between social and moral standards in the nineteenth century.

Carriger's steampunk fiction readily responds to this Victorian conflict, offering previously unattainable possibilities for women characters. However, as observed beforehand by Jeff VanderMeer, steampunk recognizes and mirrors the present day rather than the past (13). Thus, it is the privilege of the neo-Victorian women characters to openly manifest their inner states and bravely venture into the literarily constructed semi-Victorian world.

A grave social injustice indirectly influenced the origins of Carriger's work. Alexia Tarabotti is based on a historical figure—the protofeminist Arcangela Tarabotti (1604–1652), who in 1643 brought forth a monograph entitled *Paternal Tyranny*, in which the authoress argues against men who confine women to unjust suffering and solitude. Secluded in a convent herself, Arcangela Tarabotti shared her bitter reflections concerning the predatory patriarchal world. "Dear Reader," she writes, my heart has never had any personal reason for growing angry against the male sex, although it cannot bear to recall without irritation those devious words proffered by the first man when he blamed the woman given to him by God as a partner (Gn 3:12). (40)

In her work, Arcangela Tarabotti uses the word "partner" to refer to Eve. As *Oxford English Reference Dictionary* states, "partner" is "a person who shares" (1061). Thus, "partnership" implies equality and mutual understanding, the notions escaping such critics as William Rathbone Greg. "Partnership" as such appears practically unattainable for an average Victorian woman whose life was dominated by the ideology of "separate spheres."

In *Soulless*, the issues of courtship, partnership, and marriage receive particular prominence. When a long-term spinster, Alexia Tarabotti, suddenly marries Lord Conall Maccon, it seems to many that the match is based on carefully arranged social and economic criteria. However, Alexia is not an average Victorian woman who craves society's favor. As an overly assertive and pragmatic character residing between two divergent historical realms, Alexia cannot come to terms with the fact that it is Lord Maccon who occupies the dominant (patriarchal) place instead of herself. She enjoys her share of supremacy and gladly performs the role of her husband's leader and adviser. In the person of Lord Maccon she encounters a definitional partner who matches her strong, domineering personality. Before their marriage, Lord Maccon imagines "seeing her [Alexia] across the dining table, discussing science and politics, having her advice on points of pack controversy and BUR difficulties" (173). Apparently, he is enchanted by the spiritual connection of their minds. In this sense, the relationship between Lord Maccon and Alexia resembles the tie between Mr. Rochester and Jane Eyre which manifests itself through the communion of minds. Nonetheless, the tie between the characters in Brontë's novel stands for a romantic and heart-wrenching connection, whereas *Soulless* is filled with postmodern irony.[5]

There is no place for melancholy and romantic yearning in Alexia's reason-governed world. Similarly, spirituality, as presented in *Soulless*, is devoid of the pure fascination with the unknown and unfathomed. Even though *Soulless* hosts a vast number of supernatural characters (ghosts, werewolves, vampires), their existence is scientifically explained, thus depriving the literary Victorian world of its nostalgic and spiritual dimensions.

In *Soulless*, the postmodern irony is skillfully implemented by means of the language as well: Carriger blends the elevated and ornamental discourse of the bygone with numerous contemporary forms of expression deliberately interspersed within the pages of the novel. Such step allows Carriger to position *Soulless* as simultaneously a semi-Victorian and modern text. In Bakhtinian terms, Carriger resorts to "hybridization," that is, to the mixing, within a single concrete utterance, of two or more different linguistic consciousnesses, often widely separated in time and social space. Along with dialogization of languages and pure dialogues, this is a major device for creating language-images in the novel. Novelistic hybrids are intentional . . .; their double-voicedness . . . is not meant to resolve. (Bakhtin, *The Dialogic Imagination*, 429)

"The style will always give [the novelist] away," Bakhtin believes (327). While implementing linguistic hybridization in *Soulless*, Carriger bridges the literary bygone with the present, while, at the same time, playfully winking at her readers. The postmodern linguistic irony lays bare the shortcomings of Alexia's Victorian "reality" as well as the weaknesses of modernity. Certainly, it enables the rereading of the nineteenth century from contemporary angles. For instance, in chapter 14, when Queen Victoria offers Alexia the post of the muhjah, she expresses herself in a partly contemporary manner:

> The queen nodded happily. "Your future husband indicated you would not be averse to the position. Most excellent! We convene twice a week, Thursday and Saturday nights. . . . "
>
> Alexia smiled foolishly and looked at Professor Lyall from under her lashes. . . . The werewolf grinned. "He [Lord Maccon] *recommended you to the job* months ago." [emphasis added] (276)

In *Soulless*, Queen Victoria represents the mainstay of the Victorian world. Yet, "recommending one to the job" introduces a contemporary context and posits Professor Lyall as the mouthpiece of modernity. Adhering to Phelan's terminology, Alexia figures in the text as a "synthetic" character who blends both Victorian and modern "realities." This leads one to think about Ryszard Nycz's "text-reality" interdependency: Carriger's novel draws on the nineteenth-century model of femininity and, yet, shrewdly transforms this conventional image while adhering to a twenty-first-century cultural background.

The overwhelmingly logical, fictional world of *Soulless* filled with postmodern irony constitutes the background for Alexia's encounter with her future husband. The meeting takes place after the opening scene, during which Miss Tarabotti defeats an impolite vampire who strives to bite her without applying the rules of Victorian etiquette. "Manners!," Miss Tarabotti bravely instructs the unfortunate creature (2). The vampire (a potential representative of the patriarchal world) is not prepared to meet a Victorian lady who can be so self-controlled. After the bloodcurdling adventure, Alexia does not faint, nor does she need smelling salts or masculine support. She appears even displeased when Lord Maccon comes to her belated rescue. "Do not give me instructions in that tone of voice, you . . . puppy," she informs the earl (11). Alexia straightforwardly criticizes poor quality of service at the party at which she is a guest: "I was promised food at this ball. In case you had not noticed, no food appears in the residence" (12).

When the heroine becomes Lord Maccon's wife, she gains a new status of a "female-Alpha" who governs the household inhabited by other werewolves, including the earl of Woolsey himself. Elevated above women's traditional domestic routine, she performs an almost military function of a leader, as depicted in the sequel to *Soulless, Changeless* (2010). After her marriage, Alexia's social status stands in a sharp contrast to Greg's radical assumption concerning women's redundancy and their presumably ideal married life. Without a doubt, Lord Maccon is immensely proud of his dexterous wife. He readily acquaints her with the particularities of his work as a BUR (Bureau of Unnatural Registry) agent. In the course of events, Alexia receives the already-mentioned post of Queen Victoria's muhjah, a position of the greatest importance. As the fictionalized Queen Victoria explains, the muhjah is the third, preternatural member of the Shadow Council, "whose attention is solely on the Crown's concerns" (275). Most importantly, according to the Queen, muhjah is "the voice of the modern age" (275). This statement epitomizes Alexia's role in Carriger's text: Alexia Tarabotti is the voice of modern logic, invited into a discursive dialogue with the imaginary, nineteenth-century past. Thus, in Gail Carriger's novel, Alexia's intelligence gains prominence, rather than her supposed feminine vulnerability or unreasonableness. The focus on the heroine's unique qualities positively alters the traditional perception of women as passive, unintelligent, and incapable of making decisions for themselves. In numerous Victorian novels, intelligence is an aspect of femininity pushed aside as a virtue of secondary importance, hardly ever receiving enough attention. However, if intelligence is given any notice, it prevalently figures as a "cunning type" (as in Thackeray's *Vanity Fair*) or as "intelligence unemployed," (because the heroine is bound to lose anyway), as in the case of Thomas Hardy's *Tess of the d'Urbervilles*.

In *A Room of One's Own*, Virginia Woolf argues that the nineteenth-century woman was "snubbed, slapped, lectured and exhorted. Her mind must have been strained and her vitality lowered" (71). What Woolf appears to imply is the claim that, from the male perspective, the Victorian woman was essentially inferior to the man in order to convince him of his superiority. As Woolf indicates,

> we come within range of that very interesting and obscure masculine complex which has had so much influence upon the woman's movement; that deep-seated desire, not so much that *she* shall be inferior as that *he* shall be superior, which

plants him wherever one looks, not only in front of the arts, but barring the way to politics too. (71)

The woman's answer to this "masculine complex," Woolf argues, should be a "room of one's own"[6]—a private space to cultivate the woman's mind. In the case of Carriger's ingenious character, it is both the privacy of Alexia's room and, eventually, the pursuit of her political career that encourage her individual development. After marriage, Alexia emerges as a semi-contemporary woman who fulfills herself in the domestic space as well as outside its boundaries. In contrast, a professional career is an almost unattainable dream of an average Victorian woman. In Charlotte Brontë's *Shirley*, Caroline Helstone untiringly dreams of a professional occupation. It was Brontë's wish to highlight nineteenth-century women's isolation and mental incapacitation imposed on them by the constraints of the Victorian system. In the chapter entitled "Old Maids," Caroline Helstone wonders:

> Is this enough? Is it to live? Is there not a terrible hollowness, mockery, want, craving, in that existence which is given away to others, for want of something of your own to bestow it on? I suspect there is. Does virtue lie in abnegation of self? I do not believe it. (133)

Victorian women, as described in nineteenth-century texts, seem to be desperately ensnared by tedious domestic routines, so praised by William R. Greg. Their decisions, Brontë implies, appear to be the decisions of others. The eponymous protagonist of Brontë's *Shirley*, a young, orphaned mistress of Fieldhead, openly opposes submitting to "traditional" standards. Yet, as already mentioned, her social position dramatically differs from that of Caroline Helstone: she is lucky enough to possess her own fortune, which, in turn, offers her relative freedom and free will. Deep inside, Shirley is a warm and good-hearted person who longs for love and affection, yet carefully guards her independence. Eventually, Shirley marries her former tutor, Louis Gérard Moore. Hence, on the one hand, she conforms to the conventional Victorian pattern while, on the other hand, her relationship with Louis is also unconventional while based on the notion of partnership. S. N. Singh argues that Shirley

> represents those few women who exercise their individuality and keep their identity as lovers and wives, and who desire to be ruled and governed and passionately loved by their "exacting" and "rigid" husbands. . . . Charlotte Brontë advocates that men should be physically and intellectually superior to their women to protect and guide their destiny. (164)

Indeed, in Brontë's novels, men turn into guides and protectors, yet, at the same time, their relationships with women are essentially based on notions of respect, partnership and negotiation. While Louis proposes to Shirley, she is ready with a speech simultaneously filled with self-assertion and anxiety:

"And are we equal, then, sir? are we equal at last?"

"You are younger, frailer, feebler, more ignorant than I."

"Will you be good to me, and never tyrannise?" (464)

"Dear Louis, be faithful to me; never leave me. I don't care for life unless I may pass it at your side." . . . "Sir," she said, starting up, "at your peril you ever again name such sordid things as money, or poverty, or inequality. It will be absolutely dangerous to torment me with these maddening scruples. I defy you to do it." (465)

On the one hand, Shirley articulates her expectations with the confidence resembling that of the protomodern, independent woman, especially while stating that "it will be absolutely dangerous to torment [her] with these maddening scruples" connected with "sordid" matters of "money," "poverty, or inequality" (465). On the other hand, the reader senses anxiety in her words, as she asks Louis to respect her and treat her as an equal. Essentially, in Brontë's novels, characters such as Shirley or Jane preserve their identity and individuality of mind while stepping into the conventional framework of Victorian domestic lives. In this way, they preserve their metaphorical independent space while being drawn into traditional nineteenth-century patterns. Brontë's heroines do not have to resign from a satisfying private life in order to remain fully "themselves," which makes them quite revolutionary on the Victorian literary scene dominated by dualisms.

The "Woolfian room" not only offers women the opportunity to develop as independent and valuable thinkers, but also becomes the place of repose. In *Soulless*, Alexia delights in the solitude of her own space, because it allows her to engage in personal affairs, enjoying the company of books and her favorite cup of tea. However, primarily, the privacy of her own sphere allows Alexia to escape an overbearing parental influence.

It is one of the heaviest charges against the nineteenth-century New Woman that, while pursuing her new image, residing in the "room of her own" and engaging in intellectual debates, she abandons her womanly side:

When people wrote and spoke about the "New Woman" in the 1890s, they were usually referring to a very different figure: the unsexed, terrifying, violent

Amazon ready to overturn the world (Richardson, ed., 39), Talia Schaffer explicates.

Authors such as Quida and magazines such as *Punch* eagerly criticized the New Woman for wearing obnoxious, masculine garments. Moreover, "*Punch* never wearied of the chance to caricature New Women in cartoons, or to parody their fiction," indicates Elaine Showalter in *Daughters of Decadence: Women Writers of the Fin-de-Siècle* (ix). Due to their professed lack of womanliness, New Women were perceived as disrupting the functioning of the traditionally sanctioned family order. "Yet to many outraged male reviewers, the New Women writers were threatening daughters of decadence," observes Showalter. "They saw connections between New Women and decadent men, as members of avant garde attacking marriage and reproduction" (ix).

However, New Women's narratives usually originated and operated merely within the fictional, literary framework. As we already know, there were numerous fictional and often contradictory narratives concerning the literary figure of the New Woman. Therefore, Talia Schaffer argues that "the New Woman's literary status was the most challenging aspect of her identity, not a way of making it any 'safer'" (Richardson, ed., 47). The New Woman constituted a fluid construct, suspended between "reality" and fiction. Hence, nineteenth-century narratives occupied with the New Woman endowed her with numerous, often contradictory characteristics, concurrently claiming that the New Woman was a fearless Amazon, a noble scholar, a cyclist, or a threatening tomboy. Neo-Victorian fiction responds to these Victorian narratives with the vision of the New Woman akin to that proclaimed by Amy Cruse in her 1935 study *The Victorians and Their Reading*. Catherine Golden recalls Cruse's description of the New Woman as the "one who, courageously and hopefully, stepped off the beaten, easy track and forced a way through the thick growth of prejudice and established custom to the open regions where development was possible" (27).

According to Cruse's definition, the New Woman is as a self-assured individual who confidently strives to continue her personal development. So does Alexia Tarabotti in Carriger's *Soulless*. Moreover, while pursuing her scholarly interests, she invariably cultivates her womanly side by showing a deep interest in fashion. In the twenty-first century, Alexia provides a dialogical response to Quida's claims that the New Woman's "self-knowledge" is "very small" (616) and that her clothes contain abominable "balloon-sleeves" and "a bodice tight to bursting" (613). Alexia combines reason with femininity, challenging thereby Quida's assumption that the New Woman abandoned her womanly side at the expense of the "unfeminine" pursuit. Carriger's *Parasol Protectorate* series is occupied with fashion recalling the Victorian decorum and, oftentimes, serving as a dangerous weapon. In this sense, neo-Victorian

Figure 12.3. "The Bicycle Suit," cartoon from *Punch* magazine (1895), unknown author (Public Domain).

literary fashion blends trend-setting with utilitarianism. Likewise, the neo-Victorian New Woman mirrors the modern reader who, oftentimes, also finds herself oscillating between the latest fashion trends and practicality. Thus, neo-Victorian fiction displays a self-reflective potential, commenting on the modern balance between the beauty and usefulness of garments.

Soulless abounds in descriptions of fashionable and useful items, gadgets, accessories, and garments. For instance, Alexia treasures her inseparable parasol—an elegant artifact, but also a disguised weapon used against the rude vampire. Additionally, Alexia skillfully uses her parasol to attain privacy: she "deployed her trusty brass parasol and tilted in such a way she would not have to look any more at her family" (111). The parasol, a practical and exquisite item, is omnipresent in the heroine's life:

> It was terribly tasteless for her to be carrying a parasol at an evening ball, but Miss Tarabotti rarely went anywhere without it. It was of a style entirely of her own devising: a black frilly confection with purple satin pansies sewn about, brass hardware, and buckshot in its silver tip. (2)

The parasol manifests Alexia's originality and her potential for "self-creation" as an individual (the parasol is "entirely of her own devising"). In nineteenth-century England, parasols played significant roles in the overall female outfit. "It was just possible to hold another Victorian accessory, a parasol, while clamping one's arms to one's bust to anchor one's shawl," indicates Liza Picard in *Victorian London: The Life of a City 1840–1870* (214). In 1840, Picard indicates, the parasol was

> small, frequently frilled and embroidered, with jointed ivory or wood sticks to swivel and tilt so as to keep the sun from the complexion, as you sat in your carriage. They [parasols] grew in size and altered in shape, from the even curve to the ogee-shaped "pagoda" shape. They were, of course, no use in rain. (215)

For Alexia, her parasol has no use in the sun. *Soulless* parodies Victorian preference for pale complexion and opposes the traditional canon of beauty while endowing the main heroine with a naturally olive skin. While taking a walk with her friend, Ivy, Alexia holds her parasol, yet she is aware that "such an effort [is] wasted on her complexion" (28). However, she values the object as a useful, personal weapon. Accordingly, in *Soulless*, decorative nineteenth-century objects gain practical value and lose their purely theatrical qualities. Even Alexia's hairpin—"the one of wood and the other of silver"—is "deadly" (210). In *Soulless*, technology turns Victorian accessories into arcane, precarious objects. Decorativeness goes hand in hand with practicality, and there is almost no space for meaningless gadgets and accessories, if only one excuses Ivy's tastelessness and her "large red and white striped shepherdess hat, with a curved yellow ostrich feather" (138).

In the twenty-first century, steampunk strives to combine Victorian craftsmanship with environmentally friendly, individualized, ingenious technology. This intention is reflected in Carriger's *Parasol Protectorate* series. As argued by Jeff VanderMeer,

> Steampunks seek to reject the conformity of the modern, soulless, futureless design of technology—and all that implies—while embracing the inventiveness and tech origins of Victorian machines. . . . Similarly, Ruskin's movement sought to return to the creative freedom exemplified for him by the medieval workshop. (99)

Apart from the introduction of the alluring and functional items, *Soulless* revisits the Victorian wardrobe. As already mentioned, although regarded as an outsider and an odd woman, Alexia exemplifies a fashionable Victorian lady. Before the party given by Lord Blingchester, Miss Tarabotti pays particular attention to her appearance with a view to entrapping Lord Maccon:

> She had dressed with particular care. Given the earl's apparent partiality for her physique, she had chosen an evening dress of deep rose with a daringly low décolletage and the latest in small bustles. She had arranged her hair to fall over the side of her neck. . . . Her mama had even commented that she looked very well for a spinster. (101)

Soulless contradicts the nineteenth-century presumption that spinsters are uninteresting, unfeminine, or plainly dressed. Charlotte Brontë's *Shirley* features such distressing images of old maids as that of Miss Mann, sitting "primly and somewhat grimly-tidy in a cushioned rocking-chair, her hands busied with some knitting," (136) or that of Miss Ainsley, an ugly and formal person (139). Although Miss Mann and Miss Ainsley are good-hearted and widely respected for their charity, feelings of hopelessness and ridicule linger over these forlorn figures. Alexia Tarabotti intertextually revisits the literary image of the Victorian spinster, releasing her from this conventional and spiteful narrative. Although set in the Victorian era, Carriger's novel features the twenty-first-century single woman—an attractive and thriving (initially single) one instead of an actual spinster. At the same time, *Soulless* redeems the figure of the New Woman, accused of lack of femininity at the fin-de-siècle of the Victorian era. In fact, neo-Victorian revision serves as a comment on modern society, where singlehood ceases to be "odd." This new perception of womanhood is incorporated into the modern literary narratives reshaping the Victorian discourse: while striving to rewrite the past, they use contemporary tools. Hence, the revisioned Victorian past is filled with our contemporaneous mentality, envisaged by such characters as Miss Tarabotti with her scholarly inclinations and fashionable dress codes.

Alexia's inquisitive personality not only "redeems" her from the precarious passivity of her nineteenth-century counterpart, but also places her in the center of dangerous events. However, Alexia remains conscious of her femininity even in moments of great danger. When kidnapped by unknown individuals, Miss Tarabotti deplores the damage done to her dress and appearance:

> Her ivory taffeta dress was a little worse for the experience; one of the puffed sleeves and some of the gold lace had ripped, and it was stained beyond redemption in several places. Alexia was annoyed. True, it was out of fashion, but she liked the gown. She sighed and did her best to smooth out the wrinkles while looking with interest around the dressing room. There was no means of escape, but there was a bit of ribbon for her to tie back her unruly hair and a looking glass in which she could check up on the generally disreputable state of her appearance. (214)

Neither a quiet life, nor selfless charity are among Alexia's aspirations (unlike in the case of the "old maids" in Brontë's *Shirley*). On the contrary, *Soulless* reveals the heroine's detective potential, turning itself into a neo-Victorian sensation novel with the plot debating the enigmatic case of disappearing vampires. At last, Alexia embarks on a highly adventurous quest leading her to the discovery of a pseudoscientific Hypocras Club.

"Detective fiction offered a particularly effective field for portrayal of the popularized New Woman heroine," acknowledges Chris Willis, writing about the literary beginnings of the independent woman figure in "Packaging the New Woman for Mass Consumption" (Richardson, ed., 59). Willis offers an example of Matthias McDonnell Bodkin's Dora Myrl, a detective heroine in the early twentieth-century novel *The Capture of Paul Beck* (1909) (59). Dora Myrl, who is independent, attractive, and professional, paves the way for such literary New Women as Carriger's Alexia. In his article, Willis traces the pattern of Dora's developing career:

> Her chequered career provides a virtual roll-call of the professions regarded as typical of the New Woman: before taking up detection, she says that she has been "a telephone-girl, a telegraph-girl" and "a lady journalist" (Bodkin: DM, 6). Dora remains single at the end of the first book of her adventures, but in the sequel she shows an uncharacteristic wish to be "a real womanly woman" with a husband and children. Bodkin marries her off in this second volume, *The Capture of Paul Beck*. The title refers not to Dora's capture of a criminal, but to her capture of a husband. Paul Beck is a male detective who is one of Dora's professional rivals until they marry. Like the New Woman, the professional

female detective represents a threat to the convention that women should be financially dependent on men. (59)

Similarly to Dora, at first, Alexia is in rivalry with Lord Maccon, finally entrapping him as a husband. Thereby, her success is double: it is both professional (the discovery of the intrigue at the Hypocras Club) and private (the longed-for relationship with the Earl of Woolsey). Hence, Alexia combines "womanliness" with professional gratification.

The news regarding Alexia's approaching marriage immensely impress Mrs. Loontwill: "'You caught him!' she breathed in delight" (277). In *Soulless*, in contrast to such Victorian novels as Brontë's *Shirley*, the conventional Victorian ending interweaves with modern readerly expectations. Therefore, after her happy, reconciling marriage, Alexia embarks on a new career as the Queen's muhjah. In this respect, the neo-Victorian ending offered in *Soulless* is revitalizing and revisionary: it strives toward the traditionally desired resolution, yet it does not threaten to limit women's potential. Marriage—the traditional solution for Victorian women—is intertextually revisited, as the heroine attains both private and professional happiness. Alexia's choice is not detrimental to her integrity. On the contrary, her marriage appears to be fulfilling and, thus, mutually inspirational.

Louisa Hadley argues along similar lines in "Feminine Endings: Neo-Victorian Transformations of the Victorian," positing that Antonia Byatt's *Possession* (1990) "adapts the conventions of romance to demonstrate that a 'happy ever after' ending is not necessarily inimical to female independence" (Tredennick, ed., 188). Undoubtedly, Carriger's *Soulless* follows the convention of the romance as well, establishing what Heidi Hansson terms the "common ground" for modern writers and readers (3). As already mentioned in the previous chapter, postmodern literature possesses an intertextual potential inherent in romantic conventions. This intertextual potential of the romance enables one to think about literature in a wider context, reaching beyond presentism. *Soulless*, as an example of the postmodern, paranormal romance, preserves the conventions of a quest, trail, alienation and reconciliation pattern. By the same token, *Soulless* incorporates the pattern of the Cinderella story, analogous to that presented in *Jane Eyre*: Alexia, initially a social outcast, receives her final reward. However, in this postmodern tale, the prize comes with assertiveness rather than with the heroine's virtue: hence, the universally recognized conventions of archetypal female righteousness inscribed in the romance are revised and reanalyzed in the postmodern context.

The New Woman, Alexia Tarabotti, blurs the boundaries between traditional feminine and masculine spheres. Consequently, Alexia perfectly matches Virginia Woolf's claim that "it is fatal to be a man or woman pure and simple; one must be woman-manly or man-womanly" (136). Sandra Gilbert and Susan Gubar also challenge the nineteenth-century perception of women characters as either angelic or demonic figures. In their seminal work *The Madwoman in the Attic* (1979), Gilbert and Gubar argue that purely angelic or demonic women characters are phantasmagoric literary creations:

> Before the woman writer can journey through the looking glass toward literary autonomy, however, she must come to terms with the images on the surface of the glass, with, that is, those mythic masks male artists have fastened over her human face both to lessen their dread of her "inconstancy" and—by identifying her with the "eternal types" they have themselves invented—to possess her more thoroughly. Specifically, as we will try to show here, a woman writer must examine, assimilate, and transcend the extreme images of "angel" and "monster" which male authors have generated for her. (16–17)

Precisely, *Soulless* reexamines the binary roles of angels and monsters imposed on Victorian women while revealing the complex nature of the main protagonist. Alexia is neither angelic nor demonic. In the novel, the heroine shows her multifaceted personality, making her appearance as an eccentric individual, a fearless adventurer, an aspiring scholar, a down-to-earth rationalist, an unflappable skeptic, a confident friend, a daring lover, a delicate, feminine woman, and a tender companion. These contradictory features delineate Alexia as a full-fledged character who questions the limiting choice between angelic and demonic literary creations. Escaping the "eternal types," Carriger's heroine defines herself as an individual—a "madwoman in the library," unlocked, liberated, and rewritten anew by the neo-Victorian discourse.

Throughout her turbulent history, the New Woman was usually defined against the figure of the man. Interestingly enough, in *Soulless*, Gail Carriger introduces a variety of engaging masculine characters who, contrasted with Alexia's inner strength and presence of mind, lack the unshaken patriarchal reputation. Yet, Carriger's masculine characters do not serve as a modern critique of patriarchal tyranny. Instead, stripped of patriarchal despotism, they inspire deep sympathy and understanding as they are apparently well-meaning but, oftentimes, imperfect.

The most prominent male character, Lord Conall Maccon, amuses the reader with his inept courtship of Alexia. The Earl of Woolsey is a big, good-natured, although often uncultivated and rough werewolf of Scottish origin with "unreasonably pretty tawny eyes, mahogany-colored hair," "a particularly nice nose," (7) and "black and thick" eyelashes (128). Such description brings out the "feminine" side of the character and points to Maccon's gentler features contrasted with Alexia's appearance, including, among others, her prominent nose. What is more, Alexia's presence brings into prominence Maccon's soft side and his imperfections. Usually stern and decisive, he appears confused in Alexia's presence:

> Lord Maccon was quiet for a few long minutes. He examined his emotions. While admitting that at that moment—her small hands in his, the smell of vanilla and cinnamon in the air, the neckline of that damnable dress—his mind possessed all the clarity of pea soup full of ham-hock-sized chunks of need, there was something else lurking in said soup. Whatever it was, it made him angry, for it would desperately complicate everything in his well-ordered life, and now was not the time to tackle it. (165)

Hegemonic and coarse only on the surface, Lord Maccon is not a patriarchal tyrant, but rather an ordinary man with weaknesses and doubts that make him even more appealing as a character. Maccon's Beta and deputy at the Bureau for Unnatural Registration office, Professor Randolph Lyall, is yet another interesting male-werewolf figure. In the novel, he is the mainstay of wisdom and self-command, who repeatedly proves to be Alexia's indispensable adviser and Lord Maccon's right-hand man. As humorously described in the text, he is "a professor of nothing in particular and several subjects in broad detail" (59).

Apart from Lord Maccon and Professor Lyall, the novel features Alexia's friend—Lord Akeldama, an eccentric vampire. He emerges as an unconventional male figure pervasively obsessed with fashion. In chapter 9, the vampire's garments are described in detail:

> Lord Akeldama was dressed to the pink for the evening. His coat was exquisite plum-colored velvet paired with a satin waistcoat of sea-foam green and mauve plaid. His britches were of a perfectly coordinated lavender, and his formal cravat a treble bow of white lawn secured with a massive amethyst and gold pin. His Hessian boots were polished to a mirror shine, and his top hat was plum velvet to match the coat. (179)

Faultlessly dressed, life and soul of the party and a perfect gentleman, Lord Akeldama charms one with his refined manners and kindheartedness. His speech is also extravagantly elaborate and ornamental, positioning him in the novel as an effeminate and overdrawn advocate of the bygone:

> "Pardon me, my *fluffy cockatoo*," he [Lord Akeldama] said, pretending to rein in an excessively emotional state. "Please ignore my ramblings as those of a madman. . . . It is a little like having those *disagreeable* shivers running up and down one's spine. Something does not feel right with the *universe* when one's

territory is invaded. I *can* bear it, but I do not *like* it. It makes me quite edgy and off kilter." Lord Akeldama put the fan down. (182)

However, Lord Akeldama's eccentricity lies not only in his obsession with clothes and lavish home decorations or in his oratorical abilities, but also in the habit of surrounding himself with a circle of handsome male vampires and dandies. A semi-feminine[7] character, Lord Akeldama takes lively interest in the domestic routine performed by his male vampire servants.[8] Paying a visit to Lord Akeldama's house, Alexia notices outrageously luxurious furnishings and designs:

> Everything was to the height of style, if one were thinking in terms of style round about a hundred years ago. Lord Akeldama possessed real, substantial wealth and was not afraid to display it openly. Nothing in his home was substandard, or faux, or imitation, and all of it was well beyond the pale. The carpets were not Persian but were instead vibrant flower-ridden images of shepherds seducing shepherdesses under intense blue skies. . . . The vampire led her through to his drawing room. It contained none of the style clutter but instead harkened back to a time before the French Revolution. The furniture was all white or gilded gold, upholstered in cream and gold striped brocade and riddled with fringe and tassels. Heavy layers of gold velvet curtains shielded the windows, and the plush rug on the floor sported yet another proximate shepherding event. . . . For all its gilt pomposity, the room had a feeling of regular use. . . . "It is also very, uh, Rococo," she [Alexia] said, attempting not to intimate she found it at all old-fashioned. Lord Akeldama clapped his hands delightedly. "Isn't it just? I am afraid I never quite left that particular era. It was *such* a glorious time to be alive, when men *finally* and *truly* got to wear sparkly things, and there was lace and velvet everywhere." (182–83)

The vampire's apparent fondness of domesticity and his semi-feminine nature allow one to envisage Lord Akeldama as a peculiar "angel in the house" or the modern inhabitant of Ruskin's garden. Thus, in *Soulless*, men's and women's roles are reversed, and Ruskin's retreat is no longer an exclusive domain of women.

In the nineteenth century, men also venture into Ruskin's garden, one of them being Prince Albert, responsible for the management of Queen Victoria's household. As indicated by Jennifer Phegley, in Albert and Victoria's relationship

> the roles were in many ways reversed. Victoria called Albert her "Angel," and he became the overseer and organizer of the home, while she attended to the business of the nation. Though the "Angel in the House" . . . was supposed to be a woman, Albert embodied the role perfectly. (4)

Hence, in the nineteenth century, the actual division of gender roles might have been different from what the prevalent discourse professed it to be. Written in the twenty-first century, neo-Victorian texts strive to highlight this divergence between "reality" and fiction while creating highly individualized characters such as Lord Akeldama. As stated before, John Reed notices in his *Victorian Conventions* that in nineteenth-century fiction "characters . . . exhibit predictable combinations of attributes which result in conventional types" (5). Neo-Victorian fiction employs contemporary mentality in order to revisit these types. In Carriger's novel, Alexia—as the New Woman—and the "New Men" surrounding her—are open to change and novelty. Alexia Tarabotti proves that femininity is not a set of rigorously imposed features or, using Gilbert and Gubar's terminology, the "mythic masks" (17) but, rather, it is a blend of characteristics resulting in a unique persona understood as a "woman." Moreover, Alexia abolishes the myth of an ignorant and helpless Victorian lady, a spiteful spinster, as well as that of a mannish and ignorant New Woman.

I believe Alexia to be a Woolfian "woman-manly" figure rather than a character either completely devoid of feminine qualities or entirely passive. At the same time, I oppose Virginia Woolf's claim that we should "'kill' the 'angel in the house'" for the sake of abolishing the patriarchal monsters (*The Madwoman in the Attic*, 17). Rather than that, I believe that "angelic" qualities of neo-Victorian women characters can benefit the twenty-first-century image of the New Woman: Alexia is strong, endlessly rational, and independent, which does not prevent her from being womanly, sensitive, and warmhearted. Neo-Victorian fiction offers a recipe for combining womanliness with reason and independence. While Chris Willis aptly indicates that the fin-de-siècle Victorian New Woman "loses out to the 'womanly'" female (Richardson, ed., 58), the "loss" (either in personal or professional life) is no longer the malady of her present-day counterpart.

In *Soulless,* the alleged female oddity becomes a celebrated asset, enabling one to remain unrestricted and self-confident in the corrupted world. While examining Alexia's persona—self-sufficient, independent and unique—one might agree with Arcangela Tarabotti's statement: "Mary, a woman like all others, was not obliged to beg for her existence from a man's rib! She was born before time itself. . . . Woman was created *ab eterno*" (45).

Last but not least, while reading *Soulless,* it is important to recognize that, according to Phelan's terminology, Alexia is a "synthetic" character. Her "unrealness" and "unnaturalness" as a character challenge the "veracity" of the presented nineteenth-century world and question "traditional" narratives concerned with the literary past. Such questioning encourages the reader to reflect upon the past from different undiscovered angles that blend the bygone with the modern sociocultural perspective. Alexia's "artificial" presence in the text—her peculiar "suspension" between the twenty-first century "reality" and the realm of nineteenth-century London—evinces itself not only in her intrepid behavior and unconventional moral code, but also in her language. The language in the novel, oscillating between nineteenth-century discourse and present-day speech, points to the purposeful artificiality and inconsistence of the textually created world. It is what Bakhtin recognizes as hybridization, the "double-voicedness" which "is not meant to resolve." (*Dialogic Imagination*, 429). Hence, the "conflict" between the two consciousnesses residing in Alexia's language remains purposefully unsolved. This lack of resolution enables the reader to negotiate between the two differing planes: the literary past and the reader's contemporaneity. Both of these areas are equally important and equally contribute to the decoding of the text (*Dialogic Imagination*, 429). In *Soulless*, hybridization not only appears in the characters' speech, but also on the narrative level—the opening chapter of the novel introduces modern, colloquial narration which prepares the reader for the encounter with the unconventional heroine:

> Miss Alexia Tarabotti was not enjoying her evening. Private balls were never more than middling amusements for spinsters, and Miss Tarabotti was not the kind of spinster who could garner even that much pleasure from the event. To put the pudding in the puff: she had retreated to the library, her favorite sanctuary in any house, only to happen upon an unexpected vampire. (1)

As already indicated, the setting in the novel also contributes to the overall "inconsistence," introducing even more confusion into the initial readerly expectations: in *Soulless*, nineteenth-century London turns into an unfamiliar place, significantly departing from the reader's "traditional" assumptions. A particular emphasis is placed on the issue of science, which not only reflects the desire to "technologize" the past, but also attests to nineteenth-century concerns revolving around the concept of progress and discoveries. *Soulless* responds in an intertextual (hence, challenging) vein to the nineteenth-century notion of commuting: Alexia's world is filled with carriages and dirigibles enabling her to travel in a free and uncontrolled way. This freedom, both precarious and liberating, posits Alexia on the literary scene as a self-sufficient and daring woman character who readily explores all the possibilities of the New Woman.

NOTES

1. The pen name of Elizabeth Thomasina Meade Smith (1844–1914).

2. Marie-Luise Kohlke and Christian Gutleben mention the supernatural elements in *Soulless* in their *Neo-Victorian Gothic: Horror, Violence and Degeneration in the Re-imagined Nineteenth-Century* (24).

3. In *Soulless*, the lack of soul is univocal with the lack of manners.

4. As an example, the nineteenth century's strict moral standards concerning marriage are presented in Wilkie Collins's detective novel *The Law and the Lady* (1875), where Eustace Macallan enters into marriage in order to preserve the honor of the lady who appeared unchaperoned in his house.

5. "To Alan Wilde, irony is a positive and defining characteristic of the postmodern; to Terry Eagleton, irony is what condemns postmodernism to triviality and kitsch," observes Linda Hutcheon in *The Politics of Postmodernism* (17). "The past is something with which we must come to terms and such a confrontation involves an acknowledgement of limitation as well as power. We only have access to the past through its traces—its documents, the testimony of witnesses, and other archival materials. In other words, we only have representations of the past from which to construct our narratives or explanations. . . . Postmodern art acknowledges and accepts the challenge of tradition: the history of representation cannot be escaped but it can be both exploited and commented on critically through irony and parody" (Hutcheon, 56). "Postmodernism's irony is one that rejects the resolving urge of modernism toward closure or at least distance" (Hutcheon, 95).

6. A thorough study of women's spaces in Virginia Woolf's works can be found in Urszula Terentowicz-Fotyga's work *Semiotyka Przestrzeni Kobiecych w Powieściach Virginii Woolf*. As the author of the study observes, women's spaces in Woolf's works are built beyond the traditions or are redefining the current traditions (150).

7. The expression "semi-feminine" used in the description of Lord Akeldama points to the fact that in *Soulless* men are defined in relation to women and not otherwise.

8. The image of Lord Akeldama departs from the "traditional" notion of the vampire as, for example, presented in Bram Stoker's *Dracula* (1897). The protagonist of Stoker's novel, Count Dracula, is a domineering, bleak, courteous but also volatile character who rather inscribes himself in the patriarchal pattern instead of the one represented by the feminine Akeldama, who offers an "intertextual challenge" to his nineteenth-century counterpart.

Chapter Thirteen

Women and their Apparel in Victorian and Neo-Victorian Texts

Constructing Women Characters by Means of Fashion

Fashion is what one wears oneself.

—Oscar Wilde, *An Ideal Husband* (459)

Cinderella, notwithstanding her mean apparel, was a hundred times handsomer than her sisters, though they were always dressed very richly.

—Charles Perrault, *Cinderella, or a Little Glass Slipper* (64) in *The Blue Fairy Book* (1889)

Manifesting originality by means of attire was far from the primary goal of Victorian women. Rather than that, in the nineteenth century, clothes constituted a socially normative "fashion statement": a message confirming a refined, moderate taste and the particular social standing of the wearer. During the 1860s, female clothing acquired a subversive potential, negotiating between the wearer's individuality and social standards. The 1880s and 1890s saw the emergence of the so-called "aesthetic socialities," advocated and promoted by such figures as Oscar Wilde:

What can also be interpreted as progressive and feminist about aesthetic dress is its appeal to the wearer to self-stylization, which is not only a potentially feminist statement in Victorian culture, but also an anti-consumerist gesture. Further, there is a feminist history of dress reform . . . that is "embedded" in the dress reform designs of late Victorian dress reformers including Wilde who were well aware of the feminist forerunners. (Rose, ed., 184)

The overall change was highlighted in popular sensation fiction, which depicted women characters as multidimensional individuals, endowed with dangerous and theatrical qualities. Laurence Talairach-Vielmas observes:

> In the 1860s the Victorian ideal was more and more self-made, seeking public exhibition, therefore far less "natural" and, as a result, more likely to verge on waywardness. In this way, Coventry Patmore's Angel in the House came hazardously close to the equivocal figure of the actress or even the blatant figure of the prostitute. Hence, in the second half of the nineteenth century, female fashion, female role-play, and female sexuality mingled, fusing polarized versions of femininity. (134)

Talairach-Vielmas associates the predominant, normative discourse concerned with nineteenth-century female attire with the Victorian desire to categorize and explain. According to her, similarly to dualisms, "clichés" dominated Victorian society, since "the systematic quest towards categorization and dichotomies shaped the Victorian frame of mind" (40). "The wide circulation of clichéd description in Victorian fiction," Talairach-Vielmas argues, "participates in a reassuring normalizing process: it illustrates the idea of femininity as sameness, as predictability and obedience to fixed patterns and prescribed roles" (40–41). Thus, nineteenth-century fashion demands that the feminine body be shaped into a "predictable" object.

As noted by Caroline Goldthorpe, "throughout the period from 1837 to 1877, the silhouette sought by the lady of fashion was an artificial one, created by various undergarments designed to give additional volume to one area or reduce undesirable fullness in another" (23). Arguing along these lines, it can be asserted that the nineteenth-century notion of femininity was constructed and sustained by garments rather than otherwise. The woman's silhouette, shaped in the process of artificial creation, emphasized unnaturalness, turning her body into a theatrical image. At the same time, Victorian attires remolded women into symbolic figures, endowing them with a collective identity of the "angel in the house." "By following fashion codes, women learnt to fit their bodies into a social mold," observes Marcus (143). Talairach-Vielmas argues in a similar vein, positing that Victorian society creates

> fictions of the domestic ideal to such an extent that feminine identity becomes a feminine representation, a layout in a fashion magazine, a caption in an advertisement, or a set of elusive signs all pointing towards a feminine ideal. (138)

While, on the one hand, Victorian fashion restrained and actively molded the female body, it also promoted the idea of beauty and enhanced the notion of the universal, feminine perfection. Gradually, the female body lost its originality, eventually being presented as a replicated pattern. In Goldthorpe's study, corsets and crinolines play a paramount role in adjusting women's silhouettes to the nineteenth-century standards of beauty. A visible change in these standards took place in 1860, when "the circular shape of the crinoline began to alter, becoming flatter at the front and larger at the back" (Goldthorpe, 26). Finally, in 1868, "the crinoline shrank drastically to a modest cone foundation" (26).

Concurrently with the gradually liberating alterations in women's fashion, there was a change in the nineteenth-century literary world, accentuated by the popularity of the sensation novel, which offered its women protagonists more personal freedom. Fashion and the sensation novel of the period were closely related, since they were both concerned with the changing figure of the woman and her potential for subversion, instability, masquerade, and performativity. These phenomena can be analyzed in terms of Nycz's intertextuality (as discussed in his work *Tekstowy Świat. Poststrukturalizm a wiedza o literaturze*). Nycz observes that interdependence between the text and reality[1] allows for the reading of texts in a wide sociocultural context (95). The correlation between the sensation novel dominated by women characters and the "emancipation" of women's fashion in 1860s points to the fundamental intellectual and psychological change in Victorian society. Beginning in 1860s, the new developing discourse on femininity exemplified by a profound change in literature and fashion can be perceived as an intertextual response to the previous cultural constraints of the era, which diminished the woman's role by means of the confining domestic discourse and restrictive attire.

On the whole, sensation novels began to feature mysterious, chameleon-like women characters, endowed with alternative identities, artificially constructed by means of clothes and cosmetics. The woman's attire, initially meant to entrap and keep the woman on her "angel in the house" pedestal, proved to be subversive when used skillfully by female characters in the sensation novel.

Lynn Pykett, in her engaging work *The Sensation Novel: From 'The Woman in White' to 'The Moonstone'* observes that the appearance of a subversive heroine anticipated the emergence of a new discourse on femininity:

> In the 1860s, woman, womanhood and womanliness all became contested terms, as did the institutions of marriage and the family around which these terms were constructed. . . . The women's sensation novel was part of this developing discourse on the modern woman: it was both a response to and part of social change and a changing conceptualization of women. (44–45)

Simultaneously, Pykett argues that the Victorian sensation novel offers a particular potential for revision which is especially relevant for the "Woman Question" (42). Numerous attempts have been made to re-create the Victorian world in modern texts, including Gail Carriger's *Parasol Protectorate* series, which abounds in such women's clothing as dresses and hats. These feminine garments, presented from the modern viewpoint, acquire a new status as both decorative and serviceable objects. "Neo-Victorian novels present Victorian fashions . . . as *workable* items employed in the female subject's own interest," Amy L. Montz argues (115–16).[2] In this sense, in neo-Victorian texts, feminine clothing does not reveal women's vulnerability but, rather, takes on the roles of a cultural and power relations signs. In her article "Looking at the Victorian Fashion: Not a Laughing Matter," Margaret D. Stetz finds a marked contrast between the representation of Victorian fashion in the contemporary culture and its actual, reasonable, and practical deployment in the nineteenth century. For instance, as Stetz aptly notes, on the one hand, the corset is perceived as a "'daft' Victorian invention" (149) while on the other hand, "there has been a revolution . . . in scholarly interpretation of the corset, from a garment that represented the worst sort of oppression to one that could be, in some circumstances, empowering" (161). "The notion of respectability," Stetz explains, "is key to new scholarly understandings of the corset as an item of Victorian dress neither representative of women's subordination nor of women's inherent silliness" (162). Stetz highlights the fact that nineteenth-century women's fashion was ridiculed already in Victorian times by such satirical magazines as *Punch* and *The London Charivari*. The notion of fashion, she argues, was strictly related to women, while women's fashion itself served as a hilarious source of laughter for some of the male readers (149). Following this train of thoughts, Stetz notices that contemporary discourses perpetuate disregard for nineteenth-century women's fashion, as "generating laughter has been a frequent motive for this backward gaze—a chance to reaffirm not only the superiority of the present, but also the superiority of modern masculinity over a Victorian Age associated with the feminine" (160). In fact, Stetz argues, in the nineteenth century, women's fashion was a tool directed at obtaining elegance and respectability. As she observes, the "core idea" of fashion has not altered since Victorian times but, instead, has undergone a technological revolution and the process of "recycling" (159):

> it was also the outcome of a technological revolution, tied to scientific discoveries and the manufacture of new materials such as spandex (also known as Lycra), which was invented in 1959 and which made tights possible and cheap.
> Some of the fashion *turns* that we associate with the nineteenth century have *returned* in the twentieth, as though engaged in a series of rotations. (159)

Stetz treats the nineteenth-century dressing code as a feminine reassessment of womanly pride, beauty, and dignity, and so does Alexia Tarabotti, celebrating her female potential, beauty, and power in Carriger's *Soulless*.

The already-mentioned steampunk is yet another modern genre (and even a lifestyle) actively participating in a dialogical exchange with the Victorian past, drawing on the notions of individuality and distinctiveness while resorting to imaginative gadgetry and unique fashion. Originating in the 1980s, steampunk fiction dialogically inscribes itself in the tradition of the nineteenth-century sensation novel since, similarly to this genre, it introduces fashionable and attractive women characters who are, in contrast to their Victorian counterparts, loaded with futuristic, serviceable, state-of-the-art gadgets. Primarily concerned with the retelling of the Victorian past, steampunk can be considered as a part of the neo-Victorian genre. However, it may also go beyond these frames, directed toward a different aim than that of re-narration: according to Patrick Jagoda,

> steampunk fiction participates in the postmodern resurgence of interest in Victorian culture that has motivated what Sally Shuttleworth calls 'the retro-Victorian novel," but steampunk ultimately enacts a far stranger speculative revision of nineteenth-century history (Shuttleworth 1998; Gutleben 2001; Krueger 2002; Joyce 2007). (46–47)

As steampunk also represents a modern lifestyle, there are numerous steampunk fashion styles for both men and women, including the most prominent ones, as enumerated in *The Steampunk Bible*: the Street Urchin, the Tinker, the Explorer, and the Aesthete. The Street Urchin style is "functional, can be mucked about in, costs little to hack together, and nods smugly to the lowest classes of society" (VanderMeer, 138). The Tinker style includes "garments made of canvas, denim, leather, wool, and rubber. . . . Goggles can be acquired from a plethora of locales" (139). The Explorers "look fine in earth tones. . . . Silk, linen, tall boots, pith helmets, flying goggles—the list of explorer gear is endless" (139). The Aesthete costume can be dialogically linked with the late Victorian attempt at originality dating from the 1880s. The Aesthete represents "neo-Victorian nostalgia with elements of anachro-technofetishism and bohemianism" (141).

Currently, there is a proliferation of nineteenth-century-inspired, inventive clothing styles in steampunk detective fiction. This phenomenon can be likened to the heyday of the Victorian sensation novel and the concurrent emergence of Victorian aesthetic societies. It also proves that the past remains in a dialogue with the present and that history continuously repeats itself. Thus, the aim of this section of the chapter lies in exploring mutual relations between the Victorian/neo-Victorian women characters and their garments in intertextual light. As I believe, clothes possess a power to liberate, restrict, endow one with a new identity, and even express one's inner states and wishes for liberation. Therefore, clothes mold "Victorian femininities" both in the past and the present, with intertextuality serving as a tool to analyze women's garments from nineteenth-century texts up to the present.

"Clothing styles identify eras, and thus fashion becomes an index of history," states Sharon Marcus in *Between Women: Friendship, Desire and Marriage in Victorian England* (116). Fashion highlights each historical period, influences general public discussions and establishes a cultural point of reference. In Margaret Forster's novel *Lady's Maid* (1898), the eponymous heroine discovers during her travel back home that "it [is] quite easy to attract . . . helpfulness merely by being dignified and modest and [she] realised her new costume assisted the process" (107). Fashion is invariably linked to women characters, and, in Victorian fiction, these are women characters who are vividly constructed through their clothes or are presented in unique relations to their garments.

Such is the case in Ellen Wood's sensation novel *East Lynne* (1861), in which garments indicate the heroine's changing and disguised identities. Lady Isabel, initially the embodiment of feminine innocence, appears in the first chapter of the novel as a graceful figure with "fair delicate arms decorated with pearls, and a flowing dress of costly white lace" (11). The turbulent events of Isabel's life—her father's sudden death, her hasty marriage to Mr. Carlyle dictated by personal insecurity, and the unhappy state of domestic affairs triggered by the hostility of Mr. Carlyle's sister—contribute to the future portrayal of Isabel as a seemingly calculating and unfeeling person. Lady Isabel abandons her husband and children as a consequence of her treatment by the tyrannical Miss Carlyle (Mr. Carlyle's sister), but also as a result of her lifelong, disastrous infatuation with a cunning man who purposefully accuses Mr. Carlyle of infidelity. However, Isabel returns in a deforming disguise only to discover that she is bound to eternally forfeit her previous domestic bliss, because Mr. Carlyle is remarried to another woman, Barbara Hare.

Wood's *East Lynne* is a reversed Cinderella story, presenting the fall of a beautiful and promising woman. While Cinderella is beautiful regardless of her ragged clothes, Isabel purposefully disfigures her attire in order to remain ugly and unrecognizable. Wood's riveting novel triggers a debate concerning the domestic status of Victorian women and the disastrous consequences of a third party's interference in a marriage. However, it also draws one's attention to the fact that women, as characters of nineteenth-century fiction, are invariably associated with garments. Isabel, returning as an atoning mother and wife, adopts her elaborate disguise of a governess and a new name of Madame Vine. The disguise not only makes Isabel look much older and more insignificant than she is, but also offers her a new identity, leaving her to agonizingly watch the new Mrs. Carlyle's bliss through ugly blue spectacles. In the first chapter of the novel, her beautiful white dress "displays" Isabel sitting at the table as a passive object—a feminine ideal of beauty and goodness. On her dramatic return, Isabel is "sheltered" by her garments as if she was placed behind a shield of sadness and remorse. Hence, she remains unrecognizable, which enables her to watch Barbara Hare performing the role of a new feminine "object" in her most splendid dresses.

A storyline involving disguise and suspense can be also found in Clare Boylan's *Emma Brown* (2003), the neo-Victorian sensation novel. As one learns from the afterword, "the first two chapters of this book are the work of Charlotte Brontë. Written after the completion of *Villette* and before her marriage, it was to be her last piece of fiction" (438). Moreover, as indicated by Boylan, the excerpt from Charlotte Brontë's work was published posthumously in the *Cornhill Magazine* under "the working title of *Emma*" (438). On the onset of the twenty-first century, Boylan preserved Brontë's initial idea while, at the same time, she constructed her own imaginary narrative of an orphaned, nameless girl embarking on the quest for her lost identity.

Brontë and Boylan's heroine is surrounded by impenetrable mystery: her true name and origin remain unknown. In chapter 1, written by Charlotte Brontë and narrated by the figure of Mrs. Chalfont, the young heroine arrives at Fuchsia Lodge under the name of Matilda Fitzgibbon, accompanied by Mr. Conway Fitzgibbon, a wealthy and enigmatic attendant. However, as it is suggestively implied in the text, Matilda and Mr. Conway Fitzgibbon actually do not exist: both of these characters possess different, disguised identities. While "Matilda Fitzgibbon" is initially believed to be a rich heiress, it is eventually revealed that she does not belong to the upper class. Moreover, the heroine is unable to recall her past (and, thus, to reconstruct her true identity) during her stay in the inimical institution led by the self-interested Misses Wilcox. In the final chapters of the novel, the reader recognizes in the heroine the eponymous Emma. However, until that discovery, Emma is pressured to compromise with her assumed identity, since she feels incapable of reclaiming her true origins. Thus, Matilda Fitzgibbon serves as Emma's initial *doppelgänger*—an assumed and creative identity verging on a theatrical performance or, as stated in the novel, on a "masquerade" (62).

As posited by Laurence Talairach-Vielmas, "ideal femininity in the Victorian period was often gauged by its relationship to the world of beauty and fashion" (5). Talairach-Vielmas comments on the photograph of a little Victorian girl protesting against her daily beautifying practices:

> When I first came across Lewis Carroll's photograph of Irene MacDonald, "It won't come smooth" (July 1863), I was fascinated by the picture of this little

girl refusing to brush her hair and to hold the mirror up to her face to check her appearance. . . . As she seemingly frowns at the onlooker, the little girl asserts her refusal to be moulded to the pattern of docile femininity, just as her matted mane refuses to be plaited and tamed. This ideal little girl whom Victorian gentlemen idolized and who refuses here to sit still and learn her lesson in "beautification," tells us a lot about the notion of femininity in the Victorian period. . . . The brush and the mirror frame the little girl's femininity as a body which must be moulded and smoothed, which probably demands training and suffering, and which, once perfected, will perhaps give this little girl the keys to conquest. (5)

The "keys to conquest" mentioned by Talairach-Vielmas attest to the fact that the nineteenth-century woman constructed her social significance through compulsory "beautifying practices" that paved her way to society and marriage. Hence, in the Victorian age, obtaining "femininity" turns into a peculiar theatrical spectacle where garments and appearance play a socially normative role. In *Emma Brown*, the eponymous heroine passes unnoticed as Emma but gains importance in society's eyes as the theatrical Matilda.

Sharon Marcus extensively investigates the relationship between the nineteenth-century woman and her image reflected in fashion magazines of the era. In her work *Between Women: Friendship, Desire and Marriage in Victorian England*, she scrutinizes fashion plates in Victorian magazines, highlighting the relevance of women's appearance and clothing in their lives. The interest in other women's garments was verging, as she argues, on a homoerotic fascination. At the same time, Marcus questions the predominant importance of masculine gaze in the "beautifying process," observing that "Victorian manliness directed men to admire women's bodies while deriding the fashions that clothed them. . . . The most overt pleasure Victorian fashion offered women was looking at other women and being looked at by them" (117).

Hence, according to Marcus, the primary judgmental gaze directed at women was, paradoxically, the one initiated by other women and not by men. This assertion is illustrated on the pages of *Emma Brown*, where, based on their estimation of the girl's natural appearance, the Misses Wilcox form opinions about the heroine: "You know, I was never quite taken in by her. Her hair is cut too short for fashion," exclaims one of the sisters, expressing her dislike for Emma (62). However, it is "Matilda Fitzgibbon's" lavish attire that initially guarantees the Misses Wilcox's excessive attention. Boylan explores the interdependence between the girl's garments and her assumed high social status in the opening chapter of the novel, where she depicts the initial relations between Emma and her supervisors:

Women and their Apparel in Victorian and Neo-Victorian Texts   157

Figure 13.1. Ball gowns, late 1870s. Artist unknown (Public Domain).

It must not be forgotten that Miss Fitzgibbon's trunks, when opened, disclosed a splendid wardrobe; so fine were the various articles of apparel, indeed, that instead of assigning for their accommodation the painted deal drawers of the school bedroom, Miss Wilcox had them arranged in a mahogany bureau in her own room. With her own hands, too, she would on Sundays array the little favourite in her quilted silk pelisse, her hat and feathers, her ermine boa, and little French boots and gloves. And very self-complacent she felt when she led the young heiress (a letter from Mr Fitzgibbon, received since his first visit, had communicated the additional particulars that his daughter was his only child, and would be the inheritress of his estates, including May Park, Midland County)—when she led her, I say, into the church, and seated her stately by her side at the top of the gallery pew. (5)

After the discovery of the fraud, the heroine is deprived of her rich garments and, as if under a magic spell, she turns into a poor and scorned "Cinderella." In *Emma Brown*, clothes enhance the social expectations of the heroine.

When her lavish garments are removed and replaced with a poor gown, Emma loses her significance as a person:

> Now that Matilda was deprived of her prospects, Miss Wilcox saw what a very ordinary child she was. Common, even. A pale, undistinguished face, narrow limbs, hair that was no particular colour, and a donkeyish shade of that. No wonder someone had almost stifled her in frills to pass her off as pleasing. It irked Miss Wilcox that she had shown eagerness for a gift that was only wrapping. Worse, she was now expected to pay for it. (54)

Emma Brown is yet another version of Cinderella story with the protagonist gaining a new identity while donning a mysteriously acquired attire. However, in Boylan's text, the attire is donned unwillingly and Emma turns into a commodity "stifled . . . in frills to pass her off as pleasing" (54). According to Miss Wilcox, deprived of her riches, Emma loses her distinguished status. Even before the discovery of the fraud, Miss Wilcox acknowledges that her perception of Emma entirely depends on her status and garments: "had she been a poor child, Miss Wilcox herself would not like her physiognomy at all" (5).

On the contrary, Emma realizes that the "self" is a concept reaching beyond one's appearance. This is why during the sightseeing of the Great Exhibition, Emma remains unimpressed by an overwhelming display of extravagant fabrics:

> Emma joined a cluster of women jostling at a breathtaking spectacle of silks, damasks and brocades mounted on a tall structure of plate glass. Hers was the only sigh that was not composed of wistful envy at the splendid display of Spitalfield Silks. (394)

In Charles Perrault's fairy tale one reads that Cinderella, "notwithstanding her mean apparel, was a hundred times handsomer than her sisters, though they were always dressed very richly" (Dundes, ed., 16). Like Cinderella, Emma is ultimately rewarded for her inner beauty, strength, and righteousness: she eventually finds a home and a loving mother. Yet, unlike Cinderella, the heroine is displeased with excessively lavish garments that disrupt her integrity. Similarly, the display of silk during the Great Exhibition leaves Emma unruffled. On the other hand, when she gains financial independence, Emma finds pleasure in choosing her own garments, believing that

> [her] present persona merits some more spruce packaging. She counted out her savings, took what might be spared, and from a second-hand stall in Leather Lane furnished herself with an array of apparel. Such items as had, in another time and place, burdened her with misery now afforded her considerable

satisfaction. Yet this little wardrobe was the very opposite of showy: a dress in a dark blue check, a light shawl, a plain grey gown with garnet-coloured knots upon the bodice, a bonnet of horsehair with straw plait, a light grey shawl and some summer slippers. The entirety had cost two shillings with a diminutive white frock with a hem broaderie anglaise thrown in for luck for Jenny Drew. (349)

While Perrault's fairy tale carries a symbolic meaning, the beauty of Cinderella's heart is conventionally represented by means of her alluring attire and the famous glass slipper.[3] In Boylan's novel, garments concurrently confirm and disrupt the sense of one's identity. Rich clothes offer Emma the key to the socially constructed world, yet it is their loss that renders the girl her desired inner freedom. On gaining independence, Emma finds pleasure in purchasing her own garments, but she remains implicitly cautious in her choices, suspended between her intrinsic modesty and good taste. The clothes which are not imposed on the heroine carry a different meaning: they are willingly selected in a "visual" process of self-creation. Emma's choices of attire can be linked to those made by Brontë's Jane Eyre, who remains the humblest and, yet, the most captivating character of the novel.

In the opening chapters of *Emma Brown*, the theatrical framework of "Matilda Fitzgibbon"—a rich, distant girl who should be pampered—is unwillingly imposed on the heroine by her unknown, mysterious guardian. Yet, Emma is tired of her artificial role and feels relieved by the truth. It is a blessing for Emma to fall out of favor with the Misses Wilcox, since she does not have to "perform herself" anymore. When the Misses Wilcox cruelly deprive the heroine of her rich belongings, Emma asserts that she "prefer[s] this ragged gown [she is] wearing to those in which [she] arrived" (71). In this sense, she rejects the idea of performativity, which attracted and occupied the Victorians.

In contrast to Emma, the Misses Wilcox are portrayed as victims of fashion decorum rather than responsible and caring tutors. After confiscating Emma's clothes, thus compensating themselves for the unpaid school fees, the sisters rave thoughtlessly over her expensive garments:

> The trunk was fetched and opened on the floor of Mabel's room. The pretty garments were retrieved from Mabel's chest. There was an interlude of whispering, though Adelaide's lips were firmly compressed. The sound was that of gorgeous fabrics being sifted by rueful fingers: the Genoa velvets, the glacé silks, the spotted muslins, the French organdies. She almost moaned as she picked up a dress of antique watered silk, the bodice covered in Alençon print and the skirt ornamented with flounces of English lace. Into her clutches then came a gown of damask satinated Pekin taffeta in the new shade of garnet china rose. This was stuff in which to glide through the world; then sheen and pile of it a calling card

for admiration. The garments were an education for any handsome young lady. In them she would learn to walk and sit, to adorn. Thus festooned, she would begin to exploit her charms. (63–64)

Apparently, Emma refuses to be molded into a theatrical persona, thus manifesting her deep individualism. The concept of an independent "self," emphasized in Boylan's work, corresponds dialogically with protomodern, early manifestations of individualism displayed by Charlotte Brontë's Victorian female characters.[4] This intertextual correspondence is strengthened by the fact that the first two chapters of *Emma Brown* are coauthored by Charlotte Brontë. Hence, the novel bridges the gap between the past and the present, turning into an engaging atemporal study of correlations between one's clothes and identity.

In Charlotte Brontë's works, women protagonists are usually depicted through their complex relationships with their garments. Characters such as Lucy Snowe and Shirley Keeldar evince their disdainful attitude toward garments which deprive them of autonomy or personal integrity. In *Villette* (1853), Lucy Snowe feels uncomfortable while wearing her pink dress during the evening at the opera, while in *Shirley* (1849), the eponymous heroine manifests her disregard for the "proper behaviour," reading on the floor next to her beloved dog, Tartar:

> She lifts not her eyes; she neither stirs nor speaks—unless, indeed, it be to return a brief respectful answer to Mrs Pryor, who addresses deprecatory phrases to her now and then.
>
> "My dear, you had better not have that great dog so near you, he is crushing the border of your dress."
>
> "Oh, it is only muslin. I can put a clean one on tomorrow." (290)

Interestingly enough, while for Shirley it is "only muslin," Caroline Helstone carefully selects muslin only for special occasions, choosing a muslin dress to assist Shirley in the preparations for her wedding: "She dressed herself more carefully than usual on the day of this trading triumph, and went, attired in her neatest muslin, to spend the afternoon at Fieldhead" (475). Shirley's financial independence grants her the ability to "put on a clean" muslin dress "tomorrow" (290), while for Caroline wearing muslin is rare. Caroline takes pleasure in her muslin dress and rarely delights in it, while Shirley is more practically oriented, not paying attention to the garments and accessories traditionally deemed feminine.

Emma strongly echoes Brontë's most acclaimed protagonist, Jane Eyre, whose insignificant looks and reclusive character stand in contrast with her fascinating mind. Prematurely grown up and self-aware, Emma emerges as Jane's alter ego. While she unwillingly socializes with Miss Wilcox's guests, performing her artificial role of a rich heiress and a favorite pupil, Emma's behavior betrays her true character, and even the lavish attire and sophisticated hairstyle cannot turn her into the perfect "legatee" of fortune. Similarly to Jane Eyre, Emma is distant and dispirited, locked in her impenetrable, inner world, and only her clothes allow her to "keep up appearances." She is transformed into "a piece of furniture" or a decorative doll—Miss Wilcox's creation and pride:

> Their evenings rarely passed without Miss Fitzgibbon being introduced—all worked muslin and streaming sash and elaborated ringlets. . . . While "dear Miss Fitzgibbon," dressed up and flattered as she was, could only sidle round the circle with the crestfallen air which seemed natural to her, just giving her hand to the guests, than almost snatching it away, and sneaking in unmannerly haste to the place allotted to her at Miss Wilcox's side, which place she filled like a piece of furniture, neither smiling nor speaking the evening through. (10)

The above-presented passage appears in chapter 2 of *Emma Brown*. As Boylan indicates in her afterword, the first two chapters of the novel are "the work of Charlotte Brontë" herself (438). In *Emma Brown*, Brontë reproduces the literary type of "Jane Eyre," introducing fashion as the key concept for the unmasking of Emma's complex identity. Brontë's writing predates and anticipates contemporaneity as it constructs women protagonists who are as self-aware and persistent in asserting their independence as their neo-Victorian counterparts. In Brontë's fiction, clothes highlight the conflict between her heroines' desires and the rigid social expectations placed on them. Boylan continues to elaborate on this conflict in *Emma Brown*, presenting a heroine who rejects her protective disguise for the sake of personal integrity.

Returning to Ellen Wood's nineteenth-century *East Lynne*, it is interesting to note how the notion of disguise is used in this particular text. In contrast to such characters as Emma, Lady Isabel willingly resorts to her carefully arranged camouflage, because the disguise enables her to stay close to her family. A similar, deliberate deployment of disguise appears in Charlotte Brontë's *Villette*: Lucy Snowe readily disguises herself during the carnival night in order to derive pleasure from her anonymous presence in the crowd. These examples indicate that a disguise can function in a work of fiction as a symbolic burden forcefully imposed on the heroine (Emma Brown) or, on the contrary, as a deliberately applied, self-negating mechanism (Lady Isabel, Lucy Snowe).

Apart from their ambiguous, self-abnegating, and liberating potential, textually constructed garments, as well as the descriptions of activities involving garments, are capable of manifesting and externalizing characters' inner states. Caroline Helstone in Charlotte Brontë's *Shirley* resorts to sewing in order to overcome the overwhelming feelings of apathy and sorrow: "She did sew. She plied her needle continuously, ceaselessly, but her brain worked faster than her fingers. Again, and more intensely than ever, she desired a fixed occupation, no matter how onerous, how irksome." (179). Sewing a dress represents the protagonist's desire for occupation. Simultaneously, it mirrors Caroline's inner restlessness and the purposelessness of her existence as a merely decorative "angel in the house": rejected by Robert Moore, she cannot occupy herself by work which would be, in her uncle's opinion, disgraceful for the family. Hence, for Caroline, sewing turns into a form of escapism.

The notion of sewing as a monotonous and spiritually unrewarding feminine occupation—a substitute for unattainable happiness—is also explored in Margaret Forster's modern work *Lady's Maid* (1990). The eponymous female character endowed with a masculine name, Wilson, dutifully watches upon her mistress, the poet Elizabeth Barrett Browning. Placed in her mistress's tomb-like room, Wilson is mechanically mending clothes, reflecting on her incapacity to become free:

> She sat darning a stocking, as near to the window as she could get (though the blind being down not much sun struggled through) and looked round the room and found herself shivering. It was like a tomb, a very well appointed tomb, with everything the dead person could want gathered together for their enjoyment in the next world. (26)

Wilson feels physically restricted by her mistress' surroundings, but back at home she also experiences mental limitation. She realizes that, while sharing space with Miss Browning, she gradually becomes intellectually demanding as well. Hence, Wilson's family no longer satisfies her intellectual needs, which finds expression in her comment on the monotony of such activities as "scrubbing clothes" or "sewing":

> So much time and energy were spent on simple tasks necessary to run the household, tasks she was no longer much aware of in Wimpole Street. Hours spent heating water and scrubbing clothes and floors . . . , hours devoted most of all to the sewing which provided mother's income. Nobody ever sat and read all day as Miss Elizabeth, nor did they converse. (110)

As Wilson observes, sewing provides her mother with income, yet it is not a mentally rewarding task. Both texts, Brontë's *Shirley* and Forster's *Lady's Maid*, present sewing as an exclusively feminine occupation merely filling one's time with mechanical and monotonous work. Both the nineteenth-century novel *Shirley* and the contemporary text *Lady's Maid* present sewing as associated with feminine passivity, immovability, dependency, and incapacitation. In both novels, sewing expresses the unspoken feminine desire to be liberated from domestic constraints, as it provides a feeble substitute for truly desired and intellectually motivating activities.

Contrastively, in steampunk novels[5] such as Carriger's *Soulless*, designing and wearing the designed garments and accessories acquires a creative and emancipating meaning: it is Alexia Tarabotti herself who designs the pattern on her inseparable parasol, thus constructing her unique attribute and her own identity at the same time. However, in contrast to the previously presented modern novels (*Lady's Maid*, *Emma Brown*) in which the Victorian past provides the only space for the characters' lives, the world depicted in Carriger's *Soulless* fluctuates between the nineteenth-century "reality" and the high-tech urban environment: Alexia's nineteenth-century London is haunted by inconsistent traces of modernity, which creates a diversified and thought-provoking collage of the "bygone" and "now." While neo-Victorian novels such as *Emma Brown* and *Lady's Maid* try to retell the possibly "veritable" Victorian "realities," Carriger's steampunk text primarily concentrates on creating an imaginative narrative blend constructed from the relics of the nineteenth-century past and samples of futuristic technologies. "Steampunk is funeral theater," Jeff VanderMeer explicates. "It is a pageant. A pageant selectively pumps some life into the parts of the past that can excite us, such as . . . peculiar brass gadgets" (13). Importantly, he claims, "steampunks are modern crafts people who are very into spreading the means and methods of working in archaic technologies" (13). In *Soulless*, designing one's accessories turns into a liberating experience of recreating "archaic" items in a futuristic vein. Designing becomes a creative means of arriving at the nineteenth-century simplicity combined with the gadgetry and showiness of the modern era. Handmade creations express the nostalgia for the plain mode of life, where each garment and gadget possessed a unique history of production. Moreover, they offer the freedom of self-expression, so celebrated and praised in the twenty-first century. Thus, in steampunk novels, designing and sewing become fashionable and enjoyable, contrastively to those neo-Victorian texts which draw the reader's attention to the daily quandaries faced by Victorian women.

Wide Sargasso Sea (1966) offers yet another example attesting to the psychological dimension of women's clothing in literary texts. In Rhys's novel, it is the dress which enables the incapacitated heroine to express her so-far unvoiced desires, as it brings back comforting memories.

Deprived of her humanity and confined to a secluded room by an undeserving husband, Antoinette Cosway finds comfort in the physical texture of her dress. For Antoinette, the red dress is meaningful because she can "touch and hold" it:

> As soon as I turned the key I saw it hanging, the colour of fire and sunset. The colour of flamboyant flowers. "If you are buried under a flamboyant tree," I [Antoinette] said, "your soul is lifted up when it flowers. Everyone wants that." . . . The scent that came from the dress was very faint at first, then it grew stronger. The smell of vetiver and frangipani, of cinnamon and dust and lime trees when they are flowering. The smell of the sun and the smell of the rain. (119–20)

The red dress enables Antoinette to experience a metaphysical encounter with the past. Retrieving the dress from the wardrobe turns into a spiritual ritual and becomes a liberating moment of recollection. The past becomes tangible: the dress reshapes into a spiritual oracle, allowing Antoinette to recall vivid memories and realistic scents. Hence, the red dress provides emotional reassurance and reminds Antoinette of being a free and independent individual before her imprisonment by Rochester. Moreover, the dress revives Antoinette's memories of her homeland: it allows the heroine to detach herself from the current location in England and embark on a spiritual journey to the beloved home.

The lively color of the dress mirrors Antoinette's vigorous personality before her dreary marriage to Rochester. Moreover, the color red[6] evokes Antoinette's last meeting with her dear cousin Sandi (120). The scents invoked by the apparel remind the heroine about her deep love for Caribbean nature. On the whole, removing the dress from the press can be likened to a resurrection of Antoinette's soul. According to the heroine, if one is buried under a flamboyant tree, their soul will be uplifted. The dress of the flamboyant color, filled with vivid and persistent memories, guarantees a metaphysical sustenance of Antoinette's past and relieves her soul from the imprisonment imposed on her.

At the same time, Antoinette worries whether the dress is not a counterfeit, which would disable the spiritual revival of the past:

> I held the dress in my hand wondering if they had done the last and worst thing. If they had *changed* it when I wasn't looking. If they had changed it and it wasn't my dress at all—but how could they get the scent? (120)

The dress is the only source of reference to the heroine's past and origin. While Antoinette's husband deprives her of her name and identity (calling her "Bertha" instead), the dress allows the heroine to reconstruct, develop, and preserve her self-knowledge. However, when the "spiritual spectacle" comes to an end, the dress is dropped to the floor and it is as if the soul abandoned Antoinette's body again:

> I let the dress fall on the floor, and looked from the fire to the dress and from the dress to the fire. I put the grey wrapper round my shoulders. . . . I looked at the dress on the floor and it was as if the fire had spread across the room. It was beautiful and it reminded me of something I must do. (121)

The vision of the dress, spreading across the room like fire, foretells Antoinette's fate and prefigures that her memories and identity will be eventually obliterated. The gray "wrapper" donned by Antoinette brings her back to the present situation and signifies her seemingly insane state.

Before her marriage and imprisonment, Antoinette experiences a disturbing dream in which she walks with a man who guides her to the place where she is meant to climb the steps leading into the unknown. In this prophetic vision, Antoinette is "holding up the skirt of her dress" while following the strange man (34). She sees his face filled with hatred and no longer tries to hold up the dress, as if resigning herself to the impending doom:

> I follow him, weeping. Now I do not try to hold up my dress, it trails in the dirt, my beautiful dress. We are no longer in the forest but in an enclosed garden surrounded by a stone wall and the trees are different trees. I do not know them. There are steps leading upwards. It is too dark to see the wall or the steps, but I know they are there and I think, "It will be when I go up these steps. At the top." I stumble over my dress and cannot get up. (34)

The dress in the dream signifies the heroine's disgraced identity. Trailing in the dirt, it foreshadows the bleak future when Antoinette is humiliated by her husband. Antoinette stumbles over her "beautiful dress," knowing that she cannot remonstrate against the stranger from her dream. The "beautiful dress" reflects Antoinette's personality before her marriage, when, despite her family's misfortunes, she was a vivacious and noble-hearted girl. Eventually, the dress will remain after Antoinette is gone, thus offering visual evidence of her complex and tragic presence.

The complex relationship between heroines and their attire confirms that textual garments deserve a particular place in the study of female literary characters. As already explicated, women's clothes can be used in the text as indicators of liberation or restriction, as a willingly donned disguise or as camouflage concealing one's identity. Clothes can also express unvoiced desires or point to the heroine's unrealized needs. In the text, they often provide the reader with an indirect characterization of the protagonist. Additionally, in *Wide Sargasso Sea*, the red dress underlines Antoinette's individuality, distinctiveness, and fragility.

NOTES

1. Reality is understood as the subject's experience.

2. More information concerning Amy L. Montz's analysis of fashion in Carriger's series can be found in Margaret D. Stetz's article "Looking at Victorian Fashion: Not a Laughing Matter" (147–69) in *Neo-Victorian Humour: Comic Subversions and Unlaughter in Contemporary Historical Re-visions* (Kohlke and Gutleben, eds.).

3. It is important to observe that while Cinderella is undoubtedly a "perfect" character, her ultimate reward (marriage to the prince) is attained not merely by means of her goodness but, first and foremost, by means of her garments. In Charles Perrault's *Cinderella, or: The Little Glass Slipper* (1697) one reads:

> Ladies of all ranks were permitted to make a trial of the slipper; but it was of no use. Cinderella now said, "Let me try—perhaps it may fit me." It slipped on in a moment. Great was the vexation of the two sisters at this; but what was their astonishment when Cinderella took the fellow slipper out of her pocket! At that moment the godmother appeared, and touched Cinderella's clothes with her wand. Her sisters then saw that she was the beautiful lady they had met at the ball, and, throwing themselves at her feet, craved her forgiveness. A short time after, she was married to the Prince, to the intense gratification of the whole Court. (10)

The ending thus proves that not only Cinderella's goodness is unrewarded per se, but also that she has to produce tangible proofs in order to obtain the deserved "happy ending." Cinderella reshapes into the beautiful and generous lady from the ball only after trying on the slipper, producing "the fellow slipper out of her pocket" and altering her ragged clothes by means of magic. Only then are the mean sisters capable of recognizing in Cinderella the "beautiful lady." Similarly as in Cinderella's case, Emma Brown struggles with social rejection, even though she is beautiful inside. The act of buying new clothes offers Emma self-awareness and a subtle feeling of importance. While analyzing the above-presented excerpt from *Cinderella*, it is interesting to refer to the word "lady." Cinderella turns into a "beautiful lady" when she dons her lavish attire. In Wilkie Collins's novel *No Name* (1862), one of the characters explains to her servant what it means to be a lady in the following words: "Shall I tell you what a lady is? A lady is a woman who wears a silk gown, and has a sense of her own importance" (503). Hence, it seems that it is one's attire that grants this special status.

4. Charlotte Brontë's female characters, such as the eponymous heroine in *Shirley* and Lucy Snowe in *Villette*, are portrayed as "protomodern" women being at odds with the conventional Victorian life. Endowed with the masculine nickname of "Captain Keeldar," Shirley is an independent heiress who manages her own household affairs and does not conform to the social expectations of the era. Lucy Snowe, on the other hand, isolates herself from society in order to analyze it and thus expose its shortcomings and absurdities. Both these heroines are characterised by individuality and independence, while their rich inner life and deep self-awareness of their nineteenth-century limitations and possibilities attest to the fact that they can be counted among the literary New Women.

5. According to Patrick Jagoda, "even as steampunk has expanded in numerous directions, weaving through weird interstices between techno-science and history, the majority of works belonging to this category have taken the conventions of fantasy and science fiction and relocated them in worlds that run on steam power. The most prominent novels that fall under this heading draw consistently from such disparate sources as nineteenth-century culture, the early science fiction of Jules Verne and H. G. Wells, and the late twentieth-century subgenre of cyberpunk fiction. Covering a diverse historical spectrum, many of these neo-Victorian futurist texts draw parallels between the industrial revolution of the nineteenth century and the Information Revolution of the late twentieth century. Major steampunk writers have included Tim Powers, Paul Di Filippo, and China Miéville. Other literary authors who have employed certain elements of steampunk, without working entirely within the genre, include Neal Stephenson (in *The Diamond Age* [1995]) and Thomas Pynchon (in *Against the Day* [2006])." (47)

6. As John Gage observes, the sociocultural context of the color red has a lengthy history. Red was "the chromatic representative of fire and of light. Red had, since the earliest times and in many cultures, heralded the divine. It was used in Ancient Greece as a colour to sanctify weddings and funerals and as a military colour in both Greece and Rome to strike awe into the enemy" (26). It is interesting to implement these observations into the analysis of the color red in *Wide Sargasso Sea*: removing the red dress from the wardrobe turns into a "divine ritual" which mentally restores Antoinette to her blissful past. Moreover, the red dress accompanies Antoinette throughout her married life and until the day when she perishes in flames. Fire in *Wide Sargasso Sea* also carries a "divine" meaning: it is all-embracing and all-consuming, spiritually liberating and destructive—while it entraps and destroys the heroine, it simultaneously offers her the only plausible escape from the oppressive [patriarchal] world.

Chapter Fourteen

Diving Deeper into Fashion

Clothes in Wilkie Collins's The Woman in White *and in* Gail Carriger's Soulless

Garments, as depicted in novels, are purely textual constructs devoid of a tangible fabric.[1] Yet, thanks to their "readability," they remain vivid and explicitly meaningful. Clothing "transformed into language," Barthes notes in his *The Fashion System,* possesses a structure separated from its true image. Moreover, as Barthes claims, fashion is a pretext for unmasking of the encoded meaning. In this sense, "written fashion" turns into a "sign" that can be read and interpreted in a culture-oriented way, as I will illustrate on the examples of Wilkie Collins's *The Woman in White* (1859) and Gail Carriger's *Soulless* (2009). I believe that Victorian fashion can be viewed as what Barthes terms as "the matrix"—a signifying unit which is constantly transformed through texts.

Collins's *The Woman in White*, a classic sensation novel, features a subversive heroine, Anne Catherick, whose clothing is of major significance for the reading of the text. Carriger's *Soulless* introduces an independent and challenging individual, Alexia Tarabotti, whose clothes display the modern interest in combining beauty with practicality. Both of these characters participate in a detective plot, and both of them are portrayed by means of fashion.

The generic intertextuality of both texts (detective plots) and their particular preoccupation with women's attires allows me to state that in both novels the term "fashion" is regarded as a "social" kind of "fact" (Carter, 144) which cannot be separated from the social life (Carter, 153). According to Carter, fashion "should not be regarded as something having a singular identity" (145). Thus, clothes can turn into a sign with multilayered meanings.

In *The Fashion System*, a work based on the study of fashion magazines, Roland Barthes posits that fashion is "the phenomenon of initiation" (14). In textual works, he asserts, instead of the "plastic form" and the material that would establish and preserve synchrony, one encounters a literary representation of clothes—"written fashion." In order to investigate the meaning of textual fashion, one has to, according to Barthes, distinguish between "garment" and "clothing." Barthes divides "clothing" into three types of garments: "the real garments"—dependent on *production*, "the represented garments"—correlated with *distribution* and "the used garments"—subject to *consumption* (Carter, 146). The transition from the "raw material" to "finished goods" endows clothing with "meanings and symbolism" (146).

According to Barthes, "the represented garments" can be further decomposed into *written clothing* and *image-clothing* (Carter, 149). *Image-clothing* "is closer to the real garment because both share 'forms, lines, surfaces, colors' and both reside within an order that is spatial and plastic" (Carter, 149). In contrast, indicates Barthes, the written fashion, introduced by means of description, serves as "an instrument of structuration" (*The Fashion System*, 16). As one cannot see the texture of the material, "the limits of written clothing" remain the "limits of value" (15). The difference between what is an "essential item" and what is an "accessory" is expressed in language (14) which endows textual clothes with meaning, as well as with the possible limitations of this meaning. While reading a given text, Barthes argues, one is faced with a "fragmentary garment" (14) which "unveils" according to an "order" inevitably implying certain goals of the text (16). Thus, a gradual presentation of a textual garment is correlated with the specific task of description.

In addition to the above mentioned notions of clothes and fashion, Barthes introduces the aforementioned concept of "the matrix"—"an ideal and optional unit, provided by the examination of privileged utterances" (63). The matrix consists of *the object*, *the support*, and *the variant*, which may all interact in various ways. I believe that Victorian fashion can be viewed as the matrix that undergoes numerous transformations in Victorian and neo-Victorian texts. In effect, fashion emerges in each text as a new signifying unit.

The relation between women and fashion itself appears to be a diversified and intimate phenomenon, as clothes simultaneously entrap and liberate, depending on a given context. In this respect, it is relevant to evoke Roland Barthes's assumption concerning "the motivation of the garment." "The motivation of the garment as a sign" can be purely functional, partly functional or entirely dependent on the socio-cultural context (217–18). "This means that the motive for the relation of signification is either a utilitarian function or the imitation of an aesthetic or cultural model," Barthes observes (219).

However, it is the cultural context that predominantly motivates the sign. Thus, fashion strives to emphasize cultural motivations under the guise of pseudo-usefulness (for instance, while presenting garments which are [supposedly] practical and yet it is possible to do without them). Neo-Victorian novels not only offer a new awareness of fashion, but also encourage various literary interpretations of the bygone, achieved through the textual portrayals of material objects. As Nadine Boehm-Schnitker and Susanne Gruss claim, "the performative reiteration of neo-Victorian lifestyles is based on material objects, visual display and contemporary desires" (8). Apart from technology, clothes seem to adopt a privileged space in neo-Victorian literary culture. Hence, the cultural semiotics of fashion can influence and intertextually enrich contemporary perceptions of Victorian women as depicted in literary texts.

In literature, it is the textual fashion that negotiates new meanings or performs a utilitarian function. The title of Wilkie Collins's novel—*The Woman in White*—foregrounds clothes, as the eponymous heroine (essentially, "the woman") is pictured against her white garment. During the first encounter with the novel, it is predominantly the color white that grasps the reader's attention and encourages one to discover its raison d'être. The color white is held to symbolize perfection, grace, death and rebirth, spirituality, purity, and eternal life, as well as the beginning and the end. These culturally based meanings seem to apply to the color white as used in the novel. Talairach-Vielmas explicates that whiteness was also a desired color of the female complexion, since in the nineteenth century, "even if at the time body plumpness and rosy cheeks were praised in women, beauty manuals favoured pale, bloodless models verging on sickness—which were seen as pure, virginal, and self-contained" (170). On the other hand, she observes, "in most Victorian novels, plump and healthy women are frequently sexually assertive women" (170). Literary female characters such as Arabella Donn from Hardy's *Jude the Obscure*—plump, healthy, sexually assertive, reckless, and immoral—readily attest to Talairach-Vielmas's claim.

Hence, the ideal Victorian woman was associated with whiteness and transparency, which influenced her ambiguous status, since the color white symbolizes angelic innocence and purity but also, at the same time, it signifies death, coldness, and lack of feelings. It also turns the Victorian woman into an illusory, semitransparent construct. Lyn Pykett argues in a similar vein: "woman, as constructed in Victorian ideology, is asexual and passionless, and yet she is the repository of feeling and the source of affectivity" (62).

In *The Woman in White*, Wilkie Collins experiments with the socially normative idea of whiteness, portraying the eponymous heroine subversively dressed in white. In chapter 4, the heroine, Anne Catherick, appears "dressed from head to foot in white garments" (*The Woman in White*, 14). The narrator,

William Hartright, encounters a "solitary woman" who asks the way to London (14). The unexpected appearance of a ghostly, white-clothed figure introduces a startling twist into the text. Paradoxically, it is not the unexpected meeting that causes Mr. Hartright's confusion (even though it is dark and the woman appears on a solitary road), but rather the fact that the strange person is entirely dressed in white (14). The visual perception proves to constitute the strongest impulse for the first glance evaluation. Anne Catherick—as the wearer of clothes—takes on the function of a "determined sign." As Barthes claims, "fashion resolves the passage from the abstract body to the real body," while clothes become "the signified" (258). In the excerpt introduced below, the woman's garments strongly influence Hartright's perception, granting the scene a mysterious overtone and awakening the observer's curiosity:

> She held a small bag in her hand: and her dress—bonnet, shawl and gown all of white—was, so far as I could guess, certainly not composed of very delicate or very expensive materials. (15)

There are several components of the dress which form the whole of the presented attire. The most prominent ones include: the bag, the bonnet, shawl, gown, the color white, and the materials whose value is questioned. According to Barthes, in the description of textual garments the substance is always "broken off" (62). In effect, such clothing is necessarily "fragmentary" (15). The textual, potentially endless garment is divided into units of varying importance. As a result, the textual fashion is gradually revealed to the reader as a set of separate items.

As stated before, one of the basic assumptions of Barthes's *The Fashion System* is the decomposition of signifying units into *the object, the support*, and *the variant* (81). *The object* is the element which receives signification in the linguistic unit (for example, a dress) (64). *The support* is the part of *the object* (for instance, a collar), while *the variant* possesses a "non-material" character and "modifies" the support (for example, a "white" collar) (67). In the above-cited quotation, the color white takes on the role of *the variant* which modifies the perception of the units singled out in order of importance.

The supposedly "low quality" and "inexpensive" materials change the meaning of *the object* as well. The description attains a vertical character, as the object (the dress) is revealed to the reader in a fragmentary fashion starting from the top—mentioning the bonnet first, then, moving down to the shawl, and ending with the gown. The perplexity of the description lies in the gradual revealing of the dress. The parts of the textual image, singled out one after another in order to grasp the reader's attention, introduce suspense and highlight the importance of each item. Hartright, as the observer of the "feminine spectacle," is in doubt whether the strangely clad individual is an innocent lady or a wayward woman. His uncertainty confirms the assumption that the socially constructed line between whiteness as the attribute of "the angel in the house" and whiteness as the expression of death and insanity is very thin. It also attests to the transgressive potential of Anne Catherick as a character. The transformative power of fashion turns Anne into a "text" and allows others to "read" her as a helpless, victimized angel or a potential villain at the same time, which, looked at in a broader perspective, further attests to the instability of the image of the Victorian feminine ideal. This double-edged dichotomy arises as a consequence of what Talairach-Vielmas terms as "clichés" (40). Anne Catherick, fully clothed in white, is not a Victorian angel but rather an embodiment of an excessive, "dangerous femininity."[2] This subversive potential embodied by Anne threatens Hartright's integrity, since he does not know how to respond to the peculiar vision. According to Lynn Pykett,

> one of the reasons that the woman in white presents a challenge to Walter's identity is that her appearance challenges and blurs the gender categories upon which masculine identity was constructed. Walter's divided response to the woman is indicative of the contradictions of her appearance. Walter initially responds as a chivalrous gentleman to those aspects of her appearance which signify respectable, middle-class femininity: self-control, vulnerability, guardedness, "loneliness and helplessness." Having helped her to avoid recapture, he is racked with guilt that he has let loose that uncaged femininity that it is the duty of every respectable man to control. (18)

"Is Anne Catherick a Victorian Cinderella, disinherited and cruelly abused by Glyde, or is she simply another fallen woman driven insane by her wanderings in the streets?" asks Talairach-Vielmas, commenting on the ambiguous meaning of the heroine's appearance (2). By implying that Anne Catherick can be framed as a "Victorian Cinderella," she simultaneously places Hartright at the heart of a chivalric tale:

> When Hartright first meets the woman in white, the realistic text shifts into romance: as he helps her flee the men who are trying to bring her back to the asylum, the dream-like atmosphere fashions the woman into a strange, distressed damsel and turns Hartright into a golden-hearted knight. Cinderella-like, the mysterious Anne Catherick, dressed in white by some godmother whose tombstone she keeps cleaning, haunts the text, making the narrative hover between fairy tale and Gothic romance. (2)

While intertextually framing *The Woman in White* as yet another Cinderella story, Talairach-Vielmas implies that the protagonist is "dressed in white by some godmother." This godmother, as the plot reveals, is the deceased Mrs.

174   Chapter Fourteen

Figure 14.1. *Lady in White* by Edmund H. Garrett (1895) (Public Domain).

Fairlie, who provided Anne with care and attention during her childhood. Since Mrs. Fairlie dressed Anne in white, the eponymous heroine cultivates this tradition in her adult life in order to preserve Mrs Fairlie's memory. Thus, whether truly insane or not, Anne Catherick is decidedly "insanely original" and individualistically persistent in her choice of attire, since this choice is nobly motivated by the memory of a person who is especially dear to her. Taking this argument into account, the excessive perplexity caused by Anne Catherick's appearance seems ungrounded. What may appear to Hartright as a spectacle of helplessness and insanity is, in fact, Anne's conscious decision to cherish Mrs. Fairlie's memory. Freed from the normative constraints of the current fashion, this peculiar motivation paradoxically places Anne among protomodern characters for whom fashion is a statement of individuality and, decidedly, places her among the literary New Women of the era.[3] Whether Anne Catherick is entirely sane in her motives is yet another question which, however, does not deny her originality and distinctiveness. It is of no importance to the heroine what others may think about her appearance: she remains true to herself, which reminds one of the modern assertion of independence attained through original appearance. The eponymous Woman in White cultivates a peculiar tradition of individualism, which can be epitomized in the famous quotation from Oscar Wilde's play, *An Ideal Husband*: "Fashion is what one wears oneself" (459).

Importantly, Anne Catherick bears striking resemblance to another character in the novel, Laura—Mrs. Fairlie's daughter. In the course of events it is revealed that Anne is Mr. Fairlie's illegitimate child. While Laura is a talented young lady, Anne remains a miserable refugee. Laura's dress is made of muslin, while Anne's gown is visibly of inferior quality. Clearly, Anne symbolizes Miss Fairlie's imperfect twin—a mirror reflection of whom she might have been. However, there are selected components which bring these two characters together. Strikingly enough, the women are strongly connected by their physical likeness. The resemblance is especially striking when Laura, just like Anne, wears white clothes. This act shatters Hartright's emotional integrity once again: "Miss Fairlie, a white figure, alone in the moonlight; in her attitude, in the turn of her head, in her complexion, in the shape of her face, the living image . . . of the woman in white!" (50).

Wearing white clothes seems to symbolically enslave Laura in the "prescribed" feminine roles of a daughter and wife, just as it entraps Anne in the patriarchal world which regards her as insane or, in Pykett's words, as the femininity "uncaged" (18). Laura's feminine, almost angelic appearance, also carries an ambiguous message: it turns Laura into a respectable Victorian lady, but also emphasizes her vulnerability and inability to make decisions for herself. Therefore, she easily falls victim to the cunning man, Percival Glyde. The symbolic white dress, indicating innocence and the purity of mind, inevitably connects Laura with Anne's fate. In this sense, the garment embodies a link or a "medium" through which the fates of the two women are interconnected. Apart from that, Laura ties under her chin a white handkerchief which is also similar to the one which Anne possesses. While both Laura and Anne are vulnerable to masculine attacks, they achieve their ultimate victory as well: at the end of the novel their enemies are punished and justice is done. Nonetheless, Anne Catherick is bound to die in a very unequal struggle with the patriarchal world. Talairach-Vielams discusses the double-edged, sacrificial female victory, arguing that

> sensation novels feature women's anesthetization textually and literally, playing with stereotypes and constructing the female bodies as illusory and shaped in conformity with dominant models. . . . Although the female characters attempt to counteract male-preferred definitions of ideal femininity, nearly all of them are, nonetheless, destined to death, taking to their tombs mysteries and contradictions of femininity and sometimes leaving only an angelic foot crystallized in glass as a souvenir of woman's ambiguous perfection. (175–76)

Following the thread of this argument, it can be asserted that in Collins's novel the white dress takes on the role of the sign "aestheticizing" both Laura and Anne. It is the sign as symbolic and metaphysical as the elusive "glass slipper," attesting to the heroines' anterior presence in the text and their influence on the plot. Moreover, it is the sign of strength and individuality, but also a worrisome indicator of weakness, social "transparency," and dependence.

While the "untamed" femininity is bound to perish in the normatively constructed world, Laura does not share Anne Catherick's fate. However, she also faces a "fall" and needs to be rescued from an asylum by William Hartright and Marian Halcombe, her half-sister. Nevertheless, as Pykett notices, "even when she is liberated from the asylum and her husband's tyranny into the care of Hartright and Marian, Laura is still subject to strict controls and is kept more or less a prisoner for her own protection" (19). Hence, Laura, the new woman in white, is, in turn, incapacitated by her rescuers.

The female characters in *The Woman in White* become slaves of the socially sanctioned fashion which, in turn, ties them to the world of patriarchal expectations. For instance, the description of Eleanor Fairlie as a married woman exposes the tyranny of fashion dictated by the Victorian world:

> As Eleanor Fairlie (aged seven-and-thirty), she was always talking pretentious nonsense. . . . As Madame Fosco (aged three-and-forty), she sits for hours together without saying a word, frozen up in the strangest manner in herself. The hideously ridiculous love-locks which used to hang on either side of her face are now replaced by stiff little rows of very short curls, of the sort one sees in old-fashioned wigs. A plain, matronly cap covers her head, and makes her look, for the first time in her life since I remember her, like a decent woman. . . . Clad in quiet black or grey gowns, made high round the throat—dresses that she would have laughed at, or screamed at, as the whim of the moment inclined her, in her maiden days—she sits speechless in corners. (191)

The picture of the woman emerging from Wilkie Collins's novel is that of an entrapped creature, dependent on social conventions and masculine desires. The act of wearing inconvenient and unwomanly clothes deprives Eleanor of her identity and leaves her literally speechless, robbing her of the most precious gift—the voice. The only woman character in Collins's work who escapes (to some extent) the normative social constraints (and, thus, the symbolic influence of the white dress) is Marian Halcombe, whose unmatched self-awareness is reflected on the pages of her diary. At the same time, Marian poses a threat to Hartright's masculinity, since she appears more rational and self-possessed than the emotional male character.

In Collins's novel, Hartright, as an artist, remains especially sensitive to other instances of fashion. It is Laura's image that interests him quite a lot.

The textual construction of Laura appears to be clothes-dependent, as she is defined through her material attire. Essentially, it is the male gaze that glorifies Laura and assigns a special meaning to her looks. When Hartright is obliged to abandon Laura due to her unwanted engagement with Glyde, the exasperated heroine appears to bid him goodbye in a dark blue dress which he admires the most: "a dark blue silk, trimmed quaintly and prettily with old-fashioned lace" (103). Hartright's vision of Laura differs from the perspectives of other characters since it is essentially artistic. Hartright is a unique male narrator in the novel since, as an artist, he pays particular attention to garments and colors. In *The Art of Beauty* (1878), the Victorian guidebook of proper appearance, Mrs. Haweis states that "dark blue was the mourning colour among the ancient Romans" (177). Looked at in the light of this statement, Laura's dark blue mournful "goodbye" dress acquires a new meaning. This "historical frame of reference" (Davis, 6), established on a cultural assumption (Collins received classical education himself), may inform the reader about the author's (un)conscious borrowing from culture and history.

In *The Woman in White*, the textual garments turn into "silent statements" of the characters, revealing their personalities, inner qualities, desires, and dilemmas. Thus, they also turn into the elements of characterization (Rimmon-Kenan, 59). Likewise, neo-Victorian, textually constructed fashion assumes the role of a utilitarian object. As already stated, Gail Carriger's novel *Soulless* (2009), with the setting located in nineteenth-century England in a fictitious high-tech, urban context, readily explores the theme of clothing. Similarly to the Victorian texts, in modern revisionary fiction textual garments play a vital role in the process of framing femininity. Yet, in *Soulless*, this role is dramatically altered: the text features a strong and assertive woman, Alexia, who uses fashion as a weapon against the masculine world and, in general, against everyone who stands in her way. Steampunk novels, such as *Soulless*, dialogically challenge Victorian texts, as they portray heroines consciously and purposefully using garments and accessories to construct themselves through their attires. Steampunk clothes highlight protagonists' assertiveness, as they purposefully concentrate on the notions of femininity and original beauty, often divergent from the preferred Victorian canon. On the contrary, in nineteenth-century fiction, clothes reflect the instances of passive or incapacitated femininity. If garments expose the character's beauty, this feature is usually presented in a specific context, emphasizing potential marriage prospects or one's current social status. Moreover, if donned purposefully as a disguise, clothes, in works such as *East Lynne* or *Villette*, alter the heroine's true identity and appearance.

In Carriger's novel, it is originality that constitutes the value of her characters. Steampunk fiction is fully "accessorized," gadget-oriented and, thus, targeted at the idea of individuality. In *Soulless*, the decorative parasol, Alexia's favorite gadget, is turned into a weapon directed against an insulting vampire. Steampunk fashion endows Alexia with a power to transgress the boundary of a helpless Victorian lady and act independently as a self-sufficient, modern woman. The parasol can be perceived as *the variant* epitomizing Alexia's identity and her assertive qualities as revealed in the text. Additionally, the entire series of novels dedicated to Alexia Tarabotti has a collective title of *The Parasol Protectorate*, pointing out to the importance of this gadget—and it is precisely a "gadget," as the parasol is no longer a merely decorative accessory in Alexia's hands.

In contrast, in Wilkie Collins's *The Woman in White*, the parasol retains its socially recognized utilitarian function, as it protects against the sun (38). As already mentioned in the previous chapter, Alexia mocks the idea of using her parasol on a sunny day, since her complexion is naturally tanned. What follows, she does not try to adjust to the normative framework of beauty, celebrating her unique, natural appearance.

While the parasol proves useful in both texts, its function is radically different in each of the novels, which points to the fact that in *Soulless* Victorian fashion is replicated with a new purpose.

While in Collins's *The Woman in White* Laura's garments signify the angelic, feminine "beauty" devoid of passion and purpose, in Carriger's text this meaning is altered, and clothes are used in a purposeful, self-aware attempt at "attracting" and "seducing" others. Such a change reflects the modern preoccupation with the ideas of self-awareness and self-expression. Interestingly enough, while Laura remains unconscious of the fact that her clothes *signify*, Alexia purposefully selects garments that bring out her natural and seductive beauty. She is also the only person in charge of her wardrobe, estimating and choosing dresses according to her taste. Apart from that, Alexia's male friend, Lord Akeldama, appears much more preoccupied with fashion than Alexia herself:

> It was impossible not to grin at Lord Akeldama; his attire was so consistently absurd. In addition to the heels, he wore yellow checked gaiters, gold satin breeches, an orange and lemon striped waistcoat, and an evening jacket of sunny pink brocade. His cravat was a frothy flowing waterfall of orange, yellow, and pink Chinese silk, barely contained by a magnificently huge ruby pin. (38)

Soulless playfully echoes and alters Victorian conventions: a bizarre description of his outfit places Lord Akeldama in the role of a peculiar "angel in the house." In the course of events, he is even turned into a "gothic lady in distress" when kidnapped by the members of the Hippocras Club. Dressed for a dinner, Lord Akeldama becomes a spectacle himself. Carriger's work mirrors the present-day abilities of clothing, capable of molding and altering the character's identity. In the modern text, Lord Akeldama is justified in his extravagant fashion experiments, while such justification is impossible for such entrapped nineteenth-century characters as Anne Catherick. Such granted freedom of self-expression constitutes a new phenomenon in neo-Victorian fiction and turns into a dialogical, literary revision of the Victorian convention. In Carriger's novel, the characters consciously define and "create" themselves by means of their clothes. In contrast, in *The Woman in White*, it is only through Hartright's defining gaze that Laura's beauty is portrayed as angelic and feminine, while Anne Catherick's appearance is constructed as a disturbing vision. Hence, in Collins's novel, the masculine gaze "poeticizes" Laura as a fashionable object, while it also evaluates Anne as a potential threat to social stability. It is also through Hartright's subjective narration that the reader gets acquainted with Marian Halcombe and learns that she is partially devoid of femininity: "The lady's complexion was almost swarthy, and the dark down on her upper lip was almost a moustache. She had a large, firm, masculine mouth and jaw" (24). On the contrary, in Carriger's novel, instead of scrutinizing women characters with a defining, masculine gaze, Lord Akeldama constructs himself by means of fashion. Thus, in Carriger's work, fashion becomes the door to liberty and freedom of self-expression for every character, regardless of the character's gender.

Inevitably, visual portraits of the female characters in *The Woman in White* are built upon masculine perspectives. Therefore, the female characters in Collins's text are necessarily constructed through other characters' narrative. However, Marian refuses to be entirely molded by William's perception, creating her own narrative on the pages of her private diary, which adds a wider perspective to Hartright's rather artistic observations. There is a dialogical link between Marian Halcombe and Carriger's heroine Alexia: both of these figures are resistant to the general standards of conduct and appearance.

The complex relations between the heroines and their apparels in *The Woman in White* and *Soulless* point to the conclusion that "clothes can serve women" and "women can serve their clothes" as well. In *The Woman in White*, Anne Catherick and Laura Fairlie choose their clothes according to the decisions of others. Although Anne consciously chooses the color of her dress, it is a decision resulting from Mrs. Fairlie's previous arrangement. Thus, Anne and Laura "serve their garments" rather than the other way round. Contrastively, in Carriger's text, Alexia's femininity is performed by means of clothing, while clothes assign the desired meaning to her body and personality. As a modern, literary New Woman Alexia is offered a chance to consciously play with fashion and create her own identity. This process, according to Barthes, is the major theme of "human consciousness" (257).

Clothes evoke gender relations, and Alexia consciously chooses femininity (as opposed to masculinity) as shown in her carefully selected garments.

Neo-Victorian clothes endow particular characters with qualities (weapon accessories, seductive designs) allowing them to influence others. Thus, the purpose of a garment lies in its attractiveness and usefulness. Accordingly, the shift towards usefulness reveals the current nature of the milieu in which neo-Victorian texts emerge, providing an intertextual response to the nineteenth-century works.

The sartorial habits of the heroines presented, when looked at in the light of Barthes's theory, become an invaluable source of information about the characters and power relations in society. Although at first glance fashion appears to be an "innocent" phenomenon, its power to entrap can be easily traced in the descriptions of such characters as Eleanor Fairlie or Anne Catherick. Instead, for the neo-Victorian character like Alexia, fashion possesses a saving power—it becomes a self-defining tool.

Clothes gain meaning only through their poetic description and a gradual uncovering of the attire in the text. Their meaning remains vague until it is highlighted in a particular textual context. Temporal backgrounds in which neo-Victorian texts emerge provide a valuable field for investigation into the modern perception of Victorian women and their fashion. They allow for a dialogical "recapturing" of textual garments and their placement in new cultural frameworks.

When analyzing textual fashion, it is possible to look at such characters as Laura Fairlie, Anne Catherick, and Alexia Tarabotti from the perspective of the "thematic" component of the character. James Phelan posits that the "thematic" component of the character represents a general idea ascribed to a group or community. Carriger's Alexia—with her inventive dressing code—represents an independent, self-defining femininity of the modern day. Her unusual presence in the Victorian context redefines the literary past and epitomizes the nineteenth-century struggle for female independence as well as for the twenty-first century assertiveness. Anne Catherick, with her unconventional white garments, embodies the idea of the nineteenth-century woman opposing the patriarchal order and failing in this daring attempt. Her literary presence and unconventional appearance epitomize the struggle of numerous Victorian women. In contrast, Laura Fairlie represents the notion of a feeble, subdued femininity which passively and, perhaps unconsciously, conforms to the patriarchal expectations. What brings these characters together is a powerful message contained in their textual clothes. As Roland Barthes indicates, the meaning of fashion lies on the "rhetorical level" (42). Therefore, fashion and language constitute the major part of our culture which cannot be ignored when presented in the form of a literary experience.

NOTES

1. A part of this chapter was published in *Visions and Revisions: Studies in Literature and Culture*—vol. 4 (Czemiel, G., Galant, J., Kędra-Kardela, A., Kędzierska, A., Komsta, M., eds., Peter Lang, 2015, pp. 115–21).

2. "Dangerous" is understood as "potentially subversive."

3. Moreover, Anne Catherick can be perceived as a "full-fledged" protomodern New Woman, since she never performs the role of "the angel in the house."

Chapter Fifteen

Voice and Identity in the Victorian and Neo-Victorian Novel

Charlotte Brontë's Jane Eyre, *Jean Rhys's* Wide Sargasso Sea, *and Clare Boylan's* Emma Brown

"Now, tell me, my dear," I said, "what are you crying about?"
"About the years that are gone, Mr Betteredge," says Rosanna quietly.
"My past life still comes back to me sometimes."

— Wilkie Collins, *The Moonstone* (46)

In Victorian fiction and, especially in the sensation novel, identity and origins of women protagonists are usually disguised or uncertain. Appearing as irrational, compulsive, preoccupied with spirituality, or governed by "nature," women in Victorian texts often provide a "counterbalance" to rational masculinity. Neo-Victorian novels echo these literary themes, portraying mysterious women characters deprived of their roots and origins. On the other hand, neo-Victorian texts reveal their palimpsestuous nature while drawing on the previous narratives in order to endow them with a new meaning and purpose, as in the case of the already discussed *Wide Sargasso Sea*. Consequently, in neo-Victorian fiction, the narratives of female irrationality, spirituality and madness reshape into the stirring stories of women's dependency and despair. There are two relevant notions which shape the perception of the Victorian and neo-Victorian woman character: her voice and identity.

Both neo-Victorian and nineteenth-century novels with a mystery at their core host women characters lacking a clear family background. Oftentimes, the lack of family background in the lives of these characters serves as a common, dialogical link between the revisited texts and their modern counterparts. As Lyn Pykett points out,

> the motherless girl is the most important figure in the women's sensation novel. ... The lack of a mother renders the sensation heroine both more assertive and independent and/or more vulnerable than the woman who has been conventionally socialized under the surveillance and guidance of a mother. (49–50)

In Charlotte Brontë's *Jane Eyre* (1847) and Jean Rhys's *Wide Sargasso Sea* (1966), the female characters, Jane and Antoinette, are deprived of the "guidance of a mother." Moreover, these two novels are intertextually related, since Rhys's text, although written years later, offers a prequel to Brontë's work.

Brontë's Jane Eyre is an orphan, while *Wide Sargasso Sea* features a negligent mother, incapable of looking after her daughter. Interestingly enough, the fates of Jane Eyre and Antoinette Cosway intermingle, providing an atemporal dialogue of perspectives and possibilities. Paradoxically, the uprootedness of these two characters and the mysterious aura surrounding their identities offer them more narrative possibilities than disadvantages. Unconstrained by the ties of blood or detached from their families, the characters act as "blank pages" gradually filled with personal histories.

Presumably the most ignored and disadvantaged female character of Charlotte Brontë's *Jane Eyre* is Bertha Manson[1]—a vague, displaced and exotic wife of Mr. Rochester. In his article, "The Brontës: The Outsider as Protagonist," Frederick R. Karl observes that "Rochester needs the love of a good woman to cleanse him, for in marrying Bertha, he had fallen through ambition and lust into a loveless union" (ed. Bloom, 167–68). Although true, such statement positions Bertha as fully responsible for Rochester's passion and unguarded ambitions. It is usually taken for granted by the readers and critics that Bertha is insane and thus, must be imprisoned in the attic. Yet, throughout the novel, Bertha is denied the chance to comment on her presumed malady. While the document attesting to Rochester's unfortunate marriage is readily disclosed in the narrative, there are no documents or letters attesting to Bertha's past. Hence, she is a blank character without a past and a future, reduced by Rochester's testimony to an animalistic being. By the same token, Bertha's assumed monstrosity and dehumanization are left unquestioned throughout the novel. Moreover, she is portrayed in a superficial and perfunctory way as a background character not deserving further notice apart from her insanity. When Bertha sets Thornfield Hall on fire and perishes in the flames, it is almost a relief to the reader, because Jane and Mr. Rochester can be lawfully married. Bertha dies as Jane's bleak doppelgänger—a shadowy possibility of the unfathomed "female nature" which Jane, as an idealized character, skillfully avoids by employing rationality and emotional restraint. The prisoner in the attic embodies the extreme, untamed femininity which threatens masculine rationality and order. Thus, one does not find Bertha's advocates in Brontë's novel, whereas Rochester is apparently absolved from his "passion." He loses his house, sight, and a hand as a consequence of the fire and he is still presented, at least to some extent, as a victim of a mad and lustful woman.

Years later, owing to the neo-Victorian prequel to *Jane Eyre*, Bertha Manson develops and reshapes into a fascinating heroine in Jean Rhys's *Wide Sargasso Sea*. While in *Jane Eyre* Bertha Mason, an incapacitated caricature of a woman, stands in the shadow of Jane's success, *Wide Sargasso Sea* remolds Bertha into Antoinette Cosway—a delicate and feminine figure who seeks emotional and intellectual recognition. Rhys's novel portrays Antoinette's dramatic childhood in Coulibri, Jamaica, where she has to face such tragic events as her brother's death and her mother's fast-developing mental illness. Antoinette's moving narrative portrays her as a lonesome child who resorts to magic in order to protect herself from the hostile world. She is not only mentally separated from her mother, but also, as a Creole girl, remains suspended between the two worlds (the Jamaican world and the world of her ancestral origins) in which she seeks security in vain. The girl's only friend is an old Martinique nurse, Christophine, who distrusts Antoinette's future husband: Rochester's sole purpose in marriage lies in securing his financial future. The second part of the novel concentrates on Antoinette's and her husband's narratives concerning their trip to Granbois, where their marriage is quickly shattered by Rochester's love affair and his vague dealings with Daniel, a mysterious figure who claims to be Antoinette's unlawful brother. The bitter events, together with the dispiriting flashbacks from her childhood and the haunting feeling of uprootedness, contribute to Antoinette's gradual mental fall, which leads her further into depression, perceived by her husband as a dangerous mental illness. The last part of the novel presents Antoinette's thoughts on her imprisonment in the attic in Rochester's English mansion. Antoinette's narrative ends abruptly as she decides to take her own life. As Jeanette King asserts,

> novels set in [Victorian] period tend to be characterised by their engagement with gender issues. Jean Rhys' *Wide Sargasso Sea* . . . is arguably the first progenitor of this trend. In telling the story of the first Mrs Rochester, the madwoman in the attic of Charlotte Brontë's *Jane Eyre*, Rhys carried out a post-colonial and feminist reading of Brontë's canonical original, which has itself become almost canonical. Bertha's "madness" is shown to be largely Rochester's own construction. (2)

King's observation points to Rochester as to the one who is guilty of constructing the heroine's warped image, reshaping her into a villainous creature. Accordingly, it can be assumed that the notion of female maladies, including infirmity and hysteria, originates as a generalizing discourse on femininity constructed from a masculine standpoint. While Rochester certifies to Bertha's insanity in *Jane Eyre*, in Rhys's novel it is Antoinette (the counterpart of Bertha) who contributes to the narrative, introducing her story from an individualized and self-aware viewpoint. In *Wide Sargasso Sea*, the story of the "madwoman in the attic" is simultaneously narrated by Rochester (although never explicitly named in the text) and, partially, by Grace Poole—another character derived from Brontë's original story.

Closed in the attic, as if "inside cardboard covers" (*Wide Sargasso Sea*, xi), Antoinette, the Creole heiress, feels depersonalized and separated from the outer world, at times even doubting the existence of England. The dramatic endeavor to narrate her experience and to preserve her voice—the last possession not claimed by her husband—leaves Antoinette emotionally exhausted and dejected. In the last effort, she escapes from the attic with a view to setting the house on fire—the desperate act already foreseen in the prophetic dreams. The novel ends with Antoinette's plain but powerful remark: "Now at least I know why I was brought here and what I have to do" (123). This ultimate statement allows Antoinette to leave the hostile world as an unapologetic woman.

From her early life, Antoinette feels like an "outsider"—the rejected one. During her childhood, her happiness is sacrificed for the sake of her handicapped brother Pierre. After the fire at Coulibri, Antoinette's mother falls prey to an incapacitating mental illness, leaving the bewildered girl to Aunt Cora. The mother is too absorbed by her own sorrows to pay attention to the daughter, asking: "why you bring the child to make trouble" (26). Having only one true friend—Christophine—Antoinette remains permanently "entrapped" by her solitude. Her loveless marriage only deepens the sorrow, since it pushes her beyond the margin of human understanding and affection.

Apparently, Antoinette's destructive relationship with the English gentleman stands in a sharp contrast to the communion of minds between Jane Eyre and Mr. Rochester. In Charlotte Brontë's novel, Jane becomes Rochester's equal—an intellectual partner. Helen Moglen notices that

> the circumstances of her [Jane's] life have created in her a psychological need for the kind of symbiotic relationship which is essential to the stability of middle-class patriarchy, and is supported and justified by the romantic myth. (120)

In contrast, Rhys's *Wide Sargasso Sea* rejects the romantic myth of symbiotic relationship, while concentrating on Antoinette's humiliation performed by her impervious and egocentric husband. As argued by Pierrette M. Frickey,

> bringing Jean Rhys' characterizations to bear on Brontë's not only develops the blank character Antoinette, but converts Rochester into a much more interesting, equivocal figure. It counteracts his flatness in Brontë's version and questions the nature of Jane's judgment. 'Why is Jane so uncritical of Rochester?' we ask as we turn from *Wide Sargasso Sea* to *Jane Eyre*. (77)

Arguably, Rhys's heroine shares numerous features with Jane Eyre: she also experiences a traumatic childhood, possesses the gift of intellect and struggles for independence. Likewise, both heroines experience persistent loneliness and emotional bereavement in their childhood. In Jane's case, the need for human affection is substituted with her devotion to a doll. In Rhys's text, Antoinette resorts to magic, picturing in her imagination an enchanted, protective wand. These similarities bind Brontë's and Rhys's texts into a dialogic whole. As indicated by Bakhtin, "the novel . . . emerges as a genre that is both critical and self-critical, one fated to revise" (*Dialogic Imagination*, 10). According to him, the novel as a genre provides an "open source" for a continuous discussion. Hence, *Wide Sargasso Sea* critically revises Brontë's work in an intertextual light.

Dialogically analyzed, Jane and Antoinette become each other's alter egos. The validity of their projections as "good" or "evil" emerges as the result of an authoritative male evaluation. It is Mr. Rochester who authorizes Antoinette's veracity and it is his myopic perception that sanctions Antoinette's "madness" as genuine. In contrast, Brontë's Jane Eyre becomes Mr. Rochester's valuable companion when faced with his approving judgment. Simultaneously, Mr. Rochester's approving gaze implements a fairytale convention, where a virtuous and modest woman is approved and vindicated by her male suitor. As Sandra M. Gilbert and Susan Gubar observe in "A Dialogue of Self and Soul: Plane Jane's Progress," the initial meeting between Jane and Mr. Rochester fulfills a fairytale pattern:

> Jane's first meeting with Rochester is a fairy tale meeting. Charlotte Brontë deliberately stresses mythic elements: an icy twilight setting out of Coleridge or Fuseli, a rising moon, a great "lion-like" dog gliding through the shadows like "a North-of-England spirit, called a 'Gytrash' which . . . haunted solitary ways, and sometimes came upon belated travellers," followed by "a tall steed, and on its back a rider." Certainly the Romanticized images seem to suggest that universe of male sexuality with which Richard Chase thought the Brontës were obsessed. And Rochester . . . himself appears the very essence

of patriarchal energy, Cinderella's prince as a middle-aged warrior (chap. 12). (Bloom, ed., 328)

Wide Sargasso Sea retains a fairy tale convention as well. However, in Rhys's text, the dreamlike vision from *Jane Eyre* shows a new dialogical potential, as it turns from a Cinderella tale into a surrealistic, overly vibrant, and disturbing story. Mr. Rochester is not a "middle-aged warrior," but a sickly, irresponsible, and selfish young man. While traveling through the Caribbean landscape with his wife, Antoinette, Rochester comments that

> everything is too much. . . . Too much blue, too much purple, too much green. The flowers too red, the mountains too high, the hills too near. And the woman is a stranger. Her pleading expression annoys me. I have not bought her, she has bought me, or so she thinks. (39)

It is through Rochester's disapproving gaze that the vivacious landscape converts into a hostile vision verging on a surrealistic dream. His scrutinizing look denies Antoinette the role of his "Cinderella." Instead, Rochester positions himself as an effeminate victim of "marriage transaction," which actually saves him from disgrace and bankruptcy. Hence, there is nothing chivalric about Rhys's character who appears not only economically dependent on his wife, but also unresponsive to her feelings.

Although Antoinette cannot gain the status of an esteemed partner in her husband's eyes, she still possesses the power to speak, rendering it possible to unveil her true, sensitive nature. On the other hand, in Brontë's *Jane Eyre*, dialogically corresponding with *Wide Sargasso Sea*, Bertha Mason is denied the gift of voice. Since Bertha lacks the power to defend her case, she becomes muted and dehumanized. It is only her laughter that resonates in Rochester's house. "Power and powerlessness, discourse and silence, prisoners, patients and the machinery that keeps society functioning: these are the dominant concerns addressed by Jean Rhys," argues Frickey in *Critical Perspectives* (73). Thus, while tracing intertextual references to Charlotte Brontë's novel in *Wide Sargasso Sea*, the issue of "discourse and silence" appears to be the dominant theme dialogically binding the two texts. Davies observes that through their engagement with the so-far marginalized voices, neo-Victorian texts offer a "reversed" dialogue:

> we see that the "silenced" Victorians are granted a "voice" by contemporary authors and this is largely perceived as a noble, politically-aware enterprise, an attempt to challenge and redress the broader social and cultural inequalities that lead to this "silencing" in the first instance. In this sense, then, neo-Victorian fiction might be interpreted as subversively "talking back" to the Victorians. (3)

Davies highlights that the dialogue between the texts is possible because nineteenth-century fiction initiated and enabled this exchange of perspectives. Hence, the intertextual dialogue is enabled because neo-Victorian texts respond to their Victorian counterparts: "we must not forget that other connotation of 'talking back' which suggests that we cannot speak until being spoken to," she asserts (3). In this sense, the initial, voiceless creation of Bertha Mason paves the way for the appearance of Rhys's complex heroine, Antoinette, and endows Rhys's postcolonial work with new layers of meaning. Davies uses the concept of the "parent/child relationship," drawing our attention to the fact that "neo-Victorian authors are challenging an authority which has necessarily formed them" (3). This interdependency between the anterior and posterior texts constitutes the basis for the current intertextual revision. It also demonstrates that the modern criticism of anterior texts should not deprive them of their value and importance, concealed in the prospective possibility of a dialogical polemic.

In order to further discuss the intertextual influence in Rhys's novel, it is indispensable to concentrate on Bertha's representation in Brontë's "hypotext." Essentially, Bertha Mason in *Jane Eyre* is not granted the voice: her overall picture emerges from other characters' accounts (Mr. Rochester's and Jane's). In chapter 25, Jane relates to Mr. Rochester her encounter with the unknown woman [Bertha]:

> It seemed . . . a woman, tall and large, with thick and dark hair hanging long down her back. I know now what dress she had on: it was white and straight; but whatever gown, sheet, or shroud, I cannot tell. . . . It was a discoloured face—it was a savage face. I wish I could forget the roll of the red eyes and the fearful blackened inflation of the lineaments! . . . the lips were swelled and dark; the brow furrowed; the black eyebrows widely raised over the blood-shot eyes. (349, 350)

Jane's description of the strange woman transforms Bertha into a monster-like figure ("the red eyes") or a ghost ("discoloured face"). In her depiction, Jane offers a collection of Bertha's features (hair, eyes, lips) which jointly create a portrait of the "spectral female." Jane concentrates on the unknown woman's terrifying eyes, which are "red" and "fierce." These adjectives are also associated with the notion of fire which, later on, becomes the prevalent motif associated with Bertha Mason in Brontë's text: a destructive, damaging, and blind force.

Fire imagery serves as an intertextual nexus bonding Brontë's *Jane Eyre* with Rhys's *Wide Sargasso Sea*: Rhys employs in her text the notions of fire and the color red, propounding them as Antoinette's symbolic attributes. "The 'affair' at the center of *Wide Sargasso Sea* is Antoinette's insane, suicidal conflagration," Frickey argues (78). This final, suicidal "conflagration" is signaled by an earlier event in Rhys's novel. In part 1, it is the fire set to Antoinette's house in Coulibri that spells impending misfortunes. The name of the Estate—"Coulibri"—implies a hummingbird. At the outset of the story, Antoinette, just like a hummingbird, is filled with vital energy and freedom. However, as her beloved house is destroyed, Antoinette is likened to a fragile bird entrapped by the fire. The hummingbird metaphor accompanies the ill-fated heroine toward the end of Rhys's story. The allusion to Antoinette's dramatic fate is also made explicit when a parrot perishes in the fire (20). The motif of the destructive fire and flames develops through the entire text of *Wide Sargasso Sea*. Yet, as an intertextual referent to Brontë's work, fire attains in Rhys's novel a new symbolic meaning of the force directed against Antoinette and not, as in the case of *Jane Eyre*, stemming from Bertha's vicious intentions. For instance, in *Wide Sargasso Sea*, during the evening conversation between Antoinette and Rochester, there is "the procession of small moths and beetles [which] fly into the candle flames" (80). As if sealing her fate, Antoinette "flick[s] a dead moth off the table" (81). At the same time, Rochester sees by the candlelight "the hollows under her [Antoinette's] eyes, her drooping mouth, her thin, strained face" (81). The flame from the candle lays bare Antoinette's weariness and insecurity. It symbolically reclaims her contentment and safety in order to finally reclaim her life.

In contrast to their destructive potential, the fire and the color red in Rhys's novel are capable of symbolically accentuating Antoinette's vitality as well. When shut in the attic, the heroine strives to retain the precious red dress, claiming that the garment might allow her to restore her lost self. "Time has no meaning. But something you can touch and hold like my red dress, that has a meaning," states Antoinette (120), only to let the dress fall down on the floor: she "let[s] the dress fall on the floor, and look[s] from the fire to the dress and from the dress to the fire" (121). The destructive theme of perishing in flames is recalled once again, invading blissful memories from the past and wiping out Antoinette's vital energies.

Fire in *Wide Sargasso Sea* epitomizes both bliss and pain: the bliss is hidden in the analogy of a homelike, "emotional warmth" produced by the fire, while the pain is pictured as the heroine's gradual perishing, helplessness and destruction. In *Wide Sargasso Sea*, the symbolism of fire often fluctuates between misery and happiness. For instance, even the act of setting the curtains on fire allows Antoinette to dream in a bittersweet way of the warmth of her home: "I laughed when I saw the lovely colour spreading so fast," she indicates (122). Similarly, during the final scenes, while calling the absent Christophine for help, Antoinette is surrounded by "a wall of protecting fire" (122). However, it is "too hot" (122). Thus, the theme of fire in *Wide*

Sargasso Sea carries ambiguous connotations, denoting both destruction and bliss. The flames are both protective and evil: they surround Antoinette with warmth and, at the same time, threaten her existence. Rhys's "hypertext" evokes the theme of fire in a different vein from that presented in *Jane Eyre*, where Bertha is held responsible for the destruction of Thornfield Hall. In *Wide Sargasso Sea*, the threat associated with fire comes to Antoinette from the outside. In *Jane Eyre*, the fire originates in the heart of Thornfield Hall. However, in both texts, the notion of fire constructs the perception of the female characters. Such dialogical reading of the theme of fire allows for a new interpretation of Bertha's (Antoinette's) character and her deeds. *Jane Eyre* and *Wide Sargasso Sea*, engaged in an intertextual exchange of perspectives, offer a new quality of interpretation, accentuating the dramatic denouement bonding the literary past with the literary presence.

Strange dreams and prophetic visions experienced by the characters are yet another feature attesting to the intertextual dimension of the two texts. In Brontë's novel, Jane has a prophetic dream revealing the fate of Thornfield Hall:

> I dreamt another dream, sir: that Thornfield Hall was a dreary ruin, the retreat of bats and owls. I thought that of all the stately front nothing remained but a shell-like wall, very high, and very fragile looking. (348)

In a similar vein, she relates to Mr. Rochester her dreamlike, bizarre meeting with Bertha: "she took my veil from its place; she held it up; gazed at it long, and then she threw it over her own head, and turned to the mirror," Jane recalls (349). The ghostly meeting between Jane and Rochester's first wife stands for the strongest intertextual link between Brontë's work and Rhys's revisionary text. It is important to note here that while in *Jane Eyre* the mirror faithfully reflects the horror of Bertha's ghastly appearance, in *Wide Sargasso Sea* it emblematically represents Antoinette's desire for love and acceptance, especially when she unsuccessfully tries to kiss her own reflection:

> I remember watching myself brush my hair and how my eyes looked back at me. *The girl I saw as myself yet not quite myself.* Long ago when I was a child and very lonely I tried to kiss her. But the glass was between us—hard, cold and misted over with my breath. Now they have taken everything away. [emphasis added] (116)

Just like Jane "dreaming awake" of the encounter with the strange woman in Brontë's text, Rhys's Antoinette has a visionary dream as well. She encounters Jane during her disturbing vision of the burning house: "It was then that I saw her—the ghost. The woman with streaming hair" (122). Interestingly enough, in *Wide Sargasso Sea*, Jane turns into a spectral vision herself. As Jane and Antoinette meet, their narrations meet as well, mirroring each other (hence, the notion of the mirror appears again) and presenting the scene from a wider, intertextual viewpoint. With this dialogue of voices coming from the two corresponding texts, the scene of the nightly encounter turns into a multi-angled and atemporal experience. The interaction between the narrations provided by Jane and Antoinette implements Bakhtin's claim that "novelistic discourse is pregnant with an endless multitude of dialogic confrontations" (*Dialogic Imagination*, 365). The dialogue between the narratives enables the reader to perceive Brontë's and Rhys's works as an integral whole offering a multi-layered vision of the same story. Last but not least, the intertextual influence of *Wide Sargasso Sea* brings redemption to the previously obliterated and dehumanized character of Bertha: even though Antoinette perishes in flames, her own narrated story remains valid and moving, providing a meaningful revision of Brontë's *Jane Eyre*. Antoinette is victorious, because her original silence turns into a narrated experience. In this sense, Rhys's work proposes a new interpretation of the past, based on the contemporary norms and social standards. Antoinette's story offers a new, conscious rereading of otherness:

> In dialogism, the very capacity to have consciousness is based on otherness. The otherness is not merely a dialectical alienation on its way to a sublation that it will endow it with a unifying identity in higher consciousness. On the contrary: in dialogism consciousness is otherness. . . . For him [Bakhtin] self is "dialogic." . . . self/other is a relation of simultaneity. (Holquist, 17, 18)

> Dialogism assumes that intertextuality and inter-textuality are the novel's hallmarks, and therefore that otherness is at work in the genre's very heart. (Holquist, 86)

Rhys's novel thoroughly draws on the dialogue and boundaries between the "self" (Antoinette) and the other (Bertha, or: Antoinette through Rochester's gaze). Through Antoinette's account, the other (Bertha) becomes disentangled from Rochester's central, condemning narrative: she perishes in flames, but it is her re-narrated image that remains in the reader's consciousness. Above all, *Wide Sargasso Sea* provides an empathetic reading which stands for, as it has been already argued, one of the predominant tasks of neo-Victorian fiction.

NOTES

1. According to Elaine Showalter,

Bertha's origin in folk history and literature are interesting in themselves. There are numerous literary precedents in the Gothic novel, particularly Mrs. Radcliffe's *Sicilian Romance*, for mysterious captives; the situation, in fact, is repeated to the point of appearing archetypal. Other explanations for Bertha depend upon real case histories that Brontë had encountered. Mrs. Gaskell mentions one in her *Life of Charlotte Brontë*; Q. D. Leavis refers to another, a Yorkshire legend about North Lees Hall Farm, where a mad wife had allegedly been incarcerated. . . . The legends themselves express a cultural attitude toward female passion as a potentially dangerous force that must be punished and confined. In the novel, Bertha is described as "the foul German spectre—the vampire," "a demon," "a hag," "an Indian Messalina," and "a witch." Each of these is a traditional figure of female deviance with its own history in folklore. (*A Literature of Their Own*, 119)

Chapter Sixteen

Nameless and Voiceless

Clare Boylan's Emma Brown *and* Jean Rhys's Wide Sargasso Sea

Wide Sargasso Sea offers an insight into childhood distresses affecting adult life. Numerous neo-Victorian texts also employ the concept of a family (and its spectral absence impacting the character's future) in their plot. The notion of a family appears to be of primary importance both in the Victorian and modern times. As aptly observed by Marie-Luise Kohlke and Christian Gutleben in their *Neo-Victorian Families: Gender, Sexual and Cultural Politics*,

> Victorian fictions are replete with the detritus of family and characters situated precariously on its margins or beyond its borders: dubious widows, derided spinsters, fallen women, confirmed bachelors, adulterous or fugitive wives, deserter husbands, mad relatives hidden away in confinement, governesses far from home bringing up other people's children, foundlings, waifs, strays and, above all, unloved and exploited orphans. (20)

At present, as the authors of *Neo-Victorian Families* notice, we are continually "haunted" by the recurring presence of the literary, (neo)-Victorian family. It is a "fantasy construction" (21) with fragile and illusive ties at its core:

> The family's representation is thus always also a representation of absence, a ghostly *trace* of the impossible, longed for ideal than the thing itself, of something that *never existed in the first place*. Unsurprisingly, neo-Victorian writers seem particularly interested in exploring the related orphan tropes of homelessness, family-lessness, and *thinglessness.* (22)

The exploration and revision of family relations in Victorian texts results in an intertextual, palimpsestuous play with the bygone. While in the nineteenth-century novel family and household are located between an idealistic idea of the domestic bliss and its actual decadence, in neo-Victorian works families openly indicate the decline of human relations, announcing the advent of the post-human era. In neo-Victorian fiction, families embody coincidental and chaotic literary constructs, providing an explicit commentary on the present-day, unstable social relations. From the authorial perspective, such a state of affairs paradoxically "aids" the uprooted protagonists who, in this sense, are not encumbered with uncomfortable legacies and appear free to make their own, independent choices. At the same time, neo-Victorian protagonists are plagued by the feeling of loss, which often affects their choices and the overall plot:

> Loss, mourning, and regeneration are prototypical preoccupations of the neo-Victorian novel, which often revolves around the re(dis)covery of a personal and/or collective history and the restitution of a family inheritance through the reconstruction of fragmented, fabricated, or repressed memories: a retracing and piecing together of the protagonist's roots which reflects, metafictionally, on the literary 'origins' of the neo-Victorian genre and the narratological traditions it seeks to reshape. (Heilmann, Llewellyn, 34)

The orphan trope constitutes the theme of the already mentioned Boylan's *Emma Brown*. Relying on the intertextual play with *Jane Eyre*, Boylan's text abounds in realistic depictions of childhood miseries and child abuse in the Victorian age. "Neo-Victorian representations of childhood predominantly figure society's ethical failures of care and protection vis-á-vis its most vulnerable members," observes Kohlke.

> Overwhelmingly, neo-Victorian childhood is depicted as traumatic, scarred by violence, poverty, exploitation, emotional and/or sexual abuse. It is possible to discern important intersections here between neo-Victorian trauma narratives and the Gothic in terms of the horrors it depicts and exploits. (Kohlke and Gutleben, 135)

While concentrating on the notion of childhood, Boylan's *Emma Brown* powerfully echoes such works by Charlotte Brontë as: *Shirley* (1849), *Villette* (1853) and the aforementioned *Jane Eyre* (1847). Boylan's work simultaneously moves and shocks the reader, as it not only re-narrates the romantic theme of Jane Eyre's search for home but, at the same time, depicts the brutal and uncompromising realities of Victorian England as seen from the modern standpoint. As Clare Boylan indicates in her afterword to *Emma Brown*, such "development of the plot was in part inspired by Charlotte's growing interest in social conditions in London" (439). The comment provided by Boylan in the afterword can be treated as an "authorial paratext," influencing the overall reading of the novel, justifying Boylan's choices, and incorporating Brontë's initial design into the final plot. The deployment of "authorial paratext" directs the reader toward the intertextual reading, creating a link between Brontë's world and the modern "reality" which incessantly draws ideas from the nineteenth-century literary base.

Emma's appearance and behavior also deliberately allude to Charlotte Brontë's heroine. The depiction of Emma abounds in numerous intertextual references to the figure of Jane Eyre. The "soulful intelligence" radiating from Emma's face attests to her adult-like qualities and can be likened to young Jane's premature intelligence (49). Additionally, Emma is described as "little" and "plain" (49), which brings her even closer to Jane's appearance, who is portrayed as "poor, obscure, plain and little" (*Jane Eyre*, 312).

The intertextual link between *Jane Eyre* and *Emma Brown*, based on the dialogically employed theme of orphanhood, offers a new, expanded vision of a young girl striving to survive in an uncompromising Victorian reality. Essentially, in *Jane Eyre*, the textual reality is filled with "fairytale events" (such as Jane's first meeting with Mr. Rochester and the dream in which she hears his voice), with the Cinderella-like heroine being lavishly rewarded for her unflinching virtue. On the contrary, Emma's world is deprived of magic, and the heroine has to fight for her existence. Jane Eyre's unbelievably perfect resolution and Emma's prosaic struggle for survival emphasize the literary dialogue of divergent perspectives between Brontë's and Boylan's texts with the theme of orphanhood at their core. Mary Ellen Bellanca posits that in a dialogue "Bakhtin's 'voice' is no privileged oracle of truth; on the contrary, a voice can deceive others or itself, can be uncertain, even deluded" (61). The dialogue of perspectives between Cinderella-like *Jane Eyre* and disillusioning *Emma Brown* is not directed at finding the "ultimate truth" but, rather, at a conscious revision of the nineteenth-century perspective in the modern light. *Emma Brown* revises *Jane Eyre*, revealing the moral crisis at the core of the Victorian world. "Much neo-Victorian fiction," Kohlke argues, "qualifies as trauma narrative, explicitly dealing with individual and collective historical crises" (Kohlke, Gutleben, 135).

Importantly, in Boylan's novel, Emma must undergo a struggle in order to retrieve her original name: she initially appears in the text under the guise of "Matilda Fitzgibbon." In the course of the novel, the reader gradually learns that Emma was captured and sold and that she had lost all memories from the past.   As a result of the childhood trauma, Emma loses the memory of her origin and her voice. While finally Emma emerges victorious and reclaims her true name and identity, her youthful story is already filled with dramatic and painful events and thoughts, so conflicting with Jane's attitude: "She was nothing. There was no one to claim her" (Boylan, 297). For instance, chapter 30 opens with Emma's suicidal thoughts during her solitary ramblings near the riverbank in London:

> Emma climbed down the steps to the river. The water slapped indifferently against the brick. "Be done with it," it seemed to say. "Yes, be done with it," she urged herself. Yet how forsaken a sphere she entered. Merely by descending that stair she had cut herself off from all the living world. Far from the clean, anonymous erasure she had craved, the water was heavy with filth and history. It breathed out a deathly stench. (313)

Boylan's nineteenth-century London is strikingly bleak and thought-provoking. The romantic spirit of *Jane Eyre* is shattered and dialogically revised through Boylan's modern, realistic depiction of poverty and pollution (both literal and metaphorical: "heavy with filth and history") which strikes the solitary heroine. Emma seems to be surrounded by nothingness and darkness. She cringes away from her suicidal attempt while discovering the dark secrets of the river and imagining "being embraced by some other recent corpse" (313). Even more shocking is Emma's discovery of a little girl, Jenny Drew, who is sitting on the river bank holding a dead child. The child looks like "a large and life-like doll," while Jenny Drew has "cold and bare" feet (313). However, the little girl wears "a hat of quaint design with shallow brim and some very decrepit flowers on it" (313). Wearing a hat with "decrepit flowers" is an attempt at preserving elegance and dignity. It contrasts with the ghastly, bleak environment and the dead body of the unknown child held by Jenny Drew. The character of Jenny Drew dialogically corresponds with Brontë's portrayal of Helen Burns in *Jane Eyre*. However, the reader is denied romantic delusions on learning that Jenny "had the face of an angel but she spoke with the hoarse and low tones of an old man" (314). Thus, Helen's subtlety and charm disappear in Boylan's revisionary work, where the bleak realities of London transpire from every page of the text.

The hostile world surrounding Emma and Jenny is not Jane's romantic manor or even Jane's detested school: workhouses, hospitals, and gloomy streets occupied by dubious characters constitute the textual reality of Emma's world. Jenny, just like Emma, appears deprived of her family background. The girl eventually narrates her recollections of a workhouse where she gains her present name:

> "In the Great House they asked me who I was," Jenny said. "I said that I was me. They seemed not to understand so I asked for pen and paper and drew a picture of myself. They picked it up and studied it and I heard one whisper to another, 'Look what Jenny drew.' And that is how I learnt my name. Jenny Drew." (322)

Jenny attains her new identity through the artistic process of drawing, which results in an accidental creation of her surname. Emma, on the other hand,

Figure 16.1. Photograph of a Glasgow slum by Thomas Annan (1868) (Public Domain).

consciously adopts the surname of her kidnapper, Eliza Brown, whom, initially, she erroneously perceives as her mother. Consequently, Eliza Brown is not only the initiator of Emma's quest, but also the figure of a presumed and disgraced parent who casts a shadow on Emma's alleged origin, as well as on her future:[1]

> The adult perpetrators stand in actual, *presumed*, or substitute close familial relationship to the child. *[emphasis added]* . . . The neo-Victorian abused child, then, is shadowed by guilt: both social guilt as producer and product of the "family crisis." (Kohlke, Gutleben, 141)

When Emma visits Eliza Brown in the Newgate prison, she is terrified by her appearance and behavior. The depiction of Eliza Brown in Boylan's work can be dialogically likened to that of Bertha Mason in *Jane Eyre*—she is a furious and beastly creature deprived of humanity, raging behind the prison bars:

> "Mother?" she [Emma] whispered nervously. The creature snarled. Like a wild beast she seized and tried to shake the bars that divided them. . . . The woman pushed her face close to the bars. Emma's eyes had adjusted to the dark and she could see her now, a grim vision animated only by hate. A dull glitter entered her eyes and twisted her mouth to a semblance of a smile. . . . She began to laugh. It was an inhuman cackle rising in pitch until it terrified Emma and she got up and ran away. (295)

The "inhuman" laughter of Emma's assumed mother dialogically connotes that of Bertha Mason's in *Jane Eyre*. However, the vicious giggle not only expresses madness (as in the case of Bertha), but also refers to the past filled with outrageous crimes. While Bertha Mason is a grim but still fascinating character, Eliza Brown is an appalling figure, terrifying the reader with her crudeness and cruelty. Hence, even the doppelgänger of Bertha, re-created in the pages of Boylan's novel, is incomparably bleaker than the figure portrayed in Brontë's *Jane Eyre*.

On her visit to the Newgate prison, Emma learns that Eliza Brown is not her mother but a villain who sold her. Yet, she remains disconsolate since the only presumably reliable connection to her past faded away:

> She [Emma] came presently to a handsome shopping street in Cheapside and pretended to admire the window of linen draper while she stilled her hammering heart. The merchant's glass threw back a blanched and featureless reflection. "Who am I?" she asked this pallid spectre. She must be relieved. Of course she must. Not to have issued from that perversion of her sex [Eliza Brown] could not be other than a blessing. Yet she found herself, lost and shuddering, in a state of the most intolerable distress. That slender thread—however tainted—which

connected her to the earth had been severed. Her guiding star gave one last flicker and expired. She was nothing. (297)

Heilmann and Llewellyn aptly observe that "the mother and the maternal home, acting as they do as sites of both alienation and ultimate reconciliation, constitute central metaphor of the legacy of Victorianism in neo-Victorian fiction" (65). In Emma's life, the mother figure signifies absence and desperate longing for reconciliation, which constantly influences the heroine's decisions and propels the plot of the novel. When reminded that "Eliza Brown brought no honour to her name," Emma explains that "it was she who sent [me] in pursuit of [myself]" (432). Ultimately, on the final discovery that Emma descends from a respectable family, she renounces her true surname—"Osborne"—and, instead, chooses "the freedom of being a nobody" (432), which confirms that neo-Victorian characters, such as Emma Brown and Jenny Drew, actively participate in the process of self-creation, paradoxically profiting from the "freedom" of uprootedness. "The freedom of being nobody" turns into a unique, although primarily harsh experience of creating the (gradually) re-narrated "self." Moreover, such peculiar freedom carries numerous possibilities of "re-narrating" Emma as a symbolic figure who epitomizes the notion of the multifaceted neo-Victorian child. Kohlke and Gutleben argue in the same vein:

> Neo-Victorian children become whatever protean symbols we, as adult interpreters, want them to be, signifying family breakdown or familial transformation and reconstruction, the inescapability of ubiquitous trauma or the consolation of human endurance in adversity, the betrayed promise of one-time futures or the redemption of our own inner child, the catalyst of (catastrophic) change or suspension in a perpetual golden age, the voyeuristic thrill of symbolic re-violation or the opportunity for cross-generational reconciliation, purveyors of symbolic justice or the materialization (and means of indulging in) our own worst nightmares. (145)

In Boylan's novel, when transformed from the pretentious Matilda Fitzgibbon into the simple Emma (another assumed but, importantly, *self-assumed* personality), the eponymous heroine reshapes into a "self-made" young woman who begins to successfully use her voice in self-defense, finding an occupation and taking care of little Jenny:

> [t]he notion now and then passed through her mind that she had found sufficient activity and purpose for her life. By her own resources she was making a living and she was caring for someone. Far better to earn a menial livelihood than to be a precarious and vulnerable thing, forever ashamed of what one was or was

not. No one questioned her about her class or her past. She was self-reliant and appreciated for her labour. (348)

The above-quoted passage positions Emma as an almost modern individual—she is anonymous in the public space: there are no questions regarding her ancestry and she is valued for the quality of her work. The experience of uprootedness endows Emma with extraordinary strength and wisdom. She is "no more the forlorn waif who sat in a corner of [Mrs Chalfont's] drawing-room and could not open her mouth for terror, no more the embattled adolescent" (433). She even embarks on "excursions":

> At sixpence a mile it was a costly indulgence but she loved to sit on the open deck where, in fine neighbourhoods, the branches of trees brushed her face with blossom. She shared her transport with people of many nationalities gathered in the capital for a great event. (349)

Emma's "indulgence" in the company of "many nationalities" shapes the textual world as a semi-modern global village, where the heroine is one of the many self-made, accomplished and intensely uprooted and lonely individuals. On the one hand, being self-made and uprooted turns the character into a strong, resolute, and self-sufficient figure but, on the other hand, it deprives Emma of her "own place" in the world filled with anonymous passersby.

Initially muted and uncommunicative, Emma turns into a character eagerly arguing her case and consciously setting her goal: "I am on a quest to restore my honour and if honour there be none, then I shall be penitent and endeavour to improve," states Emma (323). Hence, Emma's harrowing childhood experience allows her to grow as an individual, even though

> in the main, traumatic childhoods serve to foreshadow protagonists' later suffering and explain, if not necessarily vindicate, their subsequent often violent or criminal actions—whether as children or adults—as a form of retaliation or symbolic justice not otherwise attainable. (Kohlke and Gutleben, 121)

While concentrating on the development of the female protagonist and her gradual escape from the violent childhood into a successful adult life, Boylan's novel preserves the pattern of the Victorian *Bildungsroman*. Most importantly, in *Emma Brown*, the heroine's "growth" does not lead to an inevitable "regression" (Kohlke, Gutleben, 124) but, instead, realizes the more traditional Victorian pattern of a successful journey from adolescence to young adulthood. Yet, as already indicated, Boylan's vision of Emma's trials and tribulations is appalling and painfully sincere at every step; thus, entirely robbed of "magic" from *Jane Eyre*.

As Kohlke states, "neo-Victorian childhoods are not to be enjoyed but endured" (Kohlke, Gutleben, 121). One of the most terrifying visions offered in Boylan's novel is the one of the dead child held by Jenny Drew—the scene not only depicts the nineteenth-century nightmare of juvenile homelessness, but also offers an intertextual reference to Jane Eyre's doll which becomes a substitute for someone to love. In Boylan's novel, Jenny appears to be even more uprooted than Emma, since she cannot refer to or identify with anybody apart from the dead child. It is Emma who acts as Jenny's mother and sister, although she cannot identify with the adult world either. "The mother is . . . of crucial importance to the neo-Victorian genre," Heilmann and Llewellyn posit,

> She is frequently complemented by a sister figure: here, the mother (or mother-and-sister pair) is the mark of trauma, literally represented as the *Urtext* which, if recovered and read correctly, is able to furnish a resolution to the protagonist's predicament. (65)

In contrast to *Emma Brown*, in Brontë's novel, the doll provides Jane with a substitute for human affection:

> I then sat with my doll on my knee, till the fire got low, glancing round occasionally to make sure that nothing worse than myself haunted the shadowy room; and when the embers sank to a dull red, I undressed hastily, tugging at knots and strings as I best might, and sought shelter from cold and darkness in my crib. To this crib I always took my doll; human beings must love something. (31)

Brontë's Jane Eyre seeks protection from the coldness of her crib. The feeling of coldness and darkness is intensified in Boylan's portrayal of the nineteenth-century London by night. There is no place for imagination and daydreaming in *Emma Brown*, since "reality" appears obscure and terrifying. Importantly, the world remains hostile until the victorious moment when Emma retrieves her lost origin and finds her place in a loving adoptive family. Paradoxically, Emma's adoptive family provides the perfect example of the neo-Victorian, coincidental arrangement: it consists of the widowed Mrs. Chalfont, her friend Mr. Ellin, and Jenny Drew as Emma's new sister. Thus, it is the family brought together through traumatic experiences rather than through the ties of blood. At the same time, the reader is reminded that Emma, the neo-Victorian heroine, "will never belong to anyone but herself" (431).

Similarly to Boylan's *Emma Brown*, in Rhys's *Wide Sargasso Sea*, Antoinette is deprived of her name and origin. Antoinette fights for her name but, in contrast to Emma, inevitably loses the battle. The name assigned to her by Rochester—Bertha—does not bring with itself the creative strength, as it did in Emma's case. Unlike Emma, Antoinette is not able to "rise from the ashes" and re-narrate her assumed name—"Bertha"—into a vital energy.

"My name is not Bertha; why do you call me Bertha?," inquires Antoinette (86). "Because it is a name I'm particularly fond of," responds Rochester, thus depriving his wife of her very "self" and treating her like an object (86). Deprived of her roots, her name, and her voice, Antoinette gradually becomes mad. The danger of mental illness running in Antoinette's family indicates that the heroine will share her mother's debilitating fate. Mental illness "repeats itself" in Antoinette's family and, in neo-Victorian texts, the "threat of repetition" is serious enough to irreversibly influence the character's future life (Heilmann, Llewellyn, 44). Antoinette gradually reshapes into a different being and, finally, it is only the red dress that reminds her of the person that she was before.

In chapter 26 of *Jane Eyre* the reader gets acquainted with a mysterious document which states:

> I can affirm and prove that on the 20th of October, A.D. . . . Edward Fairfax Rochester, of Thornfield Hall . . . was married to my sister, Bertha Antoinetta Mason, daughter of Jonas Mason, merchant, and of Antoinetta his wife, a Creole — at — church, Spanish Town, Jamaica. . . . Signed, Richard Mason. (358)

The information attesting to Rochester's marriage to "Bertha Antoinetta Mason" provides yet another central point for the intertextual dialogue between Brontë's and Rhys's texts. Rhys aptly uses the information from Brontë's novel, incorporating into the plot of *Wide Sargasso Sea* Bertha's second name—Antoinetta (and reshaping it into "Antoinette"). This intertextual shift allows Rhys to explicate how Rochester destroyed and warped the true image of the sensitive and delicate woman, molding her into the "madwoman in the attic."

In *Wide Sargasso Sea*, Rochester tries to silence Antoinette and turn her into a dehumanized being. In *Jane Eyre*, dehumanized and silenced Bertha cannot even stand for herself. Yet, Rochester himself has a lot to say about his muted and repressed wife:

> "Go," said Hope, "and live again in Europe: there it is not known what a sullied name you bear, nor what a filthy burden is bound to you. You may take the maniac with you to England; confine her with due attendance and precautions at Thornfield; then travel yourself to what clime you will, and form what new tie you like. That woman, who has so abused your long-suffering—so sullied your name; so outraged your honour; so blighted your youth—is not your wife; nor are you her husband." (381)

Interestingly enough, in *Jane Eyre*, Rochester never articulates the exact cause of disappointment in his wife. Additionally, he does not use his wife's name, calling her a "filthy burden" and "maniac" instead. In his tearful rhetoric, Rochester is apparently filled with self-pity, justifying the solution offered him by "Hope." It is only in Rhys's contemporary prequel to *Jane Eyre* that Antoinette is given the chance to contradict Rochester's accusations. Nonetheless, even though her enduring and powerful narrative is preserved, it is the only token attesting to the heroine's anterior presence. The deprivation of her name signifies Antoinette's impending death.

Essentially, Antoinette's gradual degradation—her vulnerability to manipulation—is the result not only of Rochester's cunning but also of the heroine's family background (or, rather, of its absence). Similarly to the eponymous protagonists of Brontë's *Jane Eyre* and Boylan's *Emma Brown*, Rhys's heroine faces the fundamental issue of domestic instability. Primarily, Antoinette's mother is mentally absent (although physically present) and this absence causes the heroine's inner anxiety: "as Setterfield puts it, 'it is dysfunction that makes a story'" (Heilmann and Llewellyn, 65). "Dysfunction," Heilmann and Llewellyn argue, "is richly illustrated in Victorian fiction, which revolves around flawed, fractured, dissolving, newly emerging (usually no less dysphoric) families: *Wuthering Heights*, *Jane Eyre*, *Great Expectations*, *The Woman in White*, *The Turn of the Screw*" (65). This pattern is intertextually revisited and strengthened in neo-Victorian novels, *Wide Sargasso Sea* included: Antoinette's mother, Annette, is "the widow of a slave-owner" and "the daughter of a slave-owner" (14). Her bleak, slavery-related background directly influences her daughter's life. Consequently, Antoinette becomes an outsider and outcast in the community mistreated by her family in the past. Gradually, Antoinette becomes an outcast in her mother's eyes as well. The mental illness, severely enhanced by the fire in Coulibri, leads to the separation between the mother and her daughter:

> A coloured man, a coloured woman, and a white woman sitting with her head bent so low that I couldn't see her face. But I recognized her hair, one plait much shorter than the other. And her dress. I put my arms round her and kissed her. She held me so tightly that I couldn't breathe and I thought, "It's not her." Then, "It must be her." She looked at the door, then at me, then at the door again. . . . "But I am here, I am here," I said, and she said, "No" quietly. Then "No no no" very loudly and flung me from her. I fell against the partition and hurt myself. (26)

While Antoinette loses her mother, she gains a faithful friend in Christophine, who serves as the substitute for motherly affection. It is also Christophine who tries to reconcile Antoinette with her husband and, furthermore, it is the resolute Christophine who warns her ward against Rochester:

> Christophine was saying, " . . . Have spunks and do the battle for yourself. Speak to your husband calm and cool, tell him about your mother and all what happened at Coulibri and why she get sick and what they do to her. Don't bawl at the man and don't make crazy faces. Don't cry, either. Crying no good with him. Speak nice and make him understand." (72)

Christophine acts as a fairy godmother, accompanying Antoinette through her darkest moments and even offering her a love potion meant to restore her husband's affection. She is a stunningly complex figure, suspended between benevolence and obscurity: a practitioner of obeah magic and an almost modern advocate of womanly self-worth. As a symbolic figure, Christophine epitomizes reconciliation with her racial identity and with the world in which she has to live. Yet, she is an unsuccessful fairy godmother: the love potion appears ineffective, and Rochester is too cunning and unfeeling to be influenced by her "magic." The passage below illustrates Rochester's attitude toward Christophine:

> Of course I laugh at you—you ridiculous old woman. I don't mean to discuss my affairs with you any longer. Or your mistress. I've listened to all you had to say and I don't believe you. Now, say good-bye to Antoinette, then go. You are to blame for all that has happened here, so don't come back. (103)

Separating Christophine from Antoinette, Rochester isolates her from the last bastion of reason, which finds direct expression in her physical imprisonment in the English mansion.

Drawing on the intertextual dialogue between Rhys's and Brontë's novels, it is essential to emphasize that in *Jane Eyre* Bertha Mason is also displaced from filial affection. Apart from Mr. Mason, Bertha's brother, and Mr. Briggs, his representative, there is nobody to claim Bertha. While her filial bonds are not even sketched out within the novel (apart from her affiliation to Mr. Mason), it is difficult for the reader to envision her as a character with a rich inner life. There is no family to uplift her from this degeneration apart from the warden, Grace Poole. Consequently, Poole fulfills two contrasting roles in Bertha's life: the one of a caretaker and that of a stern supervisor. It is impossible to perceive Grace Poole as a motherly figure, even though she dutifully performs her role. She is a warden on her duty—the one who limits Bertha's world while keeping her within the four walls of the attic.

On the other hand, Jane's motherless state in Brontë's novel not only leaves her estranged, but also opens up the new possibilities of self-discovery. After leaving Thornfield Hall, she declares in her conversation with St John: "Not a tie links me to any living thing: not a claim do I possess to admittance under any roof in England" (427). At the beginning of Brontë's novel, Jane spends her childhood in the house of her unloving aunt, Mrs. Reed. However, there is also Bessy—a background "fairy godmother" in Mrs. Reed's house who supports Jane before the mature quest begins. Bessy, the nursemaid, can be dialogically linked to Christophine in her unceasing support:

> Long did the hours seem while I waited the departure of the company, and listened for the sound of Bessie's step on the stairs: sometimes she would come up in the interval to seek her thimble or her scissors, or perhaps to bring me something by way of supper—a bun or a cheesecake—then she would sit on the bed while I ate it, and when I had finished, she would tuck the clothes round me, and twice she kissed me, and said, "Good-night, Miss Jane." When thus gentle, Bessie seemed to me the best, prettiest, kindest being in the world. (32)

Just like Christophine, Bessie is never obtrusive, yet always nearby, like a true friend. Antoinette's and Jane's "fairy godmothers" provide the heroines with motherly affection which they lack, thus compensating for the void in their emotional lives. The dialogical correspondence between such figures as Christophine and Bessie is striking, testifying to the fact that Victorian and neo-Victorian texts host characters who try to compensate for the symbolic absence of the motherly figure. The dialogical model of analysis allows one for a better understanding of the Victorian and modern problematic in a broader context in which the patterns of characters' lives (Antoinette, Bertha) and roles (Christophine, Bessie) are replicated and revisited.

As remarked by Mary E. Bellanca, "The dialogical model continues valuable in the poststructuralist environment precisely because it desires that we keep talking, listening, questioning and responding" (61). "The dialogical model" inevitably involves the reader's active engagement in the reading and "revisioning" of texts. Thus, Rhys's vision of Antoinette as a sensitive and emotionally exhausted woman impels the reader to make a revision of Charlotte Brontë's text and reread Rochester's narrative in a new light. On the other hand, while reading Clare Boylan's *Emma Brown*, one revisits Jane Eyre's story from a new, painfully striking angle. Openly revealing her misery, uprootedness, and suicidal attempt, Emma contradicts and abolishes the romantic bildungsroman myth founded on Jane Eyre's story.

On the whole, the dialogical analysis of the status of women in Victorian and neo-Victorian texts provides a multilayered commentary on femininity. Once deprived of their social status, name and voice, neo-Victorian women create their own narratives and embark on the quest to rediscover their past.

The intertextual perspective on Bertha Mason from *Jane Eyre* and Antoinette from *Wide Sargasso Sea* readily responds to the general (mis) conception of madness. Both Bertha and Antoinette highlight the "thematic" aspect of the character—the female struggle with a supposed mental incapacity as defined by nineteenth-century men. Bertha's case illustrates the nineteenth-century perception of a mental illness, which is shown as a degrading, dehumanizing, and terrifying state. In contrast, in Rhys' novel, Antoinette figures as a noble and vulnerable individual who is harassed by her husband due to her presupposed lunacy which runs in the family. What obviously is Rochester's fault (his betrayal, cruelty, and lack of affection toward his wife) is reassigned to Antoinette under false pretenses of her hereditary "malady." In fact, Antoinette's "mental fall" is the consequence of her treatment by Rochester. Importantly, both Rochester and Antoinette are allowed to narrate their perspectives, which enables the reader to make a critical judgement of both characters.

Whereas in *Wide Sargasso Sea* the "thematic" aspect of madness is revisited through the character of Antoinette, there are also other crucial issues concerning Rhys's heroine, including the themes of "uprootedness" and forced "remoulding" of her identity. In Brontë's *Jane Eyre*, Bertha's "uprootedness" remains unquestioned. Like Bertha, Jane Eyre is also deprived of her roots, yet she does not fall prey to "madness" since she challenges Rochester with her unwavering virtue. Jane's virtuous conduct toward Rochester (in contrast to his previous mistresses) allows her to preserve personal integrity, which, in turn, eliminates the threat of insanity. In *Emma Brown*, virtuous behavior and untiring work allow Boylan's heroine to divert from the path of possible madness as well. Emma consciously gives up on her past and personal history in order to start her life anew and create her own "roots."

On the whole, Brontë's, Rhys's, and Boylan's texts remain in an intertextual exchange of perspectives on female madness, identity, and voice. The quest for the lost identity symbolizes, in a broader context, the task of neo-Victorian fiction: the reconstruction and re-narration of the literary past consisting of numerous narratives and stories. Such reconstruction offers a fresh outlook on the present as well.

In recognizing the value of literary revisions, one begins to recognize the importance of offering the voice to those characters who have been previously omitted or marginalized, such as Bertha Mason in *Jane Eyre*. In effect, the novel—as the only dialogical literary genre (*sensu* Bakhtin)—responds with a "timeless," constructive self-criticism. Finally, the significance of possessing one's unique voice can be encapsulated in Mrs. Chalfont's assertion in *Emma Brown*: "I must afford her [Emma] that greatest luxury known to human relations: I must listen to her" (413).

NOTES

1. In numerous Victorian novels, such as Charles Dickens's *Little Dorrit* (1857) and *Great Expectations* (1861), low or degrading filial bonds painfully shatter the characters' "great prospects." For instance, Charles Dickens's Pip in *Great Expectations* is utterly disconsolate on learning that he owes his gentlemanliness to Abel Magwitch, a convict. What is worse, Magwitch turns out to be Estella's father, hence the union between Pip and Estella appears hopeless and disgraceful. Pip, himself, cannot boast the longed-for upper-class heritage. On the other hand, in Boylan's *Emma Brown*, the assumed humiliating origins of the heroine are not only the reason for repentance, but also (and primarily)—turn out to be the source of unbending strength. Neo-Victorian characters are "self-made," hence they do not rely on affluent benefactors as much as on their own assertiveness and righteousness.

Chapter Seventeen

Neo-Victorian Biofiction

Syrie James's The Secret Diaries of Charlotte Brontë *and the Biography Retold*

Syrie James's *The Secret Diaries of Charlotte Brontë* (2009) belongs to the genre of neo-Victorian biofiction: a biography presented as a fictional story.[1] In James's work, Charlotte Brontë appears as the protagonist of "her own" diary. Thus, turning Charlotte Brontë into the narrator of her own life, *The Secret Diaries* emphasize the "mimetic" aspect of the character (*sensu* Phelan). Whereas in the previous sections of this book neo-Victorian women characters are fictitious creations, the present chapter offers the analysis of the character who is a historical figure and a writer herself. "Contemporary biofictional representations of famous public figures, as any biographical undertaking, can variously be located between the two poles of hagiography and demythologisation," Julia Novak and Sandra Mayer observe:

> The frequently proclaimed "rebirth of the author"[2] has given rise to fictional re-writings of authors' lives in the past thirty years, which testify to an on-going fascination with authorship. . . . This growing preoccupation with authorship primarily hinges on a view of the author as an extension of his/her text. . . . Most precisely, as Wenche Ommundsen argues, readers' obsession with the author can be attributed to their desire for both identification and possession and their fascination with the "paradoxical relationship between the mundane reality of the living (or once living) writer and her/his ghostly (but no less real) reality" as an "appendage to a body writing" (Ommundsen 2004:56). (25–26)

Currently, the neo-Victorian fictional biography turns into a literary "afterlife" of the author, with the emphasis on the *self* as an indispensable step toward the understanding of the historical past. To re-narrate Brontë's life,

Syrie James's novel draws on the previous biographical sources dedicated to Brontë, as well as on the literary themes borrowed from her original texts, including *Jane Eyre* (1847) and *Shirley* (1849). James's work provides a "patchwork" of information concerning Brontë's life and, in effect, it offers a fictional portrait of the writer.

Based on Mikhail M. Bakhtin's theory of dialogism, this chapter analyzes the relation between James's novel and the two biographical works dedicated to Brontë's life, written by Elizabeth Gaskell and Winifred Gérin. In the introduction to Elizabeth Gaskell's biographical work, *The Life of Charlotte Brontë* (1857), Clement Shorter argues that Gaskell's work represents "one of the best biographies in the English language" (v). The success of Gaskell's work was rooted in the long-term friendship with Charlotte Brontë. It easily merged biographical elements from Brontë's life with fictional events. As put by Shorter, "the book lost nothing . . . from the element of romance" and from "the power of heightening colours which a writer of fiction was able to provide" (v). Hence, the fictional framework enclosing Brontë's biography resulted in high popularity of Gaskell's work. As a novelist, Gaskell reshaped Charlotte Brontë into a literary character whose life was staged in twenty-eight dramatic and highly engaging chapters. In contrast, Winifred Gérin's biography, *Charlotte Brontë: the Evolution of Genius* (1967) is a detailed, comprehensive source of information concerning Charlotte Brontë's artistic and personal life, drawing on numerous original sources from Brontë's times. However, contrary to Gaskell's text, it cannot be read as a "story."

Hence, the secret of popularity with the readers appears to lie in the structuring of a given biographical work: on the one hand, in Gaskell's case, the reader is faced with a semi-novelistic tale. On the other hand, in Gérin's work, the reader is offered exhaustive, elaborate, yet highly interesting data concerning Charlotte Brontë's life. However, neither Gaskell's nor Gérin's biographical texts can be treated as the "ultimate" source of information (in the Bakhtinian sense) concerning Brontë's life. While both Gaskell's and Gérin's works deal with the same topic, each biography concentrates on a different aspect of Brontë's life. Consequently, the biography as a genre can be treated merely as an interpretation of one's life, consisting of selected "facts" and events rather than of the "truthful" textual account of one's past. For example, Gaskell's vision of Charlotte Brontë's life can be defined as "romantic" and Gérin's viewpoint, offered over one hundred years later, appears more "scholarly." In both cases, the biographer's intention richly contributes to the overall picture drawn in the text.

What makes the Victorian past so appealing to the modern reader is its inaccessibility: it is the mythical arcana surrounding the nineteenth-century, "removed from the sphere of contact" that inexhaustibly attract writers to rediscover the bygone and redefine it in narrative terms (*Dialogic*

Imagination, 20). Published in 2009, Syrie James's *The Secret Diaries of Charlotte Brontë* enables a literary revision of the previously compiled biographies. It is a contemporary attempt at retelling Charlotte Brontë's life, thus approximating it to the modern reader's zone. As explicated by the authoress of *The Secret Diaries*,

> the novel is based almost entirely on fact. All the details of Charlotte's family life, her experiences at school, her friendship with Ellen, her feelings for Monsieur Héger, the evolution of her writing career, and her relationship with her publisher, George Smith, are all true and based on information from her [Charlotte's] letters and biographies. (James, 458)

James structures Brontë's biography as a novel which, using Bakhtin's term, remains "historically active," crossing the border between the past and the present and providing a rereading of the previously sanctioned biographical texts (*Dialogic Imagination*, 3). Consequently, James strives to depict Brontë as a figure attractive in the reader's eyes. Thus, she creates a literary vision of the nineteenth-century female writer who escapes from the constraints of Elizabeth Gaskell's "saintly heroine" and from Gérin's detailed analysis. Instead, James turns Charlotte Brontë into a passionate, realistic figure with whom the modern reader can identify. As postulated by Bakhtin, in the novel

> an individual cannot be completely incarnated into the flesh of existing socio-historical categories. There is no mere form that would be able to incarnate once and forever all of his human possibilities and needs, no form in which he could exhaust himself down to the last word, like the tragic or epic hero. (Bakhtin, *Dialogic Imagination*, 37)

Such an approach opens up inexhaustible possibilities of retelling the narratives from the past.

In James's text, Brontë's imperfections and inner struggles are gradually revealed to the reader. Thus, Charlotte (for she is no longer a distant "Brontë") abandons the role of an idealized, tragic heroine and, in the course of the plot, develops her "human possibilities and needs." This process of "familiarization" appears strategic for the idea underlying the novelistic genre. While the narrative offers the retelling of the past from a specific social and historical perspective, it simultaneously enables the reader to "accommodate" the past reflected in the text in the modern consciousness. Such "domestication" triggers the understanding of the past anew: while the vision of Brontë's life may appear unintelligible to some of the modern readers, the process of retelling enables the verification of the past.

Bakhtin argues that the "reality as we have it in the novel is only one of many possible realities; it is not inevitable, not arbitrary, it bears within itself other possibilities" (*Dialogic Imagination*, 37). Thus, Syrie James's narrative is a proposal—an endeavor to bring a possible version of the past closer to the reader. In contrast to the "arbitrary reader," the model reader[3] would recognize in James's text the "intertextual echoes" of the previous biographical sources dedicated to Brontë.

While discussing the process of reducing the distance between the reader's zone and Charlotte Brontë's life by means of the narrative mode of discourse, I propose to concentrate on a single (and singular) event from Brontë's early life, depicted in the three discussed texts. In January 1831 Charlotte began her career in the Roe Head School. In her biographical work, Elizabeth Gaskell portrays Charlotte's arrival at Roe Head in the following way:

> In January 1831 Charlotte was sent to school again. This time she went as a pupil to Miss W-, who lived at Roe Head, a cheerful roomy country house, standing a little apart in a field, on the right of the road from Leeds to Huddersfield. (75)

Characterizing Charlotte Brontë at an early stage of her life, Mrs. Gaskell refers to a letter from "Mary," whom she mysteriously describes as "one of these [Brontë's] early friends" (78). Due to the fact that many of Charlotte's contemporaries were the readers of Gaskell's work, the latter restrained herself from revealing too many facts, including Mary's precise identity. In her letter to Mrs. Gaskell, Mary states:

> I first saw her [Charlotte] coming out of a covered cart, in very old-fashioned clothes, and looking very cold and miserable. . . . When she appeared in the schoolroom, her dress was changed, but just as old. She looked a little old woman, so short-sighted that she always appeared to be seeking something. . . . She was very shy and nervous, and spoke with an Irish accent. . . . We thought her very ignorant, for she had never learnt grammar at all, and very little geography. (Gaskell, 78)

A similar account can be found in Gérin's subsequent work:

> Charlotte was told to prepare herself for departure in the New Year 1831. Pocahontas cannot have felt the severance from her kingdom to receive the culture of her conquerors more acutely than the young Charlotte at that transplantation from the "Burning Clime" to the salubrious situation of Roe Head, her new school. (54)

Relating the events connected with Brontë's departure to Roe Head, Syrie James intensifies the inner anguish of the young girl while introducing the narrative mode of discourse characteristic of the novel. Offering Charlotte the voice to narrate her own story in a language stylized on that used in Brontë's original texts, James creates an impression that it is the nineteenth-century writer speaking directly from the pages of her forgotten diary. In James's novel, Charlotte reminisces on her days in Roe Head during her travel by train. Miss Brontë suddenly perceives her own reflection in the window and it reminds her of being called "ugly" in the Roe Head School. A sudden rush of emotions encourages Charlotte to begin her narration which remains intertextually related to the already mentioned passages:

> It was a stark, grey day in early January 1831, when I first learned that I was to be sent away to Roe Head School. I was adamantly opposed to the idea of going to school at all—and no wonder. For years I had taken charge of my own studies, and worked at my own pace at home. . . . Far more grievous, however, were the harrowing memories of the last school I had attended when I was eight years old. (James, 57–58)

The passage delineates Brontë's feelings arising from the ghastly perspective of being sent away to school again. It is an endeavor to recreate Brontë's language and thoughts in a highly individualized manner. James introduces the memorable event from Brontë's life by means of a flashback. The reflection in the window brings the past "back to life": the narratives from the past are intertextually revisited, whereas the act of looking at the reflected "self" offers a new narrative shift—"plunging into" the narrative, the reader creates a bond of confidentiality with Charlotte Brontë as the heroine submerged in her intimate moment of reflection.

Read dialogically, James's excerpt allows one to approach Brontë's life from a different angle: the change of perspective from third- to first-person narration turns Brontë into a literary heroine with her ideology encapsulated in the language which she adopts: as argued by Bakhtin in "Discourse in the Novel," "the novelistic plot serves to represent speaking persons and their ideological worlds" (*Dialogic Imagination*, 365). Similarly, Allen observes that "Bakhtin speaks of characters as expressing an *idea* or 'world-view' and of the *image of voice* as associated with that character's consciousness" [emphasis added] (23). In the light of these arguments, literary characters are shaped by their utterances in the text and, consequently, these utterances highlight a unique consciousnesses of these characters.

When read in a dialogue with Gaskell's and Gérin's passages, James's excerpt complements the overall description of the event. Accordingly, it can be argued that from the Bakhtinian perspective of the "addressivity of texts,"[4] Gaskell's, Gérin's and James's accounts complement each other in a timeless dialogue of perspectives. Thus, they confirm the claim that "all discourses are interpretations of the world, responses to and calls to other discourses" (Allen, 23). In James's passage, Brontë's words written on the pages of the fictional diary serve as the "two-sided act" awaiting the reader's reaction (Morson and Emerson, 15). What follows, the "dialogic exchange" (Morson and Emerson, 14) between the discussed texts creates the "possibility of encompassing differences in a simultaneity" (Morson and Emerson, 9). Hence, when analyzed dialogically, the texts offer a new, wider interpretation. Such interpretation intrinsically depends on the reader's involvement. As Morson and Emerson argue,

> Bakhtin's dialogic model represents readers as shaping the utterance *as* it is being made. That is why utterances can belong to their speakers (or writers) only in the least interesting, purely psychological sense; but as meaningful communication, they always belong to (at least) two people, the speaker and his or her listener. . . . Voloshinov compares utterances ("the word") to a "bridge," which depends on both sides. "In point of fact, *the word is a two-sided act.* It is determined equally by *whose* word it is and *for whom* it is meant. As word, it is precisely *the product of the reciprocal relationship between speaker and listener, addresser and addressee.*" (129)

Hence, it is the interpretative role of the reader that deserves particular attention in decoding the text, as it is the reader who is capable of "receiving" the words of the author and confronting them dialogically with other sources.

While Elizabeth Gaskell's and Winifred Gérin's biographies follow chronological order, James's novel consists of flashbacks and memories interspersed among the pages of the fictional diary. Such a "patchwork" technique, characteristic of neo-Victorian fiction, allows James to create the notion of naturalness inherent in a diary. While both Gaskell and Gérin aptly present (in the third-person narration) the grief expressed by Charlotte on her arrival at Roe Head, James achieves the striking effect of immediacy by introducing the first-person narration.[5] James's work becomes persuasive, awakening in the reader the feeling of empathy, which is yet another undertaking of the neo-Victorian text. Charlotte Brontë is no longer a detached, historical figure from the past but, instead, as a "semi-fictional" figure, directly communicates her suffering, using emotional and suggestive language. Resultantly, the reader can sympathize with Charlotte and "share" her recollections. Moreover, while reading the first-person narration, the reader gains numerous additional information about Brontë's character. Importantly, these additional pieces of information are the ones chosen by the authoress of *The Secret Diaries*. For example, there are indicative statements revealing the fact that Brontë was a self-taught scholar ("For years I had taken charge of my own studies."). Brontë's secret diary shows her as an independent and reserved person who eagerly communicates through her writing.

Looking at her reflection in the window, Charlotte Brontë—the diarist—continues to recall the past:

> A hired gig being too dear, I was conveyed to my destination in the back of a slow-mowing covered cart. . . . I arrived stiff-legged, nauseous, and frozen, in the fading light of the wintry afternoon. (James, 39)

Such a depiction of the event, including the account of the heroine's sensations, presents Charlotte as an ordinary person who reveals her apprehensions and weaknesses on the pages of her diary. Paradoxically, the first-person, fictional narration appears more veritable when compared with Gaskell's account of Brontë's arrival at Roe Head. While Gaskell uses Mary Taylor's letter to acknowledge that Brontë arrived at Roe Head "cold and miserable," James enumerates Charlotte's immediate feelings, describing her as "stiff-legged," "nauseous," and "frozen." At the same time, while weaving her tale, James faithfully draws on the biographical sources and conscientiously refers to the details included in the previous biographies. For instance, she mentions after Gaskell the "covered cart" and relies firmly on other works while describing Charlotte's behavior on the first day in Roe Head. The influence of Elizabeth Gaskell on James's novel is conspicuous:

> As I was admitted to the oak-panelled entrance-hall . . . and gave my name and cloak to a waiting servant, I over-heard three girls (each dressed *á la mode* and stylishly coiffed) whispering about me in a nearby doorway—and my doubts and fears returned.
>
> "She looks so old and shriveled, like a little old woman," said the first girl.
>
> "Look at her hair, it is all a frizzle," whispered another.
>
> "Her dress is so old-fashioned!" cried a third, to which they all laughed.
>
> My face grew hot, and I wrapped my thin arms around me, as if that act could somehow shield from view the sight of my old, shabby, dark green stuff dress. (James, 60)
>
> With a sigh, I changed into my best Sunday frock—knowing full well that it would make no better impression than had the first, for it was just as plain, and equally as old. (James, 61)

In the above-presented excerpts, the reference to Mary Taylor's letter in which she compares Charlotte to a "little old woman" is discernible prima facie. Moreover, James stresses the issue of Brontë's financial situation, referring, after Gaskell, to Charlotte's worn-out clothes and modest means of transportation. Additionally, the passage reveals Charlotte's continuous sense of insecurity and dissatisfaction with herself—the theme highlighted throughout James's entire novel.

In James's passage, the suffering experienced by Miss Brontë at her arrival at Roe Head is univocal with Gérin's vision of the young Charlotte deprived of her safe environment. According to Gérin,

> [Charlotte's] desolation in that strange place, its distance from home and the endless stretch of months ahead before June brought the holidays and restored her there, was borne in upon her with so intolerable an anguish that she was literally struck down to the ground with grief. Ellen Nussey, just delivered into the Miss Woolers' hands . . . , stumbled upon her [Charlotte] . . . in what was to prove the most momentous encounter in her life. (61)

The scene depicting the beginning of the lifelong friendship between Charlotte Brontë and Ellen Nussey appears in *The Secret Diaries* as well:

> The sweetness and sympathy in her [Ellen's] voice had an immediate effect; I turned and looked at her fully for the first time. She was very pretty, with a pale complexion, docile brown eyes, and dark brown hair that fell in soft curls to just below her chin. (67)

While creating the fictional character of Charlotte Brontë who tells a "revised" story of her life, James remains cautious not to misrepresent the information provided by the previous biographical sources. The portrayal of Ellen Nussey in *The Secret Diaries* can be compared to that provided by Gérin: "Ellen's own nature, as the wide-apart sleepy eyes of her portrait as a girl reveal, was soft and docile" (62). Apparently, James draws on the vocabulary from Gérin's biography. Thus, she depicts Ellen as possessing "*docile* brown eyes." At the same time, the narrative, "told" by Charlotte herself gains irresistible attractiveness through the detailed descriptions allowing the reader to "submerge" in the story world.

The reader "enters" the fictional world and follows Charlotte on the pages of her lost diary. The possibility of "submersion in the text" distinguishes Syrie James's novel from earlier biographical works devoted to Charlotte Brontë: the reader, in the Bakhtinian sense, performs an active role of the sympathetic beholder "plunging" directly into the storyline. In *The Secret Dairies*, the authoress and the characters play an important part in the overall readerly experience: "simultaneity," Holquist highlights, "is found in the dialogue between an author, his characters and his audience, as well as in the dialogue of readers with the characters and their author" (67). The first-person narration and the reader's involvement in the reading process both define neo-Victorian texts in their orientation toward the empathetic reconstruction of the literary past.

In *The Secret Diaries*, the dialogue reaching "beyond" the text relies on the assumed discovery of Charlotte's fictional diary. The diary serves as a convincing tool for introducing the actual events from Brontë's life, as the idea of the lost and discovered personal notes appears quite veritable. Significantly, the imaginary context of the lost and found diary is also explicated in James's authorial, paratextual reference in the author's foreword (xv). It is the author's foreword that directly links the "textual world" with the reader's actual world and offers the "reading guidance."

The intertextual relation between James's text and Gaskell's and Gérin's biographies, manifested through numerous quotations, allusions, and textual calques, provides the key to the reading of James's work. Consequently, the reader acquainted with Gaskell's or Gérin's works discovers a meaningful dialogue and, thus, revisits the earlier works.

Essentially, "the history of the novel is for Bakhtin a grid that provides different reference points from which to chart a history of consciousness" (Morson and Emerson, 277). Hence, while reading Brontë's biographies combined together and treated as one dialogically constructed "unit," the reader is confronted with the texts offering different viewpoints on the same subject. These diverse perspectives, rooted in a specific sociocultural and historical background, provide the reader with the knowledge about the given epoch as well. For instance, Gaskell's tragic and often passive, romantic, and helpless heroine contrasts with James's literary creation of Charlotte, who appears self-aware and highly individualized, which reflects the modern preference for assertive and active characters. While passivity embodies the nineteenth-century ideal of womanhood, self-awareness becomes the celebrated, contemporary feature incorporated in James's revisionary biography. This seems to implement the idea that "the novel became . . . the most significant force at work in the history of consciousness" (Morson, Emerson, 276). Apparently, shifting consciousness mirrors the constantly changing portrayals of historical figures. Consequently, through their intertextual reading, the texts from different epochs enable one to "accommodate" the past in a broader context and retell the same story through the prism of current social norms, perspectives, expectations, and literary fashions.

As already mentioned, James's work combines Charlotte Brontë's literary texts with her private life. For example, the use of Charlotte's semi-original narrating style captivates the reader's attention and deludes one that it is Brontë's authentic voice speaking directly from the pages of the novel. James's text enters into a dialogue between the notions of "Charlotte Brontë as an individual" and "Charlotte Brontë as an artist inscribed in her own work of art." These two layers of representation merge into "Charlotte Brontë as a fictional character" who interacts with the reader in her diary. Writing about art and "lived experience," Holquist also combines these two notions, arguing that

> both art and lived experience are aspects of the same phenomenon, the heteroglossia of words, values and actions whose interaction makes dialogue the fundamental category of dialogism. For while art and life, when conceived as abstract topics in general, have no connections between them, in the experience of particular living subjects who consume works of art, who, as it were, "utter" them, there is a possibility of effecting exchange. Art and life are two different registers of dialogue that can be conceived only in dialogue. They are both forms of representation; therefore they are different aspects of the same imperative to mediate that defines all human experience. (109)

In Brontë's fictional (auto)biography, James not only emphasizes the dialogue between life and art, but also revisits the process of artistic creation while drawing on Brontë's novelistic themes. The incessant dialogue between James's text, Charlotte Brontë's literary creations, and the reader's reality evokes the notion of Nycz's intertextual relations involving the ones between texts and texts *versus* reality. The intertextual allusions to Brontë's works included in *The Secret Diaries* turn Charlotte into the heroine "from her own novels." For instance, in chapter 1, while reflecting on her future marriage and the inevitable abandonment of her career plans, Charlotte reveals the deep-rooted desire to meet her own "Mr Rochester":

> I have written about the joys of love. I have, in my secret heart, long dreamt of an intimate connection with a man; every Jane, I believe, deserves her Rochester—does she not? Yet I had long since given up all hope of that experience in my own life. Instead, I sought a career; and having found it, shall I—*must* I—now abandon it? Is it possible for a woman to give herself fully both to an occupation and a husband? (James, *The Secret Dairies*, 3)

Charlotte's confession—her hesitation between a career and husband—appears entirely modern. The theme of the female occupation originally appearing in Brontë's novels such as *Jane Eyre*, *Shirley*, and *Villette* becomes replaced with a straightforward career dilemma: James explores the conflict between Charlotte's love for Arthur Bell Nicholls and her writerly ambitions and it is the conflict explored in a highly "contemporary fashion," drawing on the modern clash between domestic bliss and career expectations. At the same time, the solitude pervading the fictional diary, so characteristic of Brontë herself, may dialogically respond to the contemporary "malady" of loneliness in the postmodern world.

Figure 17.1. *Rochester and Jane Eyre* by Frederick Walker, A.R.A. (1899) (Public Domain).

Yet, in *The Secret Diaries*, there is also a firm romantic overtone that shapes the entire text into a fabulous love story, similar to that portrayed in *Jane Eyre*. In the interview enclosed in the final part of the novel, James explicates her decision to introduce the romance at the core of the biographical plot: she "saw the missing link: the untold story of her [Charlotte's] relationship with Arthur Bell Nicholls" and she "knew that would make a fabulous story!" (457). The information provided by James in the interview, as well as in the author's afterword, creates another integral, authorial paratext, which offers directions for the intertextual decoding of the narrative. Placing a romantic quest at the center of her novel, James creates a universal framework of reference for the potential readers (including those unacquainted with Brontë's life). Hence, while introducing a love story, she draws on the notion of generic intertextuality and the idea of the "postmodern romance." Holquist investigates the universal theme of the quest for perennial love, relating it to the "quest for self"—the enterprise which defines the purpose of life and, while exposed on the pages of the novel, brings diverse readers together in the reading experience (178).

Interestingly enough, at first glance, Charlotte's wedding in *The Secret Diaries* closely resembles the nuptial scene from Brontë's *Jane Eyre*. The analogy between the fictionalized, yet biographical event and the imaginary depiction of Jane's wedding highlights the dialogical interaction between the two texts: *The Secret Diaries* turns into a "palimpsestuous" text portraying

Charlotte's life through the prism of her own literary works. It is an interesting shift of perspective, since Brontë wrote *Jane Eyre* (1847) before her marriage (1854) to Arthur Bell Nicholls. Hence, while writing *Jane Eyre*, Brontë could not draw on her wedding experience. Reversibly, *The Secret Diaries* build the overall idea of Charlotte's life using the events from her novels in order to re-narrate Charlotte's past by means of her own literary sources. It is as if Brontë's works "reconstructed" her figure on the pages of *The Secret Diaries*, thus "authoring" their authoress. In effect, biofiction emerges as a combination of historical narratives and fictional works.

As illustrated in the passages below, unlike in *Jane Eyre*, Charlotte Brontë's wedding in *The Secret Diaries* is not interrupted, yet both ceremonies (the fictional and the fictionalized ones) are equally quiet and modest, echoing Brontë's preference for self-effacement:

The Secret Diaries:

> As I had hoped, the church was nearly empty, the sole occupants of the seats in front being Mr. and Mrs. Grant. Reverend Sowden was waiting at the altar in his white surplice. Three other men stood nearby: the sexton, John Brown; a young pupil named John Robinson (whom, Arthur whispered, he had prevailed upon at the last moment to fetch the old parish clerk); and the clerk himself, Joseph Redman. . . . The whole proceeding was unreal to me, as if I were wrapped in the middle of a dream. (James, 401)

Jane Eyre:

> We entered the quiet and humble temple; the priest waited in his white surplice at the lowly altar; the clerk beside him. All was still: two shadows only moved in a remote corner. My conjecture had been correct: the strangers had slipped in before us, and they now stood by the vault of the Rochesters. (Brontë, 356)

The initial words uttered by the clergyman (derived from the Book of Common Prayers: "I require and charge you both as ye will answer at the dreadful day of judgment") are faithfully represented in both texts as well (Brontë, 356), (James, 401). At this point, in *The Secret Diaries*, the memory of Brontë's *Jane Eyre* directly enters the wedding scene:

> Upon hearing these words, I could not help but think of *my own Jane Eyre*, and the dire circumstances which had succeeded that proclamation at her wedding to Mr. Rochester. A side glance at Mr. Nicholls—whose twinkling eyes caught mine—insinuated that he was possessed by the same thought, and we shared a silent smile. Thankfully, there was no meddling Mr. Mason present on that

occasion to declare an impediment. All at once, I was required to slip off my glove and receive the thin gold wedding band which Mr. Nicholls slipped on my finger, to join my ring of pearls; then Mr. Sowden decried, "I now pronounce you man and wife. You may kiss the bride." [emphasis added] (James, 401)

In James's text, the shadow of the Byronic Rochester lingers in the temple where Charlotte's wedding takes place. It is as if Brontë's literary world overwhelmed her life when re-narrated by James. *The Secret Diaries* appear to be texts imposed on texts: Brontë's previous biographies and her novels constitute the dialogical layer on which James weaves her "biographical tale." The "mishmash" of perspectives and narratives offers the possibility of a unique rereading—not only of Brontë's biographies, but also of her own novels.

In chapter 18 of *The Secret Dairies*, Charlotte comments on the reviews which appeared after the publication of *Villette* (1853). She remarks that some critics concentrated on her personal life instead of focusing on her literary creation:

> The reviews for *Villette* came in. They were generally very favourable, except for a few harsh criticisms from people I had considered my *friends*; they seemed to be reviewing my life as they saw it reflected in the novel, rather than the novel itself. (354)

Neo-Victorian biofiction appears to be involved in a similar process of combining the private lives of writers with their works, thus revealing the dialogical potential of literature which crosses the borders between textual worlds and "realities." The dialogical potential of the novel as a genre, involving the borrowing from and revisioning of the previous sources and cultural perspectives, positions it as "a kind of epistemological outlaw, a Robin Hood of texts" (Morson and Emerson, 276). Consequently, the dialogical potential of the novel is capable of reshaping the nineteenth-century writers into the protagonists of modern texts. This revisionary process is especially interesting in the case of those writers who played a significant role in the shaping of the nineteenth-century literary consciousness.

In *The Secret Dairies*, Charlotte Brontë represents a very specific Victorian woman—the female writer—the heroine endowed with a creative potential. Yet, in James's text, Brontë ceases to be a celebrated literary genius and, stripped of a saintly reverence, turns into a vulnerable, deeply feeling, insecure, passionate and active woman who narrates her life in her secret diary. Charlotte's life, re-narrated from the modern angle, appears to be similar to that led by numerous contemporary women. The biofictional revision of Charlotte Brontë's life offers the readers an empathetic experience which seems indispensable for the fuller understanding and sustenance both of the literary past and the modern presence. After all, as indicated by Bakhtin, the "European novel prose is born and shaped in the process of a free . . . translation of others' works" (*Dialogic Imagination*, 378).

NOTES

1. A part of this chapter was published in *Beyond Words: Crossing Borders in English Studies* (Bleinert-Coyle, M., Choiński, M., Mazur, Z., eds., Cracow: Tertium, 2015, 347–58).

2. More information concerning the return of the author can be found in Eefje Claassen's *Author Representations in Literary Reading*, where she states that the author's "rebirth" triggers the questions of "authority" and "authenticity": "there is the question of *authority*. . . . In other words, is the author telling a story in which the presented events in the fictional world are authentic? Are these events related to the writer's experience? *Authenticity* seems to be measured by the attitude of the author to the narrator" (18). In *The Secret Diaries*, the authoress endows Charlotte Brontë with a "fictional voice" allowing her to narrate the actual events from her life (hence, the notion of *authority* is preserved as far as it concerns relating authentic events in the text).

3. In *the Role of the Reader: Explorations of the Semiotics of Texts* Umberto Eco defines the model reader as "supposedly able to deal interpretatively with the expressions in the same way as the author deals generatively with them. At the minimal level, every type of text explicitly selects a very general model of possible reader through the choice (i) of a specific linguistic code, (ii) of a certain literary style, and (iii) of specific specialization indices. . . . Other texts give explicit information about the sort of readers they presuppose. . . . Many texts make evident their Model Readers by implicitly presupposing a specific encyclopedic competence" (7).

4. According to Michael Holquist, "addressivity means rather that I am an event, the event of constantly responding to utterances from the different worlds I pass through. Addressivity implies not only that consciousness is always consciousness of something but that existence itself is always (and no more than) the existence of something" (47). "Bakhtin finds an answer in language's capacity to model addressivity and dialogue. He takes the implications of dialogue to their radical extreme and assumes that at no level where communication is possible is the subject ever isolated" (55).

5. In his *Narrative Discourse Revisited*, Gèrard Genette observes that the first-person narration entails "focalization through the narrator": "what we are obviously dealing with is the restricting of narrative information to the 'knowledge' of the narrator as such—that is, to the information the hero has at that moment in the story as *completed by his subsequent information*, the whole remaining at the disposal of the hero-become-narrator" (77). Michael Holquist, in *Dialogism: Bakhtin and his World*, approaches the issue of the first-person perspective from a dialogical viewpoint, introducing the notion of "sharing existence as an event": (28). Through the first-person narration, Charlotte Brontë (as a literary character) "shares" with

the reader those selected events that are essential for the construction of her overall, textually-represented "self." Such claim finds support in F. K. Stanzel's *A Theory of Narrative*, where the author argues that "the essence of the difference between first-person narration and third-person narration lies in the manner in which the narrator views the events of a story and in the kind of motivation for the selection of what is narrated. Everything that is narrated in the first-person form is somehow essentially relevant for the first-person narrator. For this existential relevance to the first-person narrator, there is no corresponding and similarly effective dimension of meaning in third-person narration. The narrative motivation of an authorial narrator is literary-aesthetic, but never existential" (98). Thus, Gaskell and Gérin's works rely on "literary-aesthetic" narration, while biofiction addresses existential issues. In *The Secret Diaries*, the first person narration is also complicated by the fact that Brontë figures as a "semi-fictional" character. Thus, the relevant events narrated by Brontë—as a character—in the first person are the events especially significant in Charlotte's "real" biography.

Epilogue

In his *Dialogism: Bakhtin and his World*, Holquist posits:

> Novels are overwhelmingly intertextual, constantly referring, within themselves, to other works outside them. Novels, in other words, obsessively quote other specific works in one form or another. In so doing, they manifest the most complex possibilities of the quasidirect speech. . . . But in addition, they simultaneously manifest intertextuality in their display of enormous variety of discourses used in different historical periods and by disparate social classes, and in the peculiarly charged effect such a display has on reading in specific social and historical situations. (85–86)

The intertextual character of novels enables them to act as the mouthpiece of the past while, at the same time, they are capable of creating new (never-ending) literary narratives. The intertextual nature of novels (and the specific example of neo-Victorian fiction) allowed for the creation of multifaceted concepts of literary womanhood. The "variety of discourses" offered by novels invariably attests to the fact that sociohistorical framework provides fertile ground for new literary revisions. In each literary revision, the current sociohistorical framework serves as the background for a dialogical exchange mirroring the concerns of the present day.

The dialogical exchange between texts allows for experiencing literature as a continuous flow of divergent discourses emerging and reshaping into new constructs. As a literary device, intertextuality offers common ground for bridging nineteenth-century literature with its modern, neo-Victorian counterpart. Women characters can also be perceived as such meaningful figures binding these two divergent literary worlds. Throughout the centuries, literary portrayals of women triggered dialogical exchange of narratives concerned with womanhood and society. In nineteenth-century fiction, the literary heroine not only appeared as an intricate and compelling figure, but also symbolized and portrayed Victorian society at large. Nowadays, neo-Victorian revisionary fiction allows for the revival of the Victorian woman character, scrutinizing her in a new, contemporary light. In my book I resorted to Phelan's terminology, which allowed me to study the selected female characters as synthetic, thematic, and mimetic types, thus focusing on different issues connected with nineteenth-century femininity. For instance, I treat Carriger's Alexia Tarabotti as a synthetic figure, since her blended features situate her between the nineteenth century and the modern literary world. Such positioning points to the specific structure of neo-Victorian novels which are suspended between the bygone and the present, dialogically drawing on both sources. Moreover, Alexia, as a synthetic (and, thus, "artificial") figure, offers an exaggerated and shrewd outlook on Victorian femininity as perceived from the twenty-first century standpoint. Therefore, not only does she offer an astute parody of the Victorian social world, but also focalizes the modern perception of the nineteenth-century reality.

On the other hand, the thematic aspect of such characters as Emma Brown or Antoinette Cosway paves the way for the better understanding of general issues connected with Victorian femininity. Emma and Antoinette embrace a universal problem of incapacitated Victorian women and their unrealised inner potential. Hence, their modern, literary voices serve as intertextual statements of those nineteenth-century women who could not speak for themselves. Importantly, Emma's *self-created* story has a happy ending that stresses the inner potential of the Victorian women [emphasis added].

The mimetic character of Charlotte Brontë in Syrie James's work adheres to the contemporary interest in the reviving of historical figures. In James's novel, Charlotte Brontë is presented in an empathetic way as a figure familiar to the reader—almost a friend—who narrates a "universal" story of ordinary joys, hopes, failures, and successes. As the mimetic figure, Brontë "approximates" her mental world to the reader's zone, thus demonstrating that emotional lives of nineteenth-century and modern women are universally connected.

As I argued in my book, the "revived" figure of the New Woman cannot be perceived as a "one-dimensional" creation. Instead, the neo-Victorian woman is endowed with numerous "faces" and purposes. This statement is especially evident in my analysis of the New Woman or, rather, the analysis of "New Women," since the concept itself developed into numerous literary narratives which, on the whole, led to the ultimate fictionalization of the New Woman herself.

In the nineteenth-century novel, women characters were often created with a view to embodying certain emblematic types, such as the well-known "angel in the house" model. Mental qualities of women were often undermined and defined in opposition to such superior, masculine features as: reason, individuality, independence or common sense. In contrast, the neo-Victorian literary woman successfully escapes such categorization, as she is not constructed in opposition to the man and, thus, escapes her nineteenth-century "obligation" to serve others and be defined against others. Gail Carriger's novel *Soulless* aptly defines the twenty-first-century New Woman as a self-aware figure deeply connected with her feminine side and yet rational, resourceful, and independent. Carriger's heroine no longer suffers the consequences of choosing between intelligence and womanliness—the problem which her nineteenth-century counterpart had to face in the detective fiction from the fin-de-siècle of the Victorian era. Alexia Tarabotti has an Italian surname which separates her from the textual Victorian world and accentuates her alleged "oddness." Yet, as I argued, neo-Victorian fiction reshapes "oddness" into a liberating experience, as in the case of Jean Rhys's *Wide Sargasso Sea*, where the supposedly insane prisoner in the attic turns out to be a sensitive young woman, Antoinette.

While neo-Victorian fiction concentrates on offering voices to previously unheard characters, it is also largely preoccupied with the issue of restoring lost identities. Such modern works as Rhys's *Wide Sargasso Sea* and Boylan's *Emma Brown* emphasize the interrelatedness between one's voice and identity. Both Antoinette and Emma, when deprived of their voices, are incapable of defining themselves. Their quest for identity is fully completed when their past is narrated (as in the case of Antoinette) and when their voice is restored (as in the case of Emma). In their self-defining quests, both Antoinette and Emma mirror the major concern of neo-Victorian fiction, which is the literary journey toward the re-narration and rediscovery of the novelistic genre itself. In this sense, neo-Victorian fiction can be perceived as a "patchwork" of discourses which are intertextually combined in a never-ending dialogue of perspectives. While revisionary fiction of the twentieth and the twenty-first century is primarily concerned with the "resurrection" of marginalized voices and obliterated identities, it also strongly mirrors the present day. Hence, the neo-Victorian literary world remains, to a large extent, unromantic and unsentimental, as in Boylan's *Emma Brown*, where the heroine's reality becomes entirely deprived of "Cinderella-like" dimension characteristic of *Jane Eyre*.

Yet, what figures in numerous neo-Victorian texts as an almost utopian, romantic, visionary representation of womanhood is the textual fashion. Neo-Victorian clothes no longer merely signify specific social standings of women or announce the newest trends of the season but, chiefly, serve as the repository of womanliness combined with a graceful practicality, which is especially recognisable in steampunk novels, including Carriger's *Soulless*. Moreover, neo-Victorian textual garments serve as the stronghold of one's individuality. Therefore, what connects neo-Victorian texts with such nineteenth-century creations as Wilkie Collins's *The Woman in White* is the desire to define oneself by means of attire. Yet, importantly, in *The Woman in White*, this attempt at "individualism" is reduced to insanity.

Apart from fictional characters, neo-Victorian texts host historical figures, often the well-known nineteenth-century authors themselves who are transformed into the heroes and heroines of revisionary narratives. Syrie James's *The Secret Diaries of Charlotte Brontë* testifies to the claim that there is a thin line between textual representations of an author and authorial fictional world: in James's biographical fiction, Charlotte Brontë is the narrator of her own life, which is retold almost from Jane Eyre's perspective. In order to complete her revisionary work, James draws on a number of biographical sources. The new narrative mode in James's work contributes to the novelty of the readerly experience. In this sense, James remains faithful to writerly ethics, presenting Charlotte Brontë from a new perspective, yet not distorting or warping her image.

As I argued before, the fundamental problem connected with neo-Victorian revision is an ethical approach to this issue. Whereas one may dispute over the inherent features of the literary New Woman, it is absolutely necessary to recognise that neo-Victorian writing invariably incorporates ethical engagement with the past. In this light, not every pastiche related to nineteenth-century fiction can be treated as a neo-Victorian revisionary text. Neo-Victorian texts find common ground with their nineteenth-century counterparts by means of an intertextual dialogue which highlights new perspectives of the past as well as new visions of the present. However, taking an ethical stance is invariably necessary while constructing new narrative possibilities.

As observed by Christian Gutleben, literary revisions of the nineteenth-century past are influenced by Victorian historical figures:

> Again and again, the contemporary novelists feel compelled to add forewords or afterwords where they confess to the works and writers which inspired them . . .: the sources of inspiration are systematically Victorian and the great figures of contemporary culture are remarkably and totally absent from these enthusiastic acknowledgments. (66)

This one-directional influence suggests that the literary past offers help in defining our current historical position. Moreover, the literary past is, in Bakhtinian terms, distinguished and dignified, since it is remote enough from our constantly undefined, fluctuating presentism. In this sense, the past appears to be a stable foundation for depicting our present. Without nineteenth-century narratives, the neo-Victorian heroine would be unknown.

Consequently, neo-Victorian women emerge as a subverted mirror reflection of their Victorian counterparts. Therefore, even though neo-Victorian heroines often provide a harsh criticism of the Victorian world, it must be acknowledged that without this previously created literary world, the current ethical awareness would not be expressed on the pages of revisionary works.

It also must be acknowledged that, whereas one-directional influence of the past in the creation of new narratives is invaluable, neo-Victorian fiction significantly shifts the perception of the literary past. For instance, Jean Rhys's *Wide Sargasso Sea* transforms the reader's perception of such characters as Bertha Mason from Brontë's *Jane Eyre* and places the previously romantic figure of Rochester in an awkward position of the one violating his wife's rights. Accordingly, the relation between Victorian and neo-Victorian texts is essentially bi-directional, with neo-Victorian texts encouraging the reader to ask questions about the previous works. It is the circulating exchange of Brontë's and Rhys' texts that influences the creation of new, multifaceted perspectives on such characters as Bertha or Rochester. The aim of this "circulating exchange" is not a clash of dialogical intentions but the act of unfolding of the text and its possibilities.

New meanings appearing in the process of the Victorian and neo-Victorian exchange are influenced by the cultural backgrounds of both the author and the reader. Bożena Kucała highlights that "the relations between a contemporary text and textually mediated Victorian world" are paramount in the process of an intertextual exchange (242). As she indicates, intertextuality serves a larger purpose of "making a statement about the past or present, or usually both at once" (243).

Yet, finally, as observed by Eco, there can be a discrepancy between "the author's intention and the intention of the text" (*Interpretation and Overinterpretation*, 70), as the times in which the work originated may differ from the current cultural understanding of "reality." For instance, portraying Bertha, Charlotte Brontë created a conventional character type endowed with the characteristics perceived as negative in the Victorian times. Currently, the reader's decoding of the same character differs, as the readerly interpretation is influenced by the modern socio-cultural context and by Jean Rhys' revisionary text. Eco argues that the text allows its reader for the creation of "infinite" interpretative "conjectures":

> The text's intention is not displayed by the textual surface. Or, if it is displayed, it is so in the sense of purloined letter. One has to decide to "see" it. Thus it is possible to speak of the text's intention only as the result of a conjecture on the part of the reader. . . . A text is a device conceived to in order to produce its model reader. . . . A text can foresee a model reader *entitled to try infinite conjectures*. [emphasis added] (Eco, 64)

Hence, the text comprises infinite possibilities of discourses. The reader and the author remain equally relevant in this creative process as their interpretative intentions add new qualities to the same work(s). Therefore, while remembering that "dialogism is a form of architectonics, the general science of ordering parts into a whole" and "architectonics is the science of relations" (Holquist, 28), we should treat Victorian and neo-Victorian works as equally important voices in an intertextual exchange. The Victorian past, securely locked within the pages of the Victorian novel, will always serve as the reference point to our current sociocultural and historical placement and, thus, cannot be forgotten: the Victorian novel shall never be closed—at least as long as we are here. Dear Reader, thank you for traveling through the pages of Victorian and neo-Victorian works with me.

Bibliography

Ackroyd, Peter. *Wilkie Collins.* London: Vintage Books. 2012.
Adams, James E. "'The boundaries of social intercourse': Class in the Victorian Novel." *A Concise Companion to the Victorian Novel.* O'Gorman, Francis, ed. Oxford: Wiley-Blackwell. 2004.
Allen, Graham. *Intertextuality.* London: Routledge. 2000.
Amigoni, David. *Victorian Literature.* Edinburgh: Edinburgh University Press. 2011.
Aster, Jane. *The Habits of Good Society: A Handbook For Ladies And Gentlemen.* Whitefish: Kessinger Publishing. 2007.
Azim, Fridous. *The Colonial Rise of the Novel.* London: Routledge. 1993.
Baker, William, and Womack, Kenneth, eds. *A Companion to the Victorian Novel.* London: Greenwood Press. 2002.
Bakhtin, Mikhail Mikhailovich. *Dialogic Imagination: Four Essays.* Ed. Michael Holquist. Austin: University of Texas Press. 2011.
Bakhtin, Mikhail Mikhailovich. *Problems of Dostoevsky's Poetics.* Ed. Caryl Emerson. Minneapolis: University of Minnesota Press. 1984.
Bakhtin, Mikhail Mikhailovich. *Rabelais and His World.* Trans. Hélène Iswolsky. Bloomington: Indiana University Press. 1984.
Barnes, James. *Aristotle: A Very Short Introduction.* Oxford: Oxford University Press. 2000.
Barthes, Roland. *The Fashion System.* Berkeley: University of California Press. 1967.
Bellenca, Mary E. "Alien Voices, Ancient Echoes: Bakhtin, Dialogism, and Pope's *Essay on Criticism.*" *Papers on Language and Literature* 30.1 (1994): 57–72.
Birch, Dinah, and Mark Llewellyn. *Conflict and Difference in Nineteenth-Century Literature.* Hampshire: Palgrave Macmillan. 2010.
Bloom, Harold, ed. *Bloom's Period Studies: The Victorian Novel.* New York: Chelsea House. 2004.
Bodenheimer, Rosemarie. *The Politics of Story in Victorian Social Fiction.* Ithaca, NY: Cornell University Press. 1988.
Boehm-Schnitker, and Susanne Nadine Gruss. "Introduction: Spectacles and Things—Visual and Material Culture and/in Neo-Victorianism." *Journal of Neo-Victorian Studies* 4:2 (2011).
Boylan, Clare. *Emma Brown.* London: Abacus. 2004.

Brantlinger, Patrick, and William B. Thesing, eds. *A Companion to the Victorian Novel.* Oxford: Blackwell Publishing. 2002.
Brontë, Anne. *The Tenant of the Wildfell Hall.* London: Guild Publishing. 1980.
Brontë, Charlotte. *Jane Eyre.* London: HarperCollins. 2010.
Brontë, Charlotte. *Shirley.* London: Wordsworth Classics. 2009.
Brontë, Charlotte. *Villette.* London: Wordsworth Classics. 1993.
Brown, Daniel S. "'The Autobiography . . . of a Neo-Victorian': Review of Philip Davis, *Why Victorian Literature Still Matters.*" *Journal of Neo-Victorian Studies* 2:1. 2008/2009.
Brownstein, Rachel M. *Becoming a Heroine: Reading about Women in Novels.* New York: Viking Press. 1982.
Bryson, Valerie. *Gender and the Politics of Time.* Bristol: The Policy Press. 2007.
Carlyle, Thomas. *Chartism.* London: James Fraser, Regent Street. 1840.
Carriger, Gail. *Soulless: An Alexia Tarabotti Novel.* London: Orbit. 2009.
Carter, Michael. *Fashion Classics from Carlyle to Barthes.* London: Bloomsbury Academic. 2003.
Clanton, Dan W. *The Good, the Bold and the Beautiful: The Story of Susanna and its Renaissance Interpretations.* New York: Bloomsbury. 2006.
Claassen, Eefje. *Author Representations in Literary Reading.* Amsterdam: John Benjamins Publishing Company. 2012.
Collins, Wilkie. *No Name.* London: Penguin Books. 1994.
Collins, Wilkie. *The Moonstone.* London: Collector's Library 2007.
Collins, Wilkie. *The Woman in White.* London: Penguin Books. 1994.
Cote, Rachel Vorona. *Too Much: How Victorian Constraints Still Bind Women Today.* London: Sphere. 2020. *Google Books.*
Davis, Fred. *Fashion, Culture, and Identity.* Chicago: University of Chicago Press. 1992.
Davies, Helen. *Gender and Ventriloquism in Victorian and Neo-Victorian Fiction: Passionate Puppets.* London: Palgrave Macmillan. 2012.
Deane, Bradely. *Masculinity and the New Imperialism: Rewriting Manhood in British Popular Literature. 1870–1914.* Cambridge: Cambridge University Press. 2014.
Dennis, Barbara. *The Victorian Novel.* New York: Cambridge University Press. 2000.
Dentith, Simon. *Bakhtinian Thought: An Introductory Reader.* London: Routledge. 1996.
Dundes, Alan, ed., *Cinderella. A Casebook.* Madison: University of Wisconsin Press. 1988.
Eco, Umberto. *Interpretation and Overinterpretation.* Stefan Collini, ed. Cambridge: Cambridge University Press. 1992.
Eco, Umberto. *The Role of the Reader: Explorations in the Semiotics of Texts.* Bloomington: Indiana University Press. 1979.
Edmundson, Mark. *Why Read?* New York: Bloomsbury Publishing. 2004.
Ermarth, Elizabeth D. *The English Novel in History: 1840–1895.* London: Routledge. 1997.
Eskin, Michael. *Ethics and Dialogue: In the Works of Levinas, Bakhtin, Mandel'shtam, and Celan.* Oxford: Oxford University Press. 2000.

Forster, Margaret. *Lady's Maid.* London: Vintage Books. 2005.
Frickey, Pierrette M. *Critical Perspectives on Jean Rhys.* Washington, DC: Three Continents Press. 1990.
Gage, John. *Color and Culture: Practice and Meaning from Antiquity to Abstraction.* Berkeley: University of California Press. 1993.
Gaskell, Elizabeth. *The Life of Charlotte Brontë.* London: Oxford University Press. 1961.
Gates, Barbara T. *Kindred Nature: Victorian and Edwardian Women Embrace the Living World.* Chicago: University of Chicago Press. 1998.
Genette, Gérard. *Narrative Discourse Revisited.* Jane E. Lewin, trans. Ithaca, NY: Cornell University Press. 1988.
Genette, Gérard. *Palimpsets.* Lincoln: University of Nebraska Press. 1997.
Genette, Gérard. *Paratexts: Tresholds of Interpretation.* Trans. Jane E. Lewin. Cambridge: Cambridge University Press. 1997.
Genette, Gérard. *The Architext.* Trans. Jane E. Lewin. Berkeley: University of California Press. 1992.
Gérin, Winifred. *Charlotte Brontë: the Evolution of Genius.* Oxford: Oxford University Press. 1967.
Gilbert, Sandra, and Susan Gubar. *The Madwoman in the Attic*: *The Woman Writer and the Nineteenth-Century Literary Imagination.* New Haven, CT: Yale University Press. 2000.
Gissing, George. *The Odd Women.* New York: New American Library. 1983.
Glimour, Robert. *The Idea of the Gentleman in the Victorian Novel.* New York: Routledge. 2016.
Głowiński, Michał. *Intertekstualność, groteska, parabola. Szkice ogólne i interpretacje.* TAiWPN Universitas: Kraków. 2000.
Golden, Catherine. *Images of the Women Reader in Victorian British and American Fiction.* Gainesville: University Press of Florida. 2003.
Goldthorpe, Caroline. *From Queen to Empress: Victorian Dress 1837–1877.* New York: Metropolitan Museum of Art. 1988.
Goodlad, Lauren M. E. *Victorian Literature and Victorian State: Character and Governance in a Liberal Society.* Baltimore: John Hopkins University Press. 2003.
Górski, Tomasz P. *Polskie przekłady "Hamleta" Williama Shakespeare'a: Analiza Intertekstualna.* Wrocław: Oddział PAN we Wrocławiu. 2013.
Grand, Sarah. "The New Aspect of the Woman Question." *North American Review,* vol. 158, no. 448, March 1894, pp. 270–76.
Greg, William R. *Why Are Women Redundant?.* London: N. Trübner & Co.. 1869.
Gromkowska-Melosik, Agnieszka. *Kobieta Epoki Wiktoriańskiej. Tożsamość, Ciało i Medykalizacja.* Kraków: Impuls. 2013.
Guerin, Wilfred L. *A Handbook of Critical Approaches to Literature.* Oxford: Oxford University Press. 2004.
Gutleben, Christian. "Hybridity as Oxymoron." *Hybridity: Forms and Figures in Literature and the Visual Arts.* V. Guignery, C. Pesso-Miquel, F. Specq, eds. Cambridge: Cambridge Scholars Publishing. 2011: 59–70.

Gutleben, Christian. *Nostalgic Postmodernism: The Victorian Tradition and the Contemporary British Novel*. Amsterdam: Editions Rodopi B.V.. 2001.
Haberer, Adolphe. "Intertextuality in Theory and Practice." *LiteratÛra* 49(5) 2007: 54–67.
Hadley, Louisa. "Feminine Endings: Neo-Victorian Transformations of the Victorian." *Victorian Transformations: Genre, Nationalism and Desire in Nineteenth-Century Literature*. Tredennick, Bianca, ed. Burlington, VT: Ashgate Publishing. 2011.
Hadley, Louisa. *Neo-Victorian Ficton and Historical Narrative: The Victorians and Us*. New York: Palgrave Macmillan. 2010.
Hansson, Heidi. *Romance Revived. Postmodern Romances and the Tradition*. Uppsala: Swedish Science. 1998.
Hardy, Barbara. *Forms of Feelings in Victorian Fiction*. London: Methuen. 1985.
Haweis, Mary Eliza. *The Art of Beauty*. London: Chatto & Windus, Piccadilly. 1883.
Heilmann, Ann. *New Woman Fiction: Women Writing First-Wave Feminism*. London: Macmillan. 2000.
Heilmann, Ann, Llewellyn, M. *Neo-Victorianism: The Victorians in the Twenty-First Century. 1999–2009*. London: Palgrave Macmillan. 2010.
Hoffman, Michael J., and Patrick D. Murphy, eds., *Essentials of the Theory of Fiction*. Durham, NC: Duke University Press. 2005.
Holquist, Michael. *Dialogism: Bakhtin and his World*. New York: Routledge. 1990.
Houghton, Walter E. *The Victorian Frame of Mind. 1830–1870*. New Haven, CT: Yale University Press. 1985.
Hutcheon, Linda. *A Theory of Adaptation*. Oxon: Routledge. 2013.
Hutcheon, Linda. *The Politics of Postmodernism*. London: Routledge. 2002.
Ibsen. Henrik. *A Doll's House*. New York: Dover Publications. 1992.
Jagoda, Patrick. "Clacking Control Societies: Steampunk, History, and the Difference Engine of Escape." *Journal of Neo-Victorian Studies* 3:1. (2010). 46–71.
James, Louis. *The Victorian Novel*. Oxford: Blackwell. 2006.
James, Syrie. *The Secret Diaries of Charlotte Brontë*. New York: HarperCollins. 2009.
Jeffreys, Sheila. *The Spinster and her Enemies: Feminism and Sexuality 1880–1930*. North Melbourne: Spinifex Press. 1997.
Jones, Jason B. *Lost Causes: Historical Consciousness in Victorian Literature*. Donald E. Hall, ed. Columbus: The Ohio State University Press. 2006.
Jowett, Benjamin, trans. *The Four Socratic Dialogues of Plato*. Oxford: Oxford University Press. 1924.
Joyce, Simon. *The Victorians in the Rearview Mirror*. Athens: Ohio University Press. 2007.
Juvan, Marko. *History and Poetics of Intertextuality*. West Lafayette, IN: Purdue University Press. 2008.
Kahn, Charles H. *Plato and the Socratic Dialogue*. Cambridge: Cambridge University Press. 1997.
Kaplan, Cora. *Victoriana: Histories, Fiction, Criticism*. New York: Columbia University Press. 2007.
King, Jeannette. *The Victorian Question in Contemporary Feminist Fiction*. London: Palgrave Macmillan. 2005.

Kinser, Samuel. "Saussure's Anagrams: Ideological Work." *Comparative Literature* 5:94. (1979).
Kirchknopf, Andrea. "(Re)Workings of Nineteenth-Century Fiction: Definitions, Terminology, Contexts." *Journal of Neo-Victorian Studies* 1:1. (Autumn 2008).
Knox, Marisa Palacios. *Victorian Women and Wayward Reading: Cries of Identification*. Cambridge: Cambridge University Press. 2021.
Kohlke, Marie-Luise, Gutleben, Ch. *Neo-Victorian Gothic: Horror, Violence and Degeneration in the Re-imagined Nineteenth-Century.* Amsterdam: Editions Rodopi B.V.. 2012.
Kohlke, Marie-Luise, Gutleben, Ch. *Neo-Victorian Families: Gender, Sexual and Cultural Politics.* Amsterdam: Editions Rodopi B.V.. 2011.
Kopaliński, Władysław. *Słownik Symboli.* Warszawa: Wiedza Powszechna. 1991.
Kristeva, Julia. *Desire in Language.* Ed. Leon S. Roudiez. New York: Columbia University. 1980.
Kucała, Bożena. *Intertextual Dialogue with the Victorian Past in the Contemporary Novel.* Peter Lang. 2012.
Langland, Elizabeth. *Nobody's Angels: Middle-Class Women and Domestic Ideology in Victorian Culture*. Ithaca, NY: Cornell University Press. 1995.
Leavis, Frank R. *A Study of the English Novel.* New York: Doubleday. 1954.
Ledger, Sally. *The New Woman: Fiction and Feminism at the Fin de Siècle.* Manchester: Manchester University Press. 1997.
Levy, Amy. *The Romance of a Shop.* Ontario: Broadview Press. 2006.
Lightman, Bernard, and Zon, Bennett. *Evolution and Victorian Culture.* Cambridge: Cambridge University Press. 2014.
Lisak, Agnieszka. *Życie Towarzyskie w XIX Wieku.* Warszawa: Bellona. 2013.
Llewellyn, Mark. "What is Neo-Victorian Studies?" *Journal of Neo-Victorian Studies* vol. 1, no. 1, Autumn 2008.
Logan, Deborah A. *Fallenness in Victorian Women's Writing; Marry, Stitch, Die, Or Do Worse.* London: University of Missouri Press. 1998.
Loughlin-Chow, Clare M. "The Sociological Contexts of Victorian Fiction." *A Companion to the Victorian Novel*. Baker, William, and Womack, Kenneth, eds. London: Greenwood Press. 2002.
MacDonald, Tara. *The New Man, Masculinity and Marriage in the Victorian Novel.* New York: Pickering & Chatto. 2015.
Madsen, Lea H. "*Remember . . . Whose Girl You Are*: Dynamics of Domination in Sarah Waters' *Affinity* (1999)." *International Journal of English Studies* 13.1 (2013): 149–62.
Marcus, Sharon. *Between Women: Friendship, Desire and Marriage in Victorian England.* Princeton, NJ: Princeton University Press. 2007.
Mariotti, Meg. *The Lady of Shalott: Pre-Raphaelite Attitudes Towards Woman in Society. Victorian Web.* www.victorianweb.org/painting/prb/mariotti12.html.
Matthews, Steven, ed., *Victorian Literature: A Sourcebook.* London: Palgrave. 2011.
McHale, Brian. *Postmodernist Fiction.* London: Routledge. 2004.
Mill, John Stuart. *On Liberty.* London: John W. Parker & Son, West Strand. 1859.

Mill, John Stuart. *The Subjection of Women*. London: Longmans, Green, Reader, and Dyer. 1869.
Mitchell, Kate. *History and Cultural Memory in in Neo-Victorian Fiction: Victorian Afterimages*. London: Palgrave Macmillan. 2010.
Mitchell, Sally. *Daily Life in Victorian England*. Westport, CT: Greenwood Press. 1996.
Moglen, Helene. *Charlotte Brontë: The Self Conceived*. London: University of Wisconsin Press. 1984.
Montz, Amy L. "'In Which Parasols Prove Useful': Neo-Victorian Rewriting of Victorian Materiality." *Journal of Neo-Victorian Studies* 4:1. (2011). 100–18.
Moore, Grace. *The Victorian Novel in Context*. London: Continuum. 2012.
Morgan, Simon. *A Victorian Woman's Place: Public Culture in the Nineteenth Century*. London: Tauris Academic Studies. 2007.
Morson, Gary S. and Caryl Emerson. *Mikhail Bakhtin: Creation of Prosaics*. Stanford, CA: Stanford University Press. 1990.
Nelson, Claudia. *Family Ties in Victorian England*. Westport, CT: Praeger. 2007.
Nelson, Elizabeth. "Tennyson and the Ladies of Shalott." *Ladies of Shalott: A Victorian Masterpiece and Its Contexts*, Providence, RI: Brown University Department of Art. 1985.
Nelson, James G. "The Victorian Social Problem Novel" in *A Companion to the Victorian Novel*. Baker, William, and Womack, Kenneth, eds. London: Greenwood Press. 2002.
Novak, Julia, Mayer, Sandra. "Disparate Images: Literary Heroism and the 'Works vs. Life' Topos in Contemporary Biofictions About Victorian Authors." *Journal of Neo-Victorian Studies* 7:1. 2014, 25–51.
Nycz, Ryszard. *Tekstowy Świat. Poststrukturalizm a wiedza o literaturze*. Warszawa: Instytut Badań Literackich. 1995.
O'Donnell, Kevin. *Postmodernism*. Oxford: Lion Publishing Plc. 2003.
O'Gorman, Francis. *A Concise Companion to the Victorian Novel*. Oxford: Wiley-Blackwell. 2004.
Oliver, Kelly, ed. *The Portable Kristeva*. New York: Columbia University Press. 2002.
Öztürk, Rita. *The Origin of Hardy's Tragic Vision*. Cambridge: Cambridge Scholars Publishing. 2013.
Owen, Alex. *The Darkened Room: Women, Power and Spiritualism in Late Victorian England*. Chicago: University of Chicago Press. 1989.
Patmore, Coventry. *The Angel in the House*. London: Macmillan & Co.. 1863.
Pearsall, Judy, Trumble, Bill, ed. *The Oxford English Reference Dictionary*. Oxford: Oxford University Press. 1996.
Perschon, M. (2009). "*Soulless* by Gail Carriger." (Blog) *Steampunk Scholar*. Available at: http://steampunkscholar.blogspot.com/.
Perrault, Charles. *Cinderella: Or, the Little Glass Slipper*. London: George Routledge and Sons. 1865.
Phegley, Jennifer. *Courtship and Marriage in Victorian England*. Santa Barbara, CA: Praeger. 2012.

Phelan, James. *Reading People, Reading Plots.* Chicago: University of Chicago Press. 1989.
Picard, Liza. *Victorian London: The Life of a City 1840–1870.* London: Phoenix. 2006.
Pinker, Steven. *The Blank Slate.* New York: Viking. 2002.
Pirgerou, Maria. *The Vicissitudes of Victorian Masculinity: The Case of the Bachelor.* Saarbrücken: Lambert Academic Publishing. 2014.
Purchase, Sean. *Key Concepts in Victorian Literature.* London: Palgrave Macmillan. 2006.
Pykett, Lyn. *The Sensation Novel: from "The Woman in White" to "The Moonstone."* Plymouth: Northcote House. 1994.
Quida. "The New Woman." *The North American Review*, vol. 158, no. 450, May 1894, 610–19.
Reed, John R. *Victorian Conventions.* Athens: Ohio University Press. 1975.
Rhys, Jean. *Wide Sargasso Sea.* Ed. Hilary Jenkins. London: Penguin Books. 2001.
Richardson, Angelique, Willis, Chris, eds. *The New Woman in Fiction and in Fact: Fin-de-Siècle Feminism.* New York: Palgrave Macmillan. 2002.
Rimmon-Kenan, Shlomith. *Narrative Fiction.* New York: Routledge. 2002.
Rose, Anita, ed. *Gender and Victorian Reform.* Cambridge Scholars Publishing: Newcastle upon Tyne. 2008.
Ruskin, John. *Sesame and Lilies.* London: The Electronic Book Company. 2001.
Sanders, Julie. *Adaptation and Appropriation.* London: Routledge. 2006.
Schaffer, Talia. "'Nothing But Foolscap and Ink': Inventing the New Woman." *The New Woman in Fiction and in Fact: Fin-de-Siècle Feminism.* Richardson, Angelique, Willis, Chris, eds. New York: Palgrave Macmillan. 2002.
Schaffer, Talia. *The Forgotten Female Aesthetes: Literary Culture in Late-Victorian England.* Charlottesville: University Press of Virginia. 2000.
Schmitt, Cannon. "'The sun and moon were made to give them light'" Empire in the Victorian Novel." *A Concise Companion to the Victorian Novel.* O'Gorman, Francis, ed. Oxford: Wiley-Blackwell. 2004.
Seaman, L. C. B. *Post-Victorian Britain 1902–1951.* London: Routledge. 1966.
Sharon, Marcus. *Between Women: Friendship, Desire and Marriage in Victorian England.* Princeton, NJ: Princeton University Press. 2007.
Sholl, Lesa. *Translation, Authorship and the Victorian Professional Woman: Charlotte Brontë, Harriet Martineau and George Eliot.* London: Routledge. 2016.
Showalter, Elaine, ed. *Daughters of Decadence: Women Writers of the Fin-de-Siècle.* New Brunswick: Rutgers University Press. 1993.
Siddall, S. H. *Henrik Ibsen: A Doll's House.* Charles Moseley, ed. Tirril: Humanities-Ebooks. 2008.
Singh, S. N. *Charlotte Brontë: A Thematic Study of Her Novels.* Delhi: Mittal Publications. 1987.
Smajić, Srdjan. *Ghost-Seers, Detectives, and Spiritualists: Theories of Vision in Victorian Literature and Science.* Cambridge: Cambridge University Press. 2010.
Smiles, Samuel. *Self-Help; with Illustrations of Character, Conduct and Preservance.* New York: Harper & Brothers. 1871.

Stanzel, F. K. *A Theory of Narrative.* Charlotte Goedsche, trans., Cambridge: Cambridge University Press. 1984.

Stetz, Margaret D. "Looking at Victorian Fashion: Not a Laughing Matter." *Neo-Victorian Humour: Comic Subversions and Unlaughter in Contemporary Historical Re-visions*, edited by Marie-Luise Kohlke and Christian Gutleben, Boston: Brill. 2017, 147–69.

Stevenson, Angus, ed. *Oxford Dictionary of English.* Oxford: Oxford University Press. 2010.

Striedter, Jurij. *Literary Structure, Evolution and Value: Russian Formalism and Czech Structuralism Recosnidered.* Cambridge, MA: Harvard University Press. 1989.

Sutherland, John. *Victorian Fiction: Writers, Publishers, Readers.* London: Palgrave. 1995.

Talairach-Vielmas, Laurence. *Moulding the Female Body in Victorian Fairy Tales and Sensation Novels.* Hampshire: Ashgate Publishing. 2007.

Tarabotti, Arcangela. *Paternal Tyranny.* Letizia Panizza, ed. Chicago: University of Chicago Press. 2004.

Templeton, Joan. *Ibsen's Women.* Cambridge: Cambridge University Press. 1997.

Tierney, Tom. *High Victorian Fashions: Paper Dolls.* Mineola, NY: Dover Publications. 2001.

Tredennick, Bianca, ed. *Victorian Transformations: Genre, Nationalism and Desire in Nineteenth-Century Literature.* Burlington, VT: Ashgate Publishing. 2011.

Trollope, Anthony. *An Autobiography; And Other Writings.* Nicholas Shrimpton, ed. Oxford: Oxford University Press. 2014.

Tryniecka, Aleksandra. "'Adaptation' or 'Appropriation': Re-Narrating the Victorian Past as an Ethical Decision." *Athens Journal of Humanities & Arts*, vol. 5, no. 4, 2018, 469–82.

Tryniecka, Aleksandra. "Bakhtin's Dialogism, Intertextual Theories and Neo-Victorian Fiction." *Annales Universitatis Mariae Curie-Skłodowska, Sectio FF—Philologiae*, vol. 38, no. 1, 2020, 171–85.

Tryniecka, Aleksandra. "Syrie James' *The Secret Diaries of Charlotte Brontë* and the Biography Retold: Reducing the Distance Between the Reader and the Past." *Beyond Words: Crossing Borders in English Studies.* Magdalena Bleinert-Coyle, Michał Choiński, Zygmunt Mazur, eds. Kraków: Tertium. 2015.

Tryniecka, Aleksandra. "The Bakhtinian Polyphony of Voices in Wilkie Collins's *The Woman in White*." *Visions and Revisions: Studies in Literature and Culture.* Grzegorz Czemiel, Justyna Galant, Anna Kędra-Kardela, Aleksandra Kędzierska, Marta Komsta, eds. Warszawa: Peter Lang. 2015.

Tryniecka, Aleksandra. "The Revisionary Influence: Neo-Victorian Fiction and the Past Redeemed." *Athens Journal of Philology*, vol. 2, no. 4. 2015. 255–64.

VanderMeer, Jeff, Chambers, S. J. *The Steampunk Bible: An Illustrated Guide to the World of Imaginary Airships, Corsets and Goggles, Mad Scientists and Strange Literature.* New York: Abrams Image. 2011.

Vielmas-Talairach, Laurence. *Moulding the Female Body in Victorian Fairy Tales and Sensation Novels.* Hampshire: Ashgate. 2007.

Voskuil, Lynn M. *Acting Naturally: Victorian Theatricality and Authenticity.* Charlottesville: University of Virginia Press. 2004.
Watt, Ian. *The Rise of the Novel.* Berkeley: University of California Press. 2000.
Watts, Edward J. *Hypatia: The Life and Legend of an Ancient Philosopher.* New York: Oxford University Press. 2017.
Wilde, Oscar. *An Ideal Husband* (in: *The Complete Illustrated Works of Oscar Wilde*). London: Bounty Books. 2013.
Willis, Chris. "'Heaven defend me from political or highly-educated women!': Packaging the New Woman for Mass Consumption." *The New Woman in Fiction and in Fact: Fin-de-Siècle Feminism.* Richardson, Angelique, Willis, Chris, eds. New York: Palgrave Macmillan. 2002.
Wollstonecraft, Mary. *A Vindication of the Rights of Women: with Strictures on Political and Moral Subjects.* London: Printed for J. Johnson, No 72, St. Paul's Church Yard. 1796.
Wood, Ellen. *East Lynne.* Oxford University Press: Oxford. 2008.
Woodson-Boulton, Amy. *Transformative Beauty: Art Museums in Industrial Britain.* Stanford, CA: Stanford University Press. 2012.
Woolf, Virginia. *A Room of One's Own.* Oxford: Oxford University Press. 1992.
Young, Arlene. *From Spinster to Career Woman: Middle-Class Women and Work in Victorian England.* McGill-Queen's University Press. 2019.
Zappen, James Philip. *The Rebirth of Dialogue: Bakhtin, Socrates, and the Rhetorical Tradition.* Albany: State University of New York Press. 2004.

Index

Page references for figures are italicized.

adaptation, 82
Allen, 3, 6, 9, 10–11, 12, 13, 15n2, 87–88, 103, 215
appropriation, 81–85

Bakhtin, 4–10, 53, 80, 84, 91, 106, 117, 131–32, 146, 187, 192, 197, 208, 212–13, 215–16, 218–19, 224, 227, 230
Balbus, 14
Bormann, 90
Brontë, Anne, 39, 55, 130
Brontë, Charlotte, xi, 7, 12, 13, 16, 26, 27, 28, 37, 44, 46, 51, 56, 57, 64, 68, 69, 95–98, 106, 129, 134–35, 160, 161, 187, 211–24

Carriger, 11, 18–19, 45, 106, 107–9, 115, 118, 119–45, 152–53, 163, 169, 177, 178–79, 229
conclusiveness, 4

dialogism, x–xi, 4, 6–9, 20, 106, 192, 207, 212, 220, 224, 227, 231
dialogue, xi, 3–4, 9, 10, 11, 12, 17, 31, 110, 115, 220;

"A Dialogue of Self and Soul: Plain Jane's Progress," 187;
Bakhtinian dialogue of voices, 5–7, 84, 91, 117, 132, 197, 224;
between an author, characters, and readers, 218;
between Grand and Quida, 112;
between the past and the present, 153;
between the self and the other, 192;
between Victorian and neo-Victorian texts, 19, 39, 90, 107, 188–89, 192, 197, 204, 206, 215;
between Victorian and neo-Victorian women, 117, 133, 184;
intertextual dialogue, 107, 189, 204, 206, 219, 229, 230;
Socratic dialogues, 4–5
diary, 95–96, 108, 176, 179, 211, 215, 216, 217, 218, 219, 220, 223
dualities, 45, 50, 52–53

empathy, 84, 216
ethics, 83, 84

Fowles, x, 5–6, 43, 118

Gaskell, 7, 26, 38, 54, 63, 95, 193n1, 212, 213, 214, 215, 216, 217, 219, 225n5
Genette, 10–13, 15n2, 15n3, 16n4, 17, 95, 106, 224n5
Gérin, 7, 26, 95, 212, 213, 214, 215, 216, 218, 219, 225
Głowiński, 14
Greg, 66–68, 126–27, 131, 133, 134
Gutleben, 6, 19, 52–53, 91–93, 103, 105

Hadley, 88, 90, 91, 94–95, 96, 101, 102, 141
Hansson, 14, 16n5, 17, 96, 97, 141
Heilmann, 81–83, 87, 89, 91, 94, 101, 109, 110, 117, 118, 196, 201, 203, 204, 205
heteroglossia, 6, 147, 220
high genres, 4–5
Hutcheon, 81–82, 91–92, 147n5

Ibsen, 115–16, 121
inheritance, 50, 72, 196
intertextuality, xi, 3–4, 9–11, 14–20, 81–82, 147n8, 151, 154, 169, 192, 221, 227, 231

Juvan, 9, 10, 14–15

Kaplan, 87–89
Kirchknopf, 89–90, 94
Kohlke, 105, 147n2, 195, 196, 197, 200, 201, 202–3
Kristeva, 10, 15n1, 15n2, 16n4
Kucała, 3, 9, 10, 14, 231

Lewellyn, 93–94, 98, 101, 196, 201, 203, 205

Markiewicz, 14

Neo-Victorian fiction, 5, 7, 11, 19–20, 32, 41, 52, 56–57, 73, 84, 88, 90–96, 99, 101, 103, 136, 138, 145, 179, 183, 188, 192, 196–97, 201, 208, 211, 216, 227, 228, 229, 231
Neo-Victorian women, xi, 107–8, 130, 230;
    attire, 149–66, 229;
    historical figures, x, 18, 83–84, 92, 96, 130, 211–25, 228, 230;
    independence, 19, 106, 145;
    individualism, 106;
    spinster, 120, 123, 131, 139, 145, 146;
    spirituality, 101;
    the past, 207;
    voices, xi, 20, 73, 97, 101–3, 183–93, 195, 201, 204, 207–8, 214
New Woman, 70, 72–73, 108–21, 124, 135–42, 145–46, 176, 179, 228–30
nostalgia, 5–6, 80–81, 87, 97–98, 119, 153, 163
novel, x, 4–5, 10, 132, 169, 208, 227;
    bildungsroman, 202;
    biographical/biofiction, 95–96, 211–24;
    detective, 95, 147n4;
    faux-Victorian, 89;
    gothic novel, 193n1;
    historical, 89, 92;
    historiographic metafiction 89–92;
    neo-Victorian, ix–xi, 3, 6–7, 10, 12–14, 16, 17–20, 49, 52–53, 57, 83–84, 89–91, 95–99, 101–46, 152, 155–66, 171, 183–92, 196–97, 203–6, 229;
    postmodern romance, 96–97, 221;
    post-Victorian, 89;
    retro-Victorian, 89, 93, 153;
    revisionary fiction, 3, 95;
    sensation, 140, 151–53, 155, 169, 175, 183;
    steampunk, 153, 163, 167n5, 177, 229;

Victorian, ix–xi, 3, 10, 14, 17,
        21–46, 49–56, 58, 58n1,
        63–65, 67–68, 73, 76, 78, 84,
        94, 105, 114, 122, 124–25,
        128, 133, 135, 141, 154–55,
        166n3, 169, 171–80, 183–92,
        200, 203, 206, 209n1, 228, 232
Nycz, 14, 17, 132, 151

past, ix–xi, 3–7, 8n3, 12, 18–19, 21–22,
        31, 39, 41, 45, 53, 56–58, 62, 79–82,
        84, 85n1, 88–99, 101–3, 105, 119,
        133, 139, 145–46, 147n5, 153–55,
        160, 163–65, 167, 180, 184, 191–92,
        197, 200, 207, 208, 211–15, 219,
        222, 224, 227, 229, 230–32
pastiche, 13, 82, 87, 94, 95, 230
Patmore, 64, 75, 77, 109, 150
Phelan, 107, 132, 145, 180, 211, 228
Pirgerou, xiii, 41, 44, 45, 50, 67
postmodernism, 79–82, 88, 89–90, 91,
        103, 147n5

Rhys, x–xi, 12, 17–18, 43, 101, 103,
        106, 107, 108, 164, 183–92, 195,
        203–9, 229, 231
Ruskin, 47n3, 69–72, 77n3, 139;
        his garden, 109, 112–14, 116,
                121, 124, 144

Shiller, 90

Trollope, 17, 29, 31, 32, 34, 38, 39, *40*,
        42, 46, 49, 64, 67

VanderMeer, 119, 130, 139, 153, 163
ventriloquism, 93–95
Victorian women, ix, xi, 28, 33, 44, 47,
        72, 75–78, 127, 163;
        angel in the house, 61, 64, 67,
                73, 74, 75, 76, 115, 123, 124,
                144, 145, 150, 151, 162, 173,
                178, 181n3;
        attire, 149–80, 229;
        domesticity, 134, 154;
        marriage, 141;
        revisiting, 118;
        roles, 142;
        spinsters, 42, 67–69, 121, 195;
        spiritualism, 103, 124;
        their voices, xi, 20, 228, 183–92
voice, ix, x, 4–7, 9, 19, 20, 73, 94,
        117, 133, 183, 192, 197, 215, 218–
        19, 228, 230;
        double-voicedness, 10, 132, 146;
        marginalized voices, 32, 81, 84,
                176, 186, 188–89;
        unheard voices, 53, 84, 91–93,
                195, 204, 229

Women Question, 61–76
Woolf, 133–35, 141, 145, 147n6

About the Author

Aleksandra Tryniecka is an assistant professor at Maria Curie-Skłodowska University in Lublin, Poland, and a children's author and illustrator. She is especially interested in the nineteenth-century British novel and in literary women characters of this era. In her free time she writes poetry in order to accommodate her life with the right words.

www.ingramcontent.com/pod-product-compliance
Lightning Source LLC
Chambersburg PA
CBHW021351300426
44114CB00012B/1176